Transistor Physics

ANDERSONIAN LIBRARY
★
WITHDRAWN
FROM
LIBRARY
STOCK
★
UNIVERSITY OF STRATHCLYDE

MODERN ELECTRICAL
STUDIES

A Series edited by

Professor G. D. SIMS

Head of Department of Electronics
University of Southampton

402077456

Transistor Physics

K. G. NICHOLS, M.Sc.

Senior Lecturer in Electronics

and

E. V. VERNON, Ph.D

Lecturer in Electronics
University of Southampton

CHAPMAN AND HALL LTD
and
SCIENCE PAPERBACKS

First published 1966
by Chapman and Hall Ltd
11 *New Fetter Lane London* EC4P 4EE

First published as a Science Paperback 1973

Printed in The Netherlands by
Nederlands Bockdruk Inrichting N.V.

SBN 412 08680 5 *cased edition*
SBN 412 21080 0 *science paperback edition*

© *K. G. Nichols and E. V. Vernon* 1966

All rights reserved. No part of this book
may be reprinted, or reproduced or utilized in
any form or by any electronic, mechanical or
other means, now known or hereafter invented,
including photocopying and recording, or in
any information storage and retrieval system,
without permission in writing from the Publisher.

This book is sold subject to the condition that it shall
not, by way of trade or otherwise, be lent, re-sold, hired
out, or otherwise circulated without the publisher's prior
consent in any form of binding or cover other than that in
which it is published and without a similar condition
including this condition being imposed on the subsequent
purchaser.

621·3815'28
NIC

Contents

Preface

This book is intended as an introduction to the application of physical theory to the study of semiconductors and transistor devices. The book is based on lecture courses given by the authors to second and third year honours students in the Electronics Department of Southampton University, England. Some elementary knowledge of physics, circuit theory, and vector methods is assumed. The book deals almost exclusively with the theoretical aspects, but references are given to experimental work.

The first two chapters discuss classical atomic theory and quantum mechanical applications to electron energy levels in atoms, in particular the hydrogen atom, and in one-dimensional crystalline solids leading to the distinctions between metals, insulators, and semiconductors. Chapter 3 deals with statistical mechanics in some detail, so that the reader can appreciate the historical background leading to the Fermi-Dirac statistics for electrons in metals and semiconductors, and in chapter 4 these statistics are applied to determine the current carrier density in various types of semiconductor. Equations for drift and diffusion currents are obtained in chapter 5, and the results applied to uniform and graded impurity semiconductors in chapter 6. Current flow across p-n junctions is analysed in chapter 7, and the p-n-p transistor theory is developed in chapter 8. The discussion is limited to p-n-p transistors, but similar results apply for the n-p-n transistor. Attention is almost entirely confined to a one-dimensional model, as it is analytically fairly straightforward, and demonstrates most of the important features of practical transistors. Some account of majority carrier transistors will be found in chapter 9, although no attempt is made to discuss frequency effects about which little is yet known. High level injection effects have been excluded, as has also discussion of noise, as these subjects are too complex for a textbook of this type.

After careful consideration the authors decided against a list of symbols. Not only would such a list be prohibitively long but, in many cases, the same symbol would have to be used for different purposes in different parts of the text unless serious departures from common practice were to be made. As far as possible symbols are redefined in each chapter as they arise.

The authors gratefully acknowledge useful discussion with many colleagues, in particular with Mr G. G. Bloodworth and Mr H. A. Kemhadjian, and are indebted to the D. van Nostrand Company, Inc, N.J. for permission to reproduce the diagram of a diamond lattice, fig. 4.4a. They are also indebted to Miss M. A. Porter and Mrs R. McKie for typing the manuscript, and to Mr M. Broomfield for producing the drawings.

CHAPTER 1

Classical Atomic Theory and Interatomic Binding

1.1 Early Theories of Electrons in Metals

Any theory of electrons in metals must account for the experimental observations on thermal and electrical conduction, photoelectric and thermionic emission, and on the specific heat of metals. Proof, that the particles emitted from metallic surfaces when illuminated by ultraviolet light or when heated to some 2,500°K were electrons, led to the suggestion that electrical conductivity in metals may be due to the existence of a cloud of *free* electrons in the interatomic spaces. The application of an electric field would then cause the electrons to move with the consequent production of a current, the flow of electrons being in the opposite direction to that of the conventional current. This theory, known as the classical theory, was developed by Drude and Lorentz. They assumed that the electrons, when accelerated by an electric field, collided with each other and with the atomic nuclei, and had the usual Maxwellian distribution of velocities, see section 3.5, appropriate to the temperature of the metal. They also showed that these free electrons would account for the high thermal conductivity of metals, because as their masses were considerably less than those of the atoms, they would have correspondingly high velocities.

The classical theory accounts adequately for photoelectric and thermionic emission, as it is reasonable to suppose that these *free* electrons are contained within the solid by forces of attraction. If an electron escapes from a metal surface an electrical image can be considered to arise in the surface, and consequently the electron must do work to escape from the metal. This work is called the *work function* of the surface. The necessary energy can be supplied by the energy of the incident photons. The energy of a photon E is hv, according to Planck's theory 1901, where v is the frequency of the radiation and h is a universal constant known as Planck's constant. Alternatively the energy can come from heating the solid.

Difficulty was experienced in accounting for the specific heats of metals, as the specific heat of a metal is the change in the kinetic and potential energy of the whole system of atoms and electrons as the temperature is altered. According to the classical principle of the equipartition of energy the *free* electrons should contribute an additional energy equal to $\frac{3}{2}kT$ per electron, so the specific heat of metals should be greater than non-metals by $\frac{3}{2}Nk$, where N is the number of atoms

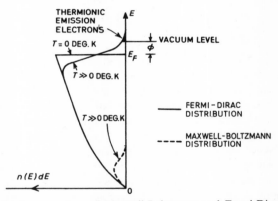

Figure 1.1a. A comparison of Maxwell-Boltzmann and Fermi-Dirac energy distributions for electrons in metals

in a gram-atom; k is Boltzmann's constant (see section 3.3). This anomaly was removed by applying Fermi-Dirac statistics instead of Maxwell-Boltzmann (see section 3.9) where it is seen that the total energy of electrons in a metal changes very little with temperature. These statistics were used by Sommerfeld in a new theory of conduction, a theory which may be considered to be the first step towards the modern theories of wave mechanics.

The two statistical distributions are shown for comparison in fig. 1.1a,

$n(E)dE$ being the number of electrons with energies in the range E to $E + dE$. The electrons in the *tail* above the vacuum level have sufficient energies for emission from the surface. ϕ is the work function of the surface.

1.2 Early Atomic Theories

Theories of the structure of the atom were first put forward at the beginning of the nineteenth century, but little definite evidence became available before Sir J. J. Thomson's discovery of the electron in 1897. It then became obvious that an atom must be made up of equal quantities of positive and negative charges. This still left unknown the number of charged particles and their arrangement.

An indication of the number of charged particles per atom was obtained from measurements on the scattering of X-rays for which classical theory provided a formula in terms of the number of electrons per unit volume. Results at first indicated that the number was of the order of the atomic weight, but Barkla [1.1] later showed that for the lighter elements, at least, the number was about half the atomic weight. Subsequently it was shown by scattering measurements that hydrogen has only one electron per atom.

The arrangement of the charged particles must fulfil two conditions: (i) they must be stable, the particles being held by forces, probably electrostatic, in equilibrium positions about which they can vibrate with definite frequencies as indicated by the frequencies of the line spectra; (ii) except when the particles are distributed by external forces they must be at rest, since an accelerating electron radiates energy.

J. J. Thomson postulated the atom as a relatively large positively charged sphere with the electrons embedded in it, fig. 1.2a(i). Experiments were performed where a narrow beam of α rays, positively charged helium atoms, was fired at sheets of gold or silver foil and the paths of the scattered particles were observed as scintillations on a zinc sulphide screen. The angular distribution of the scattered particles was obtained, and it was found that a very significant proportion was scattered through an angle greater than $90°$, the distribution being proportional to $1/\sin^4(\phi/2)$ where ϕ is the angle of deflection.

It is apparent that with the Thomson atomic model, large angles of deflection are impossible, since the charge is distributed over a large volume. A particle initially travelling to pass near the centre of the sphere would be little deflected as the electric field inside the sphere would be fairly small. However, if the positive charge is collected in a very small volume, the nucleus, fig. 1.2a(ii), a particle coming close to

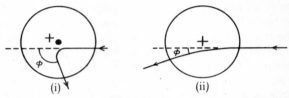

Figure 1.2a Deflection of an α-*particle by the* Thomson atom *(i), and by the* Rutherford atom *(ii).*

this charge would experience a large deflection. This was the atomic model suggested by Rutherford, and using it, he obtained a deflection distribution equation that agreed with the experimental evidence extremely well.

There then remained the question of the location of the electrons. It is obvious that the electrons could not be at rest, as they would then be attracted to the positively charged nucleus. The attraction between an electron and the nucleus can be counteracted by giving the electron angular motion round the nucleus such that the centrifugal force created equals the electrostatic force between the particles. The electron would then rotate in an orbit round the nucleus. However, classical theory requires that an accelerating electron radiates energy. This energy can come only from the system, so the electron would spiral into the nucleus giving out radiation of continuously increasing frequency. This phenomenon is not observed in emission spectra, since they consist of definite, and discrete, energies.

This impasse was not solved until Bohr in 1913 produced his theory of the structure of the atom and the origin of the spectra. He used

Planck's concept of the quanta of energy and applied it to Rutherford's model of an atom consisting of a very small positively charged nucleus with the electrons rotating in orbits about it.

1.3 The Bohr Theory of Atomic Hydrogen

Planck in 1901 postulated two conditions about the energy of oscillations which formed the beginning of the quantum theory. He assumed that the energy of an oscillator cannot vary continuously, as suggested by classical theory, but must take one of a discrete set of values: $0, hv, 2hv \ldots nhv$, where v is the frequency, h is Planck's constant $(6 \cdot 63 \times 10^{-34}$ joule sec.) and n is an integer. He further postulated that an oscillator whilst in one of its energy *states*, does not emit radiation although it is accelerating continuously, but only radiates or absorbs energy when it changes its energy state.

These assumptions, which Planck had applied successfully to radiation theory, were then used by Bohr [1.2] in 1913 as the basis of his theory of electron orbits in atoms. He further suggested that if the energy of an electron changes as a result of a change of the electron orbit, the frequency v of the radiation emitted or absorbed is given by

$$v = \frac{E_1 - E_2}{h} \tag{1.3-1}$$

where E_1 and E_2 are the energies of the electron in its initial and final orbits, respectively. If E_1 is greater than E_2 the radiation is emitted, and if E_2 is greater than E_1 it is absorbed.

In addition Bohr quantized the angular momentum in integral multiples of $\hbar$, equal to $h/2\pi$, so that if we consider an electron in a circular orbit of radius a and angular momentum ω the condition is

$$ma^2 \omega = n\hbar \tag{1.3-2}$$

where m is the mass of the electron and n is an integer called the total or principal quantum number of the orbit or state.

Further, the laws of mechanics require that the centrifugal force on the rotating electron is balanced by the electrostatic attraction between the electron and the positive nucleus. Hence we have

$$ma\omega^2 = \frac{Zq^2}{4\pi\varepsilon_0 a^2} \tag{1.3-3}$$

where Z is the atomic number of the element, equal to unity for hydrogen, q is the electronic charge, and ε_0 is the permittivity of free space.

Eliminating ω from (1.3-2) and (1.3-3) gives

$$a = \frac{4\pi\varepsilon_0 n^2 \hbar^2}{mZq^2}. \tag{1.3-4}$$

The total energy E of the electron is made up of potential energy U, equal to $-Zq^2/4\pi\varepsilon_0 a$, where the energy is taken to be zero at infinity, and kinetic energy K equal to $\frac{1}{2}ma^2\omega^2$.

Substituting for ω^2 from eqn. 1.3-3 gives

$$K = \frac{Zq^2}{8\pi a\varepsilon_0} \tag{1.3-5}$$

Therefore

$$E = U + K = -\frac{Zq^2}{8\pi a\varepsilon_0} \tag{1.3-6}$$

which, substituting for a, gives

$$E = -\left(\frac{mZ^2 q^4}{32\pi^2 \hbar^2 \varepsilon_0^2}\right)\left(\frac{1}{n^2}\right). \tag{1.3-7}$$

If the electron jumps from an orbit where the quantum state is n_1 to one where it is n_2 the change in energy of the electron $E_1 - E_2$ is

$$E_1 - E_2 = \left(\frac{mZ^2 q^4}{32\pi^2 \hbar^2 \varepsilon_0^2}\right)\left(\frac{1}{n_2^2} - \frac{1}{n_1^2}\right) \tag{1.3-8}$$

and if $E_1 - E_2$ is positive radiation is emitted, and its frequency is

$$v = \left(\frac{mZ^2 q^2}{64\pi^3 \hbar^3 \varepsilon_0^2}\right)\left(\frac{1}{n_2^2} - \frac{1}{n_1^2}\right). \tag{1.3-9}$$

If the equation is modified so that the frequency v is replaced by the wave number $\bar{v}$ of the radiation, we have

$$\bar{v} = \frac{v}{c} = \left(\frac{mZ^2 q^4}{64\pi^3 \hbar^3 c\varepsilon_0^2} \right) \left(\frac{1}{n_2^2} - \frac{1}{n_1^2} \right) \tag{1.3-10}$$

where c is the velocity of light.

The constant $mq^4/64\pi^3 \hbar^3 c\varepsilon_0^2$ is known as the Rydberg constant. The theory only applies for an atom with one orbital electron, such as hydrogen, singly ionized helium ($Z = 2$), and doubly ionized lithium ($Z = 3$).

The energies E corresponding to the various values of n are often represented diagrammatically by a series of parallel lines, fig. 1.3a. Each line in the figure is referred to as an energy level, the corresponding energy, for the hydrogen atom, is here given in *electron volts*. (An electron volt (eV) is the work done on an electron when its potential is raised by 1 volt.)

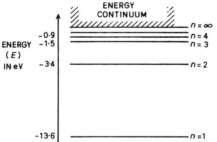

Figure 1.3a. Electron energy levels for atomic hydrogen

A small correcting factor should be applied to eqns (1.3-9) and (10) to take into account the fact that the nucleus is not at rest but that it and the electron rotate about their common centre of gravity, which is close to the nucleus since its mass M is some 1,800 times that of the electron. The correction can be made by replacing m of eqn (1.3-9) by what is called the reduced mass m', where

$$m' = \frac{mM}{m + M}. \tag{1.3-11}$$

Results obtained using Bohr's theory agree very well with the experimental values for the hydrogen spectral lines and because of this and the fact that the wave mechanical theory, see section 2.4, gives the same equation as eqn (1.3-9), the accepted value of $\hbar$ is the one obtained by fitting the experimental results to this theory.

1.4 Modifications to the Bohr Theory

Sommerfeld [1.3] generalized the Bohr theory of electron orbits to allow for the possibility of elliptic orbits in addition to Bohr's circular orbits. He considered an electron at B in an elliptical orbit with the nucleus at A (fig. 1.4a), and with the radius vector AB equal to $\mathbf{r}$. There

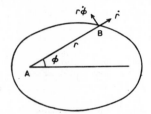

Figure 1.4a. Sommerfeld's elliptic orbit

are in this case two variable co-ordinates r and ϕ, and consequently two quantum numbers known as the radial (n_r) and azimuthal (n_ϕ) quantum numbers. The relations corresponding to Bohr's quantization of angular momentum are now

$$\oint m\dot{r}\,dr = n_r h \tag{1.4-1}$$

and

$$\oint mr^2\,\dot{\phi}\,d\phi = n_\phi h \,. \tag{1.4-2}$$

These replace eqn (1.3-2), and lead to the result that the energy E of the electron is given by

$$E = -\frac{mZ^2 q^4}{32\pi^2 \hbar^2 \varepsilon_0^2 (n_r + n_\phi)^2} \tag{1.4-3}$$

From comparison of this equation with eqn (1.3-7), it is seen that they give the same value for the energy if $(n_r + n_\phi)$ is equal to n, the total quantum number. That is, elliptical orbits of different ellipticity but with the same total quantum number have, on this theory, exactly the same energy. In this case, the various orbits are said to be degenerate. Two orbits are of particular interest; if $n = n_\phi$ the orbit is a circle – the Bohr orbit, and if $n_\phi = 0$ the ellipse becomes a pair of straight lines, which is clearly an impossible condition looked at from the physical standpoint. Hence the azimuthal quantum number can take any value from 1 to n. (A quantum number $l = n_\phi - 1$ is sometimes called the azimuthal quantum number, but when it arises in section 2.4, it will be called the orbital quantum number.)

Sommerfeld then showed that if the relativistic change of electronic mass with velocity is taken into account the energies associated with orbits of different ellipticities but the same total quantum number, have very slightly different energies, and so the degeneracy is removed. A single energy level in, say, atomic hydrogen is then replaced by a number of closely spaced levels.

The theory of atomic energy levels will be discussed in more detail in section 2.4.

1.5 Interatomic Force and Binding

We have, so far, only considered the forces acting between the nucleus and the orbital electrons, but we shall later be concerned with solid materials. It is therefore of interest to discuss briefly the forces which bind atoms together making a solid substance.

Elementary ideas of mechanics suggest that at least two types of force exist, an attractive force holding the atoms together and a repulsive force preventing the atoms from being too close. This view is confirmed by simple experiments on elasticity. Let us therefore consider a system of two atoms A and B which are bound together by these two forces. In general, the potential energy of atom B due to the field of atom A is of the form

$$V(r) = -\alpha/r^n + \beta/r^m \tag{1.5-1}$$

where r is the atomic separation. The first term produces a force of attraction and the second a force of repulsion.

Hence the interatomic force

$$F(r) = -\frac{dV}{dr} = -\frac{n\alpha}{r^{n+1}} + \frac{m\beta}{r^{m+1}}. \qquad (1.5\text{-}2)$$

Now, for a particular value of r, the two atoms must be in equilibrium, so the potential and force functions must be of the type shown in fig. 1.5a. The normal interatomic separation will then be r_0, the minimum of the resultant potential curve. The energy V_0, represents the dissociation energy of the atoms, which in practice is of the order of a few electron volts.

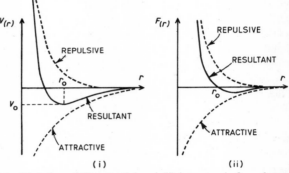

Figure 1.5a. Variation of (i) potential and (ii) interatomic force between two atoms, as a function of the distance between the atoms

The equilibrium condition by eqn (1.5-2) is given by

$$\frac{n\alpha}{r_0^{n+1}} = \frac{m\beta}{r_0^{m+1}} \qquad (1.5\text{-}3)$$

that is

$$r_0^{m-n} = \frac{m\beta}{n\alpha}. \qquad (1.5\text{-}4)$$

Hence $V(r_0)$ at equilibrium is (from eqn. 1.5-1)

$$V(r_0) = -\alpha\left(1 - \frac{n}{m}\right)r_0^{-n}. \qquad (1.5\text{-}5)$$

This equation shows that equilibrium is only possible if m is greater than n as at equilibrium $V(r_0)$ must be negative for stability. It is apparent, therefore, that the attractive force is of greater range than the repulsive force.

The interatomic forces in solids are electric, and the resulting force comes from the sum of the forces between all the outer electrons as well as the forces between the nuclei. Hence the number and distribution of the orbital electrons determines the type of atomic binding. In general the binding forces are split into four categories:

  (i) Ionic (*e.g.* NaCl)
 (ii) Valence (*e.g.* Diamond, Ge, Si)
(iii) Metallic (*e.g.* Ag, Cu)
(iv) van der Waals (organic compounds, rare gases)

However, many cases arise where the binding is the result of two or more different categories of force.

(i) *Ionic crystals.* In these crystals one or more electrons from one atom are transferred to another atom resulting in the formation of positive and negative ions. A good example of this is NaCl which becomes Na^+ and Cl^- in the crystal lattice. The binding forces are then mostly the Coulomb forces between the ions.

(ii) *Valence or homopolar crystals.* Here neighbouring atoms share their valence electrons and form covalent bonds. The hydrogen molecule is the simplest illustration of this type of bonding; the bond is made from two equal nuclei and two electrons.

From the point of view of this text, this type of bonding is most important as all the semiconductor substances in Group IV of the periodic table have four co-valent bonds at angles of 109° to each other, see fig. 4.4a; these bonds are very strong, so hard crystals are produced.

(iii) *Metallic crystals.* In these crystals the outermost electrons are very loosely bound to the nuclei. The result is that there is a lattice of positive ions in a cloud of electrons, and the binding comes from the Coulomb electrostatic forces between the ions and the cloud of electrons. For further information see references [1.4] and [1.5].

(iv) *van der Waals crystals.* Some elements, particularly the rare gases, have completely full outer shells and consequently have little tendency to share their electrons. Interatomic binding then results only from the fact that the orbiting electrons produce weak fluctuating dipoles, and the dipoles of neighbouring atoms then interact. The binding forces are consequently very weak. They are called van der Waals forces, and are found in solid and liquid forms of the rare gases and in many organic compounds.

References

[1.1] BARKLA, C. G. (1911), 'Energy of scattered X-radiation', *Phil. Mag.*, **21**, 648–52.
[1.2] BOHR, N. (1913), 'Constitution of atoms and molecules', *Phil. Mag.*, **26**, 1–25.
[1.3] SOMMERFELD, A. (1929), *Atomic structure and spectral lines*, Methuen.
[1.4] WIGNER, E. and SIETZ, F. 1933 and 1934, 'On the constitution of metallic sodium', *Phys. Rev.*, **43**, 804–10 and **46**, 509–24.
[1.5] SIETZ, F. (1940), *The modern theory of solids*, McGraw-Hill.

CHAPTER 2

Quantum Mechanics and Band Theory

2.1 Quantum Mechanics

The Bohr theory of the atom was founded on a hypothesis, that the momentum of the orbiting electron is an integral multiple of $(h/2\pi)$ (section 1.3). No justification for this was given, nor was certain finer detail of atomic spectra accurately accounted for on Bohr's theory. Justification had, in fact, to await a suggestion put forward in 1924 by L. de Broglie. He argued that if electromagnetic radiation could often be considered to be made up of particles, could not particles often be considered as waves? This suggestion was developed by de Broglie, Dirac, Heisenberg and Schrödinger in the years 1926 and 1927, and formed the basis of a new quantum theory called *quantum mechanics*.

However, before further discussion, it is interesting to mention another important case in which the fundamental constant h arises. This is in connexion with what is known as Heisenberg's Principle of Uncertainty, according to which the product of the errors in the measurement of position and momentum of a particle cannot be less than h. Hence, if the position is very accurately known, the momentum, and consequently the energy, of the particle is correspondingly known only to a low order of accuracy. There is, therefore, a certain vagueness in the orbits allowed on the Bohr theory.

If we consider a group of waves of slightly different wavelengths travelling in a dispersive medium, that is one in which the velocity u of a wave is a function of the wavelength λ then it can be shown [2.1] that the velocity v of the centre of the group is given by

$$\frac{d\omega}{dk} = v = u - \lambda \left(\frac{du}{d\lambda}\right) \tag{2.1-1}$$

13

as $2\pi\omega$ is equal to (u/λ) and k is equal to $(2\pi/\lambda)$. The velocity v is here called the group velocity, and may in certain circumstances be appreciably different from the wave velocity.

Now, if a particle is to exhibit the property of a wave packet, it is reasonable to assume that the velocity of the particle will be the group velocity of its associated waves.

We have seen that the energy E of a photon is given by:

$$E = hv \qquad (2.1\text{-}2)$$

where h is Planck's constant and v is the frequency of the radiation of the photon. But the kinetic energy of a particle is $\frac{1}{2}mv^2$.

Therefore, equating these we get:

$$E = hv = \tfrac{1}{2}mv^2 + V \qquad (2.1\text{-}3)$$

where V is the potential energy, which for the present can be assumed constant. Differentiating eqn (2.1-3) with respect to λ, which itself is equal to u/v, we have:

$$h\left(\frac{\partial v}{\partial \lambda}\right) = mv\left(\frac{\partial v}{\partial \lambda}\right). \qquad (2.1\text{-}4)$$

Substituting into eqn (2.1-1) gives:

$$v = v\lambda - \lambda\frac{\partial(v\lambda)}{\partial \lambda} = -\lambda^2\left(\frac{\partial v}{\partial \lambda}\right). \qquad (2.1\text{-}5)$$

But from eqn (2.1-4) this leads to:

$$v = -\lambda^2\left(\frac{mv}{h}\right)\left(\frac{\partial v}{\partial \lambda}\right)$$

or

$$\left(\frac{\partial v}{\partial \lambda}\right) = -\left(\frac{h}{m\lambda^2}\right). \qquad (2.1\text{-}6)$$

This integrated gives:

$$v = \left(\frac{h}{m\lambda}\right) + \text{const.} \qquad (2.1\text{-}7)$$

The constant may be set equal to zero for it is assumed that an infinite wavelength corresponds to a particle at rest. The wavelength λ of the particle is thus:

$$\lambda = \left(\frac{h}{mv}\right). \qquad (2.1\text{-}8)$$

In other words, the wavelength of the particle is equal to Planck's constant divided by the momentum of the particle. This wavelength is known as the de Broglie wavelength. That particles exhibit the properties of waves has been elegantly demonstrated by Davisson and Germer [2.2]. These workers directed an electron beam at a single crystal of nickel, and found that the reflected beam obeyed Bragg's law, a law established to account for X-ray diffraction by crystals. They therefore showed that the electrons exhibited wave properties.

2.2 Schrödinger's Wave Equation

Schrödinger was the first person to use de Broglie's idea of particle waves in connection with electron orbits in atoms. A wave motion can be expressed by the differential equation:

$$\nabla^2 \Psi = \left(\frac{\partial^2 \Psi}{\partial x^2}\right) + \left(\frac{\partial^2 \Psi}{\partial y^2}\right) + \left(\frac{\partial^2 \Psi}{\partial z^2}\right) = \frac{1}{u^2}\left(\frac{\partial^2 \Psi}{\partial t^2}\right) \qquad (2.2\text{-}1)$$

where Ψ is the amplitude of the wave and u is the wave velocity. Schrödinger proposed that the de Broglie waves associated with an electron must obey this equation, and further that if the total energy of the electron is E, then the frequency v must be such that:

$$E = hv \qquad (2.2\text{-}2)$$

where h is again Planck's constant.

The amplitude at a particular point of the wave for the electron can be represented by the equation:

$$\Psi(x, t) = \psi(x) \exp (j2\pi vt) .$$

Hence

$$\left(\frac{\partial \Psi}{\partial t}\right) = (j2\pi v) \Psi \qquad (2.2\text{-}3)$$

and

$$\left(\frac{\partial^2 \Psi}{\partial t^2}\right) = -4\pi^2 v^2(\Psi) \quad . \tag{2.2-4}$$

Therefore substituting in eqn (2.2-1) leads to:

$$\nabla^2 \psi = -\left(\frac{4\pi^2 v^2}{u^2}\right)\psi \tag{2.2-5}$$

Now, if v is the frequency of the wave, and u is the velocity of the wave, then the wavelength λ is (u/v). But the wavelength given by the de Broglie equation, (2.1-8), is

$$\lambda = \left(\frac{h}{mv}\right)$$

where v is the velocity of the electron.

Therefore: $$\left(\frac{u}{v}\right) = \left(\frac{h}{mv}\right) \tag{2.2-6}$$

and so: $$\nabla^2 \psi = -4\pi^2 \left(\frac{mv}{h}\right)^2 \psi \ . \tag{2.2-7}$$

If, as before, the total energy of the electron is E, and it is at a position where its potential energy is V, then the kinetic energy of the electron is $(E-V)$. Therefore:

$$\tfrac{1}{2}mv^2 = (E-V) \tag{2.2-8}$$

and eqn (2.2-7) becomes:

$$\nabla^2 \psi + \left[\frac{8\pi^2 m(E-V)}{h^2}\right]\psi = 0 \ . \tag{2.2-9}$$

This is known as the time independent Schrödinger wave equation.

The significance of the amplitude ψ at a point is that it is a measure of the probability of finding the particle at that particular point. The probability of finding the particle within an elementary volume $(dx\,dy\,dz)$ is proportional to $(|\psi|^2)(dx\,dy\,dz)$ or $(\psi\psi^*)(dx\,dy\,dz)$ where ψ^* is the conjugate complex of ψ. The constant of proportionality can be found,

QUANTUM MECHANICS AND BAND THEORY 17

if required, by evaluating the triple integral and equating it to unity, thus

$$\iiint |\psi|^2 \, dx \, dy \, dz = 1 . \tag{2.2-10}$$

This equation simply means that the particle must be somewhere! The amplitude ψ is often called the probability amplitude.

2.3 An Electron in a Potential Box

An example of the application of Schrödinger's equation is the investigation of the behaviour of an electron contained in a constant potential region between two reflecting planes. This could, theoretically, be realized by assuming that the electron is moving in the x-direction between two planes at which the electron potential energy suddenly becomes infinite; see fig. 2.3a(i). Whilst this is strictly an academic exercise, it sheds more light on the significance of ψ and also on the difference between classical and quantum mechanics.

For values of x between 0 and L, Schrödinger's equation becomes:

$$\left(\frac{\partial^2 \psi}{\partial x^2}\right) + \left(\frac{8\pi^2 mE}{h^2}\right)\psi = 0 . \tag{2.3-1}$$

It is convenient when handling Schrödinger's equation to replace $(h/2\pi)$ by $\hbar$, as before, so that the equation becomes:

$$\left(\frac{\partial^2 \psi}{\partial x^2}\right) + \left(\frac{2mE}{\hbar^2}\right)\psi = 0 . \tag{2.3-2}$$

This differential equation has the general solution:

$$\psi = A \exp(jkx) + B \exp(-jkx) \tag{2.3-3}$$

where k is the wavenumber (equal to $2\pi/\lambda$) and

$$k^2 = \left(\frac{2mE}{\hbar^2}\right). \tag{2.3-4}$$

The values of the constants can be related by the boundary conditions, which require that ψ is zero, at x equal to zero and at x equal to L. This leads to:

$$A + B = 0 \tag{2.3-5}$$

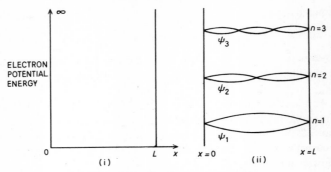

Figure 2.3a(i). The electron *potential box*
(ii). Some probability amplitude functions

and
$$A \exp(jkL) + B \exp(-jkL) = 0$$

or
$$A[\exp(jkL) - \exp(-jkL)] = 0 . \tag{2.3-6}$$

Hence
$$\sin(kL) = 0 \tag{2.3-7}$$

because A cannot be zero.

This gives values for k of $0, (\pi/L), (2\pi/L), \ldots$ or in general $(n\pi/L)$ where n is an integer. Hence:

$$\psi_n = C \sin\left(\frac{n\pi x}{L}\right) \tag{2.3-8}$$

where C is another constant, equal to $2jA$.

Substituting the condition imposed on k in eqn (2.3-4) leads to a series of allowed energies, showing that the energy is quantized. Thus:

$$E_n = \frac{(\hbar k)^2}{2m} = \frac{1}{2m}\left(\frac{\pi\hbar}{L}\right)^2 n^2 . \tag{2.3-9}$$

These characteristic values of E are often referred to as *eigenvalues.*

The constant C in eqn (2.3-8) can be determined by substituting in the one-dimensional equivalent of eqn (2.2-10). Thus:

$$C^2 \int_0^L \sin^2\left(\frac{n\pi x}{L}\right) dx = 1 \tag{2.3-10}$$

which leads to:

$$C = \left(\frac{2}{L}\right)^{\frac{1}{2}}.$$

Therefore

$$\psi_n = \left(\frac{2}{L}\right)^{\frac{1}{2}} \sin\left(\frac{n\pi x}{L}\right). \tag{2.3-11}$$

With this value of C, ψ_n is said to be normalized. Some of the allowed values of ψ_n are shown drawn in fig. 2.3a(ii), from which it is seen that there is a strong similarity between this solution and the standing waves produced by the transverse vibration of a string.

2.4 Electron Orbits and the Hydrogen Atom

A valuable application of Schrödinger's equation is to the problem of the electron orbits in the hydrogen atom, and in other elements with a single orbital electron. In this case, there is a central force between the atomic nucleus and the electron, such that the potential energy V can be represented by a function:

$$V = -\frac{Zq^2}{4\pi\varepsilon_0 r} \tag{2.4-1}$$

where Z is the atomic number, q is the electronic charge, ε_0 is the permittivity of free space, and r is the distance between the nucleus and the electron. It is convenient now to express $\nabla^2\psi$ of Schrödinger's equation in spatial polar co-ordinates r, θ, and ϕ, and so the equation becomes (see ref. [2.3]):

$$\left(\frac{\partial^2\psi}{\partial r^2}\right) + \frac{2}{r}\left(\frac{\partial\psi}{\partial r}\right) + \frac{1}{r^2}\left[\frac{1}{\sin\theta}\frac{\partial}{\partial\theta}\left(\sin\theta\frac{\partial\psi}{\partial\theta}\right) + \frac{1}{\sin^2\theta}\left(\frac{\partial^2\psi}{\partial\phi^2}\right)\right]$$

$$+ \frac{2m_0}{\hbar^2}\left(E + \frac{Zq^2}{4\pi\varepsilon_0 r}\right)\psi = 0 \tag{2.4-2}$$

where m_0 is the electronic mass.

There is a solution of this equation of the form:

$$\psi = R(r) . S(\theta, \phi) \tag{2.4-3}$$

which when substituted in eqn (2.4-2) gives:

$$\frac{1}{R} \frac{d}{dr} \left(r^2 \frac{dR}{dr} \right) + \left[\frac{1}{S \sin^2 \theta} \left(\frac{\partial^2 S}{\partial \phi^2} \right) + \frac{1}{S \sin \theta} \frac{\partial}{\partial \theta} \left(\sin \theta \cdot \frac{\partial S}{\partial \theta} \right) \right]$$
$$+ \frac{2m_0 r^2}{\hbar^2} \left(E + \frac{Zq^2}{4\pi\varepsilon_0 r} \right) = 0 . \tag{2.4-4}$$

The term in the square brackets is independent of r, and must, therefore be constant, say equal to $-A$. Therefore we have:

$$\frac{1}{S \sin^2 \theta} \left(\frac{\partial^2 S}{\partial \phi^2} \right) + \frac{1}{S \sin \theta} \frac{\partial}{\partial \theta} \left(\sin \theta \frac{\partial S}{\partial \theta} \right) + A = 0 . \tag{2.4-5}$$

Now if we write, $S(\theta, \phi)$ as $\Theta(\theta) . \Phi(\phi)$ we get:

$$\frac{1}{\Phi} \left(\frac{d^2 \Phi}{d\phi^2} \right) + \frac{\sin \theta}{\Theta} \frac{d}{d\theta} \left(\sin \theta \frac{d\Theta}{d\theta} \right) + A \sin^2 \theta = 0 . \tag{2.4-6}$$

The first term is independent of θ, so it must be constant. Hence we can write:

$$\left(\frac{d^2 \Phi}{d\phi^2} \right) + m^2 \Phi = 0 \tag{2.4-7}$$

where m is a constant.

The general solution of eqn (2.4-7) is:

$$\Phi = B_1 \exp(jm\phi) + B_2 \exp(-jm\phi) \tag{2.4-8}$$

where B_1 and B_2 are constants.

In order that Φ shall be a single-valued function of ϕ, m must be an integer.

From eqns (2.4-6) and (7),

$$\frac{1}{\sin \theta} \frac{d}{d\theta} \left(\sin \theta \frac{d\Theta}{d\theta} \right) + \left(A - \frac{m^2}{\sin^2 \theta} \right) \Theta = 0 . \tag{2.4-9}$$

Now, if θ is zero, $(1/\sin \theta)$ is infinite, and so there are only certain values of A for which Θ remains finite. It can, in fact, be shown that these values are given by $l(l+1)$ where l is zero or a positive integer. When l and m are integers, with the magnitude of m less than or equal to l, the solutions Θ of eqn (2.4-9) are, apart from a multiplicative, constant, the associated Legendre polynomials $P_l^m(\theta)$ [2.3]. Returning to eqn (2.4-4) and writing D for $[(2m_0 E)/\hbar^2]$ and C for $[(m_0 Z q^2)/(2\pi\varepsilon_0 \hbar^2)]$ we have:

$$\left(\frac{d^2 R}{dr^2}\right) + \frac{2}{r}\left(\frac{dR}{dr}\right) + \left(D + \frac{C}{r} - \frac{A}{r^2}\right)R = 0 . \qquad (2.4\text{-}10)$$

The nature of the solution depends primarily on the sign of D, and hence of the energy E, and can be either an elliptic or a hyperbolic function. This can be seen clearly if we make r large so that eqn (2.4-10) becomes:

$$\left(\frac{d^2 R}{dr^2}\right) + DR = 0 . \qquad (2.4\text{-}11)$$

When D is negative, the solution is elliptic and corresponds to a bound electron, hence letting

$$D = -\left(\frac{1}{r_0^2}\right) \qquad (2.4\text{-}12)$$

where r_0^2 is positive, the solution to eqn (2.4-11) is

$$R = K_1 \exp\left(\frac{\rho}{2}\right) + K_2 \exp\left(-\frac{\rho}{2}\right). \qquad (2.4\text{-}13)$$

Here, K_1 and K_2 are constants and ρ, a new variable, is $2(r/r_0)$. Only the term with the negative exponent is relevant for the bound electron, because the other term tends to infinity with r.

Let us assume that the general solution of eqn (2.4-10) is:

$$R = v(\rho) \exp\left(-\frac{\rho}{2}\right) \qquad (2.4\text{-}14)$$

where $v(\rho)$ is a new function of ρ.

This leads to the differential equation:

$$\left(\frac{d^2 v}{d\rho^2}\right) + \left(\frac{2}{\rho} - 1\right)\left(\frac{dv}{d\rho}\right) + \left[\left(\frac{r_0 C}{2} - 1\right)\frac{1}{\rho} - \frac{A}{\rho^2}\right]v = 0 . \qquad (2.4\text{-}15)$$

remembering that A has the value $l(l+1)$.

We now seek a solution for $v(\rho)$ in eqn (2.4-15) by assuming $v(\rho)$ is made up of the series

$$v(\rho) = \rho^k(a_0 + a_1\rho + a_2\rho^2 + \ldots + a_p\rho^p + \ldots) \qquad (2.4\text{-}16)$$

where k is not necessarily an integer. Substituting this series for $v(\rho)$ in eqn (2.4-15) gives

$$\sum_{p=0} a_p \left\{ (k+p)(k+p-1)\rho^{(k+p-2)} + \left(\frac{2}{\rho} - 1\right)(k+p)\rho^{(k+p-1)} \right.$$
$$\left. + \left[\left(\frac{r_0 C}{2} - 1\right)\frac{1}{\rho} - \frac{l(l+1)}{\rho^2} \right]\rho^{(k+p)} \right\}$$
$$= \sum_{p=0} a_p \left\{ \left[(k+p)(k+p+1) - l(l+1) \right]\rho^{(k+p-2)} \right.$$
$$\left. - \left(k+p+1 - \frac{r_0 C}{2}\right)\rho^{(k+p-1)} \right\} \equiv 0 . \qquad (2.4\text{-}17)$$

This is an identity as it must be true for all values of ρ, hence, the coefficients of every power of ρ must be zero. In particular, the coefficient of the lowest power of ρ that is $\rho^{(k-2)}$ is zero.

Therefore

$$k(k+1) = l(l+1) \qquad (2.4\text{-}18)$$

and so

$$k = l \qquad (2.4\text{-}19)$$

or

$$k = -(l+1) . \qquad (2.4\text{-}20)$$

We have already, from eqn (2.4-9), that either l is zero or a positive integer. By considering eqns (2.4-14) and (16), it can be seen that if we use the value of k from eqn (2.4-20), R tends to infinity as ρ, which is proportional to the radius of the electron orbit, tends to zero. Hence eqn (2.4-20) is not physically allowable.

If we now consider, in particular, the coefficient of $\rho^{(k+p-1)}$, which must also be zero, we have, when k equals l,

$$[(l+p+1)(l+p+2) - l(l+1)]a_{(p+1)} = \left[(l+p+1) - \frac{r_0 C}{2} \right]a_p = 0 .$$
$$(2.4\text{-}21)$$

Then $$\left(\frac{a_{(p+1)}}{a_p}\right) = \frac{l+p+1-\dfrac{r_0 C}{2}}{(l+p+1)(l+p+2)-l(l+1)}.$$ (2.4-22)

Now, the expansion of an exponential is given by the series

$$\exp(\rho) = \sum_{p=0}^{\infty} \frac{\rho^p}{p!}.$$ (2.4-23)

Therefore, for this expansion, the ratio of the coefficient of the power of $\rho^{(p+1)}$ to that of ρ^p is

$$\frac{a_{(p+1)}}{a_p} = \frac{1}{p+1}.$$ (2.4-24)

Hence, we see that for both eqns (2.4-22) and (24) $(a_{(p+1)}/a_p)$ tends to $(1/p)$ for large values of p. It follows that the series expansion of $v(\rho)$, eqn (2.4-16), is asymptotic to $\exp(\rho)$ for large values of ρ. This means that the function R, eqn (2.4-14), is asymptotic to $\exp(\rho/2)$ for large ρ. However, this is not a physically acceptable solution, as R increases with the size of the electron orbit, and ultimately tends to infinity with ρ.

Now, if the series $v(\rho)$ of eqn (2.4-16) terminates in a finite number of terms, R tends to zero as ρ tends to infinity because of the factor $\exp(-\rho/2)$ in eqn (2.4-14). This is then a physically acceptable solution. If the series terminates at the pth term, the coefficient $a_{(p+1)}$ must be zero so eqn (2.4-21),

$$\left[(l+p+1)-\frac{r_0 C}{2}\right]a_p = 0$$ (2.4-25)

is the required condition.

We then have, since a_p is non-zero,

$$r_0 C = 2(l+p+1) = 2n$$ (2.4-26)

where, as l and p are positive integers or zero, n is a positive integer.

Therefore

$$\left(\frac{C}{2n}\right)^2 = \left(\frac{1}{r_0}\right)^2$$ (2.4-27)

which, by means of eqn (2.4-12), gives

$$\left(\frac{C}{2n}\right)^2 = -D. \tag{2.4-28}$$

Now, substituting for C and D, after eqn (2.4-28), we have

$$\left(\frac{m_0 Z_q^2}{4\pi\varepsilon_0 \hbar^2}\right)^2 \left(\frac{1}{n^2}\right) = -\frac{2m_0 E_n}{\hbar^2} \tag{2.4-29}$$

where E_n corresponds to the energy for the nth integer. Hence

$$E_n = -\left(\frac{m_0 Z^2 q^4}{32\pi^2 \varepsilon_0^2 \hbar^2}\right)\left(\frac{1}{n^2}\right). \tag{2.4-30}$$

It will be seen that this equation is exactly the same as eqn (1.3-7) for the energy levels on the Bohr theory, and that n is the total or principal quantum number. We have also found that there are two additional quantum numbers l and m. The integer l can have any value from 0 to $(n-1)$ and is called the orbital quantum number. The integer m, called the magnetic quantum number, can have values such that its magnitude is less than or equal to l. For a detailed account of this topic see, for example ref. [2.4].

Table 2A

n	l	m	No. of states	Designation of states	Shell
1	0	0	1	$1s$	K
2	0	0	1	$2s$ ⎫	L
2	1	$-1, 0, +1$	3	$2p$ ⎬	
3	0	0	1	$3s$ ⎫	
3	1	$-1, 0, +1$	3	$3p$ ⎬	M
3	2	$-2, -1, 0, +1, +2$	5	$3d$ ⎭	
4	0	0	1	$4s$ ⎫	
4	1	$-1, 0, +1$	3	$4p$ ⎪	N
4	2	$-2, -1, 0, +1, +2$	5	$4d$ ⎬	
4	3	$-3, -2, -1, 0, +1, +2, +3$	7	$4f$ ⎭	

Table 2A gives the various combinations of n, l, and m which are possible, and the last two columns give the total number of states for each value of n and the designation of the electrons. Electrons in a state where l equals zero are called s electrons; where l is unity they are called p electrons and with l equal to 2, d electrons.

2.5 The Pauli Exclusion Principle

We have now an idea of the relationship governing the orbits of the electrons around a nucleus, and we come then to the question of how many electrons can have the same orbit. This will lead us to an understanding of how the periodic table is built up, and why certain groups of elements have some similar properties.

In 1925, Pauli expounded the principle that no two electrons associated with a particular atom can have the same set of quantum numbers; this is known as the *Pauli Exclusion Principle*. For further discussion see, for example, ref. [2.4]. It cannot be proved theoretically, but its application always leads to results in agreement with experiment.

2.6 Electron Spin

Table 2A indicates the number of states or orbits which can occur for various values of the principle quantum number, and we have seen from section 1.3 that transitions of electrons from one orbit to another account for the atomic line spectra; the main lines can be attributed to changes in the principal quantum number. However, the fine structure of a line results from the slight difference in the energy levels due to the other quantum numbers, but it is found that those so far mentioned are not able to account for the finest detail. It was suggested in 1925, by Uhlenberg and Goudsmit, that a further quantum number would explain this, and it was attributed to the spinning of the electron about its own axis, and the fact that it could, in a magnetic field, rotate either clockwise or anti-clockwise. The very fine structure was accounted for by giving this new quantum number s a value of $\pm\frac{1}{2}$ depending on its direction of rotation in the field. A mass of other detail of atomic structure confirms the additional quantum number, but there is doubt about it being due to electron spin.

By the use of the Pauli Exclusion Principle, we are now able to allocate two electrons to each of the states given in Table 2A.

2.7 The Periodic Table

If we investigate the elements, starting with the lightest, hydrogen, we find some interesting information on the relationship between the filled atomic orbits and the physical properties. In the case of hydrogen, for which Z equals one, it has only one electron which in its lowest state, called the ground state, has its principle quantum number n equal to one, and therefore l and m are both zero. It is thus as $1s$ electron in the K shell. Helium, with atomic number Z equal to two, has two orbital electrons, and as there are two $1s$ states corresponding to the two electron spins, they are both $1s$ electrons. The third element, lithium, with Z equal to three, has again two $1s$ electrons, but the third electron must have a principle quantum number, n equal to two, and is, therefore, a $2s$ electron in the L shell. Similarly, all the elements from lithium up to, and including, neon ($Z = 10$) have, in the ground state, their outer electrons in the L shell, but with neon the $2p$ state, or sub-shell, becomes full, and so the next element sodium ($Z = 11$), has its eleventh electron in the M shell where n equals three. Further electrons are added to the M shell until with argon ($Z = 18$) it is full; there are now 2 electrons in the K shell, 8 in the L shell and 8 in the M shell. It is found that the next element potassium ($Z = 19$) has the last electron in the $4s$ state, the N shell, rather than in the $3d$ state, that is the M shell. This is because the potential energy of an electron in a $4s$ state is lower than one in a $3d$ state. However, a $4p$ state corresponds to a higher energy than a $3d$ state, and so, after the two $4s$ electrons have been added the $3d$ state is filled. As the complete range of elements is gone through it is found that they break up into periods, the period being known by the principal quantum number of the highest s state filled. The reader is referred to books such as ref. 2.1, for a complete list of elements and a periodic table.

If the elements are grouped so that all the elements, except hydrogen, with one s-electron only in the outer shell are in Group I, those with two s-electrons in Group II, those with one p-electron in Group III, up to those with six p-electrons in Group VIII, it is found that the elements in a group, up to argon ($Z = 18$), have similar physical and chemical properties. Beyond argon the elements can still be classed in groups, but, as already pointed out, the sub-shells no longer fill in the order that might be expected from the state designation. It becomes apparent that the physical and chemical properties of the elements are

Table 2B.   *The semiconductor elements in the periodic table*

Period	Group III		Group IV		Group V	
II	B-5	$2p^1$	C*-6;	$2p^2$	N*-7	$2p^3$
III	A–13;	$3p^1$	Si-14;	$3p^2$	P-14;	$3p^3$
IV	Ga-31;	$4p^1$	Ge-32;	$4p^2$	As-33;	$4p^3$
V	In-49;	$5p^1$	Sn*-50;	$5p^2$	Sb-51;	$5p^3$

The element is followed by its atomic number, the designation of the electrons in the partly filled shell, and the superscript gives the number of electrons in the partly filled shell.
* These elements are not normally used in semiconductors.

largely determined by the extent to which a shell or sub-shell is filled. Good conductors in the main, are those with only partially filled shells, and good insulators have full shells. The part of the Periodic Table containing Groups III, IV, and V is given in Table 2B.

2.8 Semiconductor Materials

All the elements silicon, carbon, germanium and tin are in Group IV and have two s-electrons and two p-electrons in the outer shell. These elements form tetrahedral co-valent crystalline structures, as they have four electrons to make the bonds. The arrangement of the atoms and bonds in a unit cell is shown diagramatically in fig. 4.4a. One process of semiconduction, see section 4.4, arises from the breaking of these bonds by thermal energy. The elements carbon and grey tin are of no practical use as it is impossible at present to make suitable crystals of them, and in any case the energy gaps, see sections 2.19 and 4.2, are for practical purposes too large in the case of diamond and too small in the case of grey tin. This is because the co-valent bonds are too strong in diamond and too weak in tin.

Table 2C gives the important physical constants of silicon and germanium as semiconductor materials.

Table 2C

Element	Density kg/m³	Lattice constant A.U.	Melting point Deg.C	Energy gap eV	Mobility cm²/v-sec	
					holes	electrons
Si	2.33×10^3	5·431	1,420	1·12	480	1,350
Ge	5.33×10^3	5·657	936	0·75	1,900	3,900

2.9 Bloch Wave Functions

It is now proposed to develop a theory which will answer the question – What distinguishes a semiconductor from other materials? Some idea of the conduction processes in the lattice will also be forthcoming from the theory. However, to make the task reasonably manageable, the investigation will be restricted at present to a one-dimensional case – a row of equally spaced atoms, and it is then our task to investigate the behaviour of an electron when it experiences the periodically varying potential field associated with the atomic nuclei. It will be assumed that the remainder of the electrons contribute a uniform potential which will not affect the motion of the particular electron.

If the potential at a point x is $V(x)$, the Schrödinger equation for the electron can be written:

$$\left(\frac{d^2\psi}{dx^2}\right) + \frac{2m}{\hbar^2}\left[E - V(x)\right]\psi = 0 . \qquad (2.9\text{-}1)$$

This equation can be solved by a relationship for a plane wave of the type:

$$\psi = \exp(\pm jkx). \qquad (2.9\text{-}2)$$

On substituting this in eqn (2.9-1) we get the kinetic energy

$$E - V(x) = \frac{(\hbar k)^2}{2m} = \frac{p^2}{2m} \qquad (2.9\text{-}3)$$

where p is the momentum of the electron. It is therefore apparent that k is the momentum of the electron divided by $\hbar$. This quantity k is usually referred to as the wave number*. If variation with time is taken into account the solution of eqn (2.9-1) is $\exp(\pm jkx) \exp(j\omega t)$ which represents a wave propagated along the x-axis with a pulsatance ω which is equal to $(E/\hbar)$.

If the potential field is produced by the atoms, separated by a distance l it is reasonable to assume that the potential function $V(x)$ must obey the condition

$$V(x) = V(x+l) . \tag{2.9-4}$$

A theorem due to Bloch [2.5] states that if a function of this type is inserted in the Schrödinger eqn (2.9-1), the amplitude of the probability wave is a function of x namely:

$$\psi(x) = u_k(x) \exp(\pm jkx) \tag{2.9-5}$$

where

$$u_k(x) = u_k(x+l) \tag{2.9-6}$$

are known as Bloch functions. In the theory of differential equations this equation is known as Floquet's theorem, and whilst the reader is referred to Bloch's original paper for a complete statement, the following is adequate for our purposes. However, before the proof, it will be useful to note the following property of the Bloch functions that because, from eqn (2.9-5),

$$\psi(x+l) = u_k(x+l) \exp[jk(x+l)] . \tag{2.9-7}$$

Eqn (2.9-6) becomes,

$$\psi(x+l) = u_k(x) \exp(jkx) \exp(jkl) = \psi(x) . Q \tag{2.9-8}$$

where

$$Q = \exp(\pm jkl) . \tag{2.9-9}$$

* When three-dimensional considerations are involved, we refer to a wave vector **k** and its magnitude k, but in one-dimensional cases we refer to the wave number k, a scalar quantity, in order to obtain the simplicity of a non-vector form for the equations.

Because eqn (2.9-1) is a linear second order equation with real coefficients it has, in general, two independent real solutions $\psi_1(x)$ and $\psi_2(x)$. Any other solution of the equation can be expressed as a linear combination of these solutions. Hence $\psi_1(x+l)$ and $\psi_2(x+l)$ can be written

$$\psi_1(x+l) = \alpha_1\psi_1(x) + \alpha_2\psi_2(x) \tag{2.9-10}$$

$$\psi_2(x+l) = \beta_1\psi_1(x) + \beta_2\psi_2(x) \tag{2.9-11}$$

where the α's and β's are real functions of the energy of the wave.

From eqn (2.9-8), and (10) and (11), respectively

$$Q\psi_1(x) = \alpha_1\psi_1(x) + \alpha_2\psi_2(x) \tag{2.9-12}$$

and

$$Q\psi_2(x) = \beta_1\psi_1(x) + \beta_2\psi_2(x) . \tag{2.9-13}$$

Non-trivial solutions for $\psi_1(x)$ and $\psi_2(x)$ exist for this pair of linear homogeneous equations if, and only if, the determinant of their coefficients vanishes. Hence

$$\begin{vmatrix} \alpha_1 - Q, & \beta_1 \\ \alpha_2 & , \beta_2 - Q \end{vmatrix} = 0 \tag{2.9-14}$$

or $\qquad Q^2 - (\alpha_1 + \beta_2)Q + (\alpha_1\beta_2 - \alpha_2\beta_1) = 0 . \tag{2.9-15}$

Now from eqns (2.9-10) and (11), it can be shown that the determinant

$$\begin{vmatrix} \psi_1(x+l), & \psi_2(x+l) \\ \psi_1'(x+l), & \psi_2'(x+l) \end{vmatrix} = [\psi_1(x)\psi_2'(x) - \psi_2(x)\psi_1'(x)](\alpha_1\beta_2 - \alpha_2\beta_1)$$

$$= \begin{vmatrix} \psi_1(x), & \psi_2(x) \\ \psi_1'(x), & \psi_2'(x) \end{vmatrix} \begin{Vmatrix} \alpha_1, & \alpha_2 \\ \beta_1, & \beta_2 \end{Vmatrix} \tag{2.9-16}$$

where $\psi' = \dfrac{d\psi}{dx}$.

But if the solutions of a differential equation written in the form

$$\left(\frac{d^2\psi}{dx^2}\right) + f(x)\psi = 0 \tag{2.9-17}$$

are ψ_1 and ψ_2, we have

$$\psi_1 \psi_2'' + f \psi_1 \psi_2 = 0 \tag{2.9-18}$$

and

$$\psi_2 \psi_1'' + f \psi_2 \psi_1 = 0 \tag{2.9-19}$$

subtracting eqn (2.9-19) from eqn (2.9-18) gives:

$$0 = \psi_1 \psi_2'' - \psi_2 \psi_1'' = \frac{d}{dx}(\psi_1 \psi_2' - \psi_2 \psi_1') . \tag{2.9-20}$$

Therefore $(\psi_1 \psi_2' - \psi_2 \psi_1')$ is a constant, in particular it has the same value at x and $(x+l)$. Hence

$$\begin{vmatrix} \psi_1(x), & \psi_2(x) \\ \psi_1'(x), & \psi_2'(x) \end{vmatrix} = \begin{vmatrix} \psi_1(x+l), & \psi_2(x+l) \\ \psi_1'(x+l), & \psi_2'(x+l) \end{vmatrix}. \tag{2.9-21}$$

By the comparison of eqns (2.9-16) and (21) we must have

$$\begin{vmatrix} \alpha_1, & \alpha_2 \\ \beta_1, & \beta_2 \end{vmatrix} = 1 . \tag{2.9-22}$$

Hence eqn (2.9-15) becomes

$$Q^2 - (\alpha_1 + \beta_2)Q + 1 = 0 . \tag{2.9-23}$$

From the form of this equation, if the two solutions are Q_1 and Q_2, then $Q_1 \cdot Q_2$ is unity; that is Q_1 and Q_2 are conjugates.

Therefore from eqn (2.9-9)

$$Q_1 = \exp(jkl) \quad \text{and} \quad Q_2 = \exp(-jkl) . \tag{2.9-24}$$

But Q_1 and Q_2 are only complex if $(\alpha_1 + \beta_2)$ is less than 2, and as α_1 and β_2 are real functions of the energy, there are values of the energy for which eqns (2.9-24) cannot be fulfilled. When complex conjugate values of Q_1 and Q_2 exist, the corresponding functions ψ_1 and ψ_2 are then given by

$$\psi_1(x+l) = \psi_1(x)\exp(jkl) \quad \text{and} \quad \psi_2(x+l) = \psi_2(x)\exp(-jkl) \tag{2.9-25}$$

and these are Bloch functions as defined in eqn (2.9-8).

There can be no electronic energy levels in energy regions corresponding to real roots Q_1 and Q_2 of eqn (2.9-23), for then according to eqns (2.9-8) and (9), the wavefunctions could not be periodic as demanded by the physical condition of the problem. This concept of allowed and forbidden energy bands will be elaborated in the next section.

2.10 The Kronig-Penney Model

The complicated nature of the potential function $V(x)$ makes a rigorous solution of Schrödinger's equation, even for a one-dimensional array of atoms, exceedingly difficult. However, Kronig and Penney [2.6] made certain simplifications which make the mathematics manageable, and showed the important effect of a periodic potential function on the energies allowed to an electron and on its behaviour in electric fields, and it is reasonable to assume that a more rigorous treatment would still show the effects to be described.

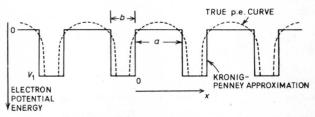

Figure 2.10a. The Kronig-Penney one-dimensional potential energy curve

Kronig and Penney simplified $V(x)$ so that it could be represented by a series of square potential wells as shown in fig. 2.10a. The period of the potential is $(a+b)$ equal to l, the separation of the atoms. In regions for which x lies between zero and a, the potential energy of the electrons is assumed to be zero, and in regions for which x lies between $-b$ and zero the potential energy is taken as V_1. The value of the Kronig-Penney model is that it enables us to take two Schrödinger equations for the different regions and by establishing continuity equations at the boundaries arrive at the electron energy considerations required.

We have, therefore, in one-dimension

$$\left(\frac{d^2\psi}{dx^2}\right) + \left(\frac{2mE}{\hbar^2}\right)\psi = 0 \; ; \qquad \text{for} \quad 0 \leqslant x \leqslant a \qquad (2.10\text{-}1)$$

and

$$\left(\frac{d^2\psi}{dx^2}\right) + \left(\frac{2m}{\hbar^2}\right)(E - V_1)\psi = 0 \; ; \quad \text{for} \quad -b \leqslant x \leqslant 0 \; . \qquad (2.10\text{-}2)$$

Writing for simplicity

$$\alpha^2 = \left(\frac{2mE}{\hbar^2}\right) \qquad (2.10\text{-}3)$$

and

$$\beta^2 = \left(\frac{2m}{\hbar^2}\right)(V_1 - E) \qquad (2.10\text{-}4)$$

we obtain for eqns (2.10-1) and (2) respectively

$$\psi'' + \alpha^2\psi = 0 \qquad (2.10\text{-}5)$$

and

$$\psi'' - \beta^2\psi = 0 \; . \qquad (2.10\text{-}6)$$

Bloch's theorem enables us to say that the form of the solutions is

$$\psi = u \exp(jkx) \; ; \qquad [\text{writing } u = u_k(x)] \qquad (2.10\text{-}7)$$

Hence

$$\psi' = (jku + u') \exp(jkx) \qquad (2.10\text{-}8)$$

and

$$\psi'' = (-k^2 u + 2jku' + u'') \exp(jkx) \; . \qquad (2.10\text{-}9)$$

Equation (2.10-9) is now substituted in eqns (2.10-5) and (6) giving

$$u'' + 2jku' + (\alpha^2 - k^2)u = 0 \qquad (2.10\text{-}10)$$

and

$$u'' + 2jku' - (\beta^2 + k^2)u = 0 \; . \qquad (2.10\text{-}11)$$

The solutions of this pair of equations are of the form

and

$$u_1 = A \exp[j(\alpha - k)x] + B \exp[-j(\alpha + k)x] \qquad (2.10\text{-}12)$$
$$u_2 = C \exp[(\beta - jk)x] + D \exp[-(\beta + jk)x] \; . \qquad (2.10\text{-}13)$$

A, B, C, and D are constants which can be determined from the conditions of continuity across the potential well walls, viz.

$$
\begin{aligned}
u_1(0) &= u_2(0) & u_1(a) &= u_2(-b) \\
u_1'(0) &= u_2'(0) & u_1'(a) &= u_2'(-b)
\end{aligned} \qquad (2.10\text{-}14)
$$

The use of these four equations enables four linear equations in A, B, C and D to be obtained. However, we are more interested in the condition that the four equations should have a non-trivial solution, that is, the condition that the determinant of the coefficients of A, B, C, and D is zero. This condition leads to the equation:

$$\left(\frac{\beta^2 - \alpha^2}{2\alpha\beta}\right) \sinh(\beta b)\sin(\alpha a) + \cosh(\beta b)\cos(\alpha a) = \cos[k(a+b)] . \quad (2.10\text{-}15)$$

To obtain a more convenient form, Kronig and Penney considered the case when the potential barriers become *delta functions*, that is, the case when V_1 is infinitely large, over an infinitesimal distance b, but the product $V_1 b$ remains finite. They let

$$\lim_{\substack{b \to 0 \\ \beta \to \infty}} \left(\frac{\beta^2 ab}{2}\right) = P . \quad (2.10\text{-}16)$$

Then eqn (2.10-15) becomes:

$$P\left[\frac{\sin(\alpha a)}{\alpha a}\right] + \cos(\alpha a) = \cos(ka) \quad (2.10\text{-}17)$$

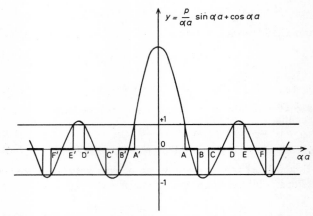

Figure 2.10b. Showing the allowed energy bands (heavy lines along αa-axis) for electrons in the Kronig-Penney model

since β is much larger than α and (βb) is very small.

This equation must have a solution for α, and hence for the energy E, see eqn (2.10-3), in order that the wave functions of the form given by eqns (2.10-12) and (13) can exist. Equation (2.10-17) is most conveniently solved graphically by plotting its left-hand side as a function of (αa), since the right-hand side of the equation is limited to the range -1 to $+1$. Figure 2.10b shows the form of the curve and the values of (αa) for which solutions of the equation exist, the values being indicated by thick lines along the (αa)-axis.

It is to be noted that the energy spectrum of the electrons is, therefore, broken up into a number of allowed energy bands separated by forbidden bands, and that the width of the allowed bands increases with the energy of the electron. It is also of interest that the width of the allowed bands decreases as P increases. Now P equals $(mV_1 ab/\hbar^2)$, and is therefore a measure of the magnitude of the potential barriers. Thus a large P corresponds to strong binding of an electron to a particular potential well, or atomic nucleus, and we see that with P tending to infinity, the energy bands are reduced to lines, and since the electrons are *infinitely* tightly bound to a particular nucleus, we have the spectrum of an isolated atom. In this case $\sin(\alpha a)/\alpha a$ tends to zero, and α equals $(n\pi/a)$ where n is a non-zero integer. Substituting for α, from eqn (2.10-3), gives

$$E_n = \frac{1}{2m} \left(\frac{\pi\hbar}{a} \right)^2 n^2 . \qquad (2.10\text{-}18)$$

This is seen to be similar to eqn (2.3-9) obtained for a particle in a box with a in place of L. This is to be expected as the electron is now absolutely confined to one well.

When P is zero, eqn (2.10-17) holds for all values of (αa). This situation corresponds to an electron in free space.

It is also very useful to plot a curve of E against k, which can also be done from eqn (2.10-17). If P equals zero we have

$$\cos(\alpha a) = \cos(ka)$$

or $$\alpha = k \qquad (2.10\text{-}19)$$

That is $$E \propto k^2 . \qquad (2.10\text{-}20)$$

If, however, P is finite, discontinuities occur at the edges of the bands. The first band AB and $A'B'$, (fig. 2.10b), extends from $\cos(ka)$ equal to one to $\cos(ka)$ equal to minus one, that is k ranges from zero to $\pm (\pi/a)$. In the second band, made up of CD and $C'D'$, k ranges from (π/a) to $(2\pi/a)$ and from $-(\pi/a)$ to $-(2\pi/a)$. It is therefore apparent that there are discontinuities at

$$k = \left(\frac{n\pi}{a}\right) ; \quad \text{for} \quad n = \pm 1, \pm 2, \pm 3, \ldots . \qquad (2.10\text{-}21)$$

We can also determine the slope of the E–k curve at the discontinuities by means of eqn (2.10-17). Let

$$f(E) = P \left[\frac{\sin(\alpha a)}{\alpha a}\right] + \cos(\alpha a) = \cos(ka) . \qquad (2.10\text{-}22)$$

Therefore

$$\left(\frac{df(E)}{dk}\right) = -a \sin(ka) . \qquad (2.10\text{-}23)$$

Now, at the band edges ka is $n\pi$, so that $\sin(ka)$ is zero. Therefore

$$\left(\frac{df(E)}{dk}\right) = f'(\alpha)\left(\frac{d\alpha}{dE}\right)\left(\frac{dE}{dk}\right) = 0 \qquad (2.10\text{-}24)$$

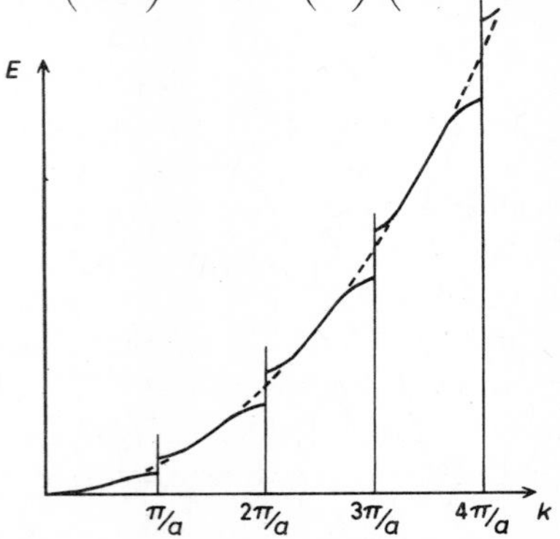

Figure 2.10c. The discontinuities in the E–k curve (The dotted curve represents $E \propto k$)

Since neither $\left(\dfrac{d\alpha}{dE}\right)$, see eqn (2.10-3), nor $f'(\alpha)$, see fig. (2.10-b), is zero at the band edges, it follows that

$$\left(\frac{dE}{dk}\right) = 0 \qquad (2.10\text{-}25)$$

at the edges of the band. Figure 2.10c shows a typical plot of the energy E against the wave number k.

Since $\cos(ka)$ equals $\cos(-ka)$, the E–k curve is symmetrical about the E-axis, and therefore the first band runs from $-(\pi/a)$ to (π/a), the second, in two halves runs from $-(2\pi/a)$ to $-(\pi/a)$ and (π/a) to $(2\pi/a)$. These bands are known as Brillouin zones, and will be dealt with more fully in sections 2.12 and 13.

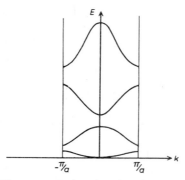

Figure 2.10d. The energy E plotted against the *reduced wave number*

From a further reference to eqn (2.10-17), it is apparent that the right-hand side of the equation has the same value if k is replaced by $(k+2\pi n/a)$ where n is an integer. Thus k is not uniquely determined, and it is often sufficient to refer to the *reduced wave number* which is limited to values of k between $-(\pi/a)$ and (π/a). The reduced wave number is plotted in fig. 2.10d.

2.11 The Maximum Number of Wave Functions per Band

So far we have not been concerned with the boundaries of the crystal, but if we now say that the crystal extends from x to $(x+L)$, a distance L in the x-direction, we must have the boundary condition

$$\psi(x+L) = \psi(x) . \tag{2.11-1}$$

This condition can be arrived at by considering the linear crystal to be bent into a circle so that the nucleus at x is the same as the one at $(x+L)$ [2.7].

Also, from the Bloch function, we have

$$\exp[jk(x+L)]u_k(x+L) = \exp(jkx)u_k(x). \tag{2.11-2}$$

But because of the periodicity of u_k, we have

$$u_k(x+L) = u_k(x) . \tag{2.11-3}$$

Therefore, dividing eqn (2.11-2) by eqn (2.11-3) gives

$$\exp[jk(x+L)] = \exp(jkx) \tag{2.11-4}$$

which leads to

$$k = \left(\frac{2\pi}{L}\right) n ; \quad \text{with} \quad n = \pm 1, \pm 2, \pm 3, \ldots \tag{2.11-5}$$

For any one band k extends over a range of $(2\pi/a)$, so we get that

$$\left(\frac{2\pi}{L}\right) n = \left(\frac{2\pi}{a}\right)$$

or

$$n = \left(\frac{L}{a}\right). \tag{2.11-6}$$

The integer n is then the maximum number of wave functions per band. If n is large, (L/a) is equal to the number of atoms in the length L, so we see that, in effect, each atom can contribute one wave function to each band. Now, each wave function is associated with a single energy level, so we arrive at the result that the number of electron energy levels in a band is equal to the number of atoms in the system. This result can be extended to the three-dimensional case. It should be noted that by the Pauli Exclusion Principle each energy level can accommodate two electrons.

2.12 The Physical Significance of the Discontinuities in the $E-k$ Curve

We will now try to see the physical reason leading to forbidden energy bands at particular values of the wave number k. The Kronig-Penney model leads to discontinuities in the $E–k$ curve at values of k of $(n\pi/a)$ for a one-dimensional lattice of atomic spacing a.

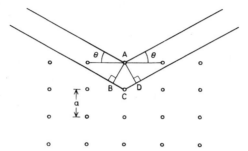

Figure 2.12a. Conditions for the constructive interference of waves (Bragg)

Let us consider a parallel pencil of rays incident on two atoms A and C, fig. 2.12a. The condition that the reflected pencil has maximum intensity is that the path BCD is an integral number (n) of wavelengths, that is

$$2a \sin \theta = n\lambda . \tag{2.12-1}$$

This is known as Bragg's Law [2.8], and was originally derived to account for the reflection of X-rays from crystals. If, now we consider a linear one-dimensional array of atoms in the direction AC, a wave incident at an angle θ of $(\pi/2)$ will be reflected if

$$2a = n\lambda . \tag{2.12-2}$$

Now, as k is $(2\pi/\lambda)$ the condition becomes

$$k = \left(\frac{n\pi}{a}\right) \tag{2.12-3}$$

which is the value of k at which the energy discontinuity occurs. It appears, therefore, that the energy is reflected for waves with this value of the wave number, and therefore, standing waves are produced instead of the travelling waves at other values of k. The region in k-space between $-(\pi/a)$ and (π/a), where n equals unity, is the first Brillouin zone. For a value of n equal to 2, we again have a standing wave, and the two regions between $-(2\pi/a)$ to $-(\pi/a)$ and (π/a) to $(2\pi/a)$ make up the second Brillouin zone.

2.13 Brillouin Zones in Two- and Three-Dimensions

So far we have considered the motion of electrons in one-dimension only, and the one-dimensional Brillouin zones. Brillouin [2.9] has emphasized the importance of the shape of the zones in **k**-space on the electrical characteristics of the material, so it is important to understand the method by which the shapes of constant energy surfaces and Brillouin zones are found in two- and three-dimensional lattices.

Now, Brillouin zone edges are determined, as we have seen in section 2.12 by finding the position and inclination of surfaces in **k**-space which reflect the electron waves normally so it is necessary to extend Bragg's law to apply to two- and three-dimensional lattices. First, it is necessary to be able to specify particular planes of atoms with respect to the major axes of the crystal. This is done by means of *Miller indices*, which are obtained in the following way. Suppose a particular plane of a set of parallel planes makes intercepts pa, qb, and rc with the three major

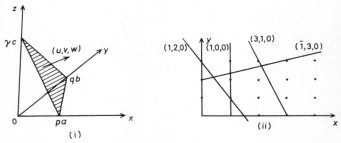

Figure 2.13a. The identification of planes in a crystal by Miller indices

axes which are not necessarily orthogonal, fig. 2.13a(i), where a, b, and c are the dimensions of the unit cell. The *Miller indices* of the planes are then given by u, v and w, where the following relation holds

$$u:v:w = \left(\frac{1}{p}\right):\left(\frac{1}{q}\right):\left(\frac{1}{r}\right). \qquad (2.13\text{-}1)$$

The quantities u, v, and w must be the smallest integers that satisfy eqn (2.13-1). The *Miller indices* of a set of parallel planes are usually enclosed in brackets thus (u, v, w). If one of the intercepts is negative the resulting index is shown thus $\bar{u}$. Some typical planes are shown in fig. 2.13a(ii), where for simplicity of representation they are all drawn

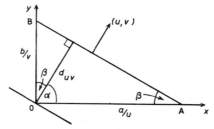

Figure 2.13b. The spacing between the parallel planes (u, v)

parallel to the z-axis. In most crystal lattices [2.10] some of the planes are equivalent, and the indices are then placed in braces thus $\{u, v, w\}$. For example the six cube faces $(1, 0, 0)$, $(0, 0, 1)$, $(\bar{1}, 0, 0)$, $(0, 0, \bar{1})$, $(0, 1, 0)$ and $(0, \bar{1}, 0)$ are written as $\{1, 0, 0\}$.

In order to use Bragg's law, it is necessary to know the spacing between the planes, which can be found by simple geometry for the two-dimensional lattice, and then extended to the three-dimensional case. Consider a plane AB, as in fig. 2.13b, with the origin of the co-ordinate system O in the next parallel plane, so that d_{uv} is the spacing between planes with Miller indices u, v. From the figure, we have

$$\cos \beta = \left(\frac{v}{b}\right) d_{uv} = \left(\frac{u}{a}\right)\left[\left(\frac{a}{u}\right)^2 - d_{uv}^2\right]^{\frac{1}{2}} \qquad (2.13\text{-}2)$$

which leads to

$$d_{uv} = \frac{1}{\left[\left(\dfrac{u}{a}\right)^2 + \left(\dfrac{v}{b}\right)^2\right]^{\frac{1}{2}}}. \qquad (2.13\text{-}3)$$

In a square lattice a and b are equal, so eqn (2.13-3) becomes

$$d_{uv} = \frac{a}{(u^2 + v^2)^{\frac{1}{2}}}$$

In a three-dimensional lattice, of lattice constants a, b, and c, the equivalent equations are

$$d_{uvw} = \frac{1}{\left[\left(\dfrac{u}{a}\right)^2 + \left(\dfrac{v}{b}\right)^2 + \left(\dfrac{w}{c}\right)^2\right]^{\frac{1}{2}}} \qquad (2.13\text{-}5)$$

and for the cubic lattice

$$d_{uvw} = \frac{a}{(u^2 + v^2 + w^2)^{\frac{1}{2}}}. \qquad (2.13\text{-}6)$$

Now, if we take the condition for standing waves obtained from Bragg's law, (eqn 2.12-3), we have

$$k_{uvw} = n\pi \left[\left(\frac{u}{a}\right)^2 + \left(\frac{v}{b}\right)^2 + \left(\frac{w}{c}\right)^2\right]^{\frac{1}{2}} \qquad (2.13\text{-}7)$$

where k_{uvw} is the magnitude of the wave vector $\mathbf{k}_{uvw}$ normal to the plane u, v, w. If $\mathbf{k}_{uvw}$ is resolved into its components k_x in the x-direction, k_y in the y-direction, and k_z in the z-direction we obtain*

* If the wave vector k_{uvw} makes angles α, β, and γ, with the wave vectors k_x, k_y, and k_z, respectively, then

$$k_x = k_{uvw} \cos\alpha, \quad k_y = k_{uvw} \cos\beta \quad \text{and} \quad k_z = k_{uvw} \cos\gamma$$

Therefore

$$k_x \cos\alpha + k_y \cos\beta + k_z \cos\gamma = k_{uvw}(\cos^2\alpha + \cos^2\beta + \cos^2\gamma) = k_{uvw}$$

Also, it can be seen from an extension to three dimensions of fig. 2.13b, that

$$\cos\alpha = \frac{d_{uvw}}{a/u}, \quad \cos\beta = \frac{d_{uvw}}{b/v}, \quad \text{and} \quad \cos\gamma = \frac{d_{uvw}}{c/w}$$

$$\left(\frac{u}{a}\right)k_x + \left(\frac{v}{b}\right)k_y + \left(\frac{w}{c}\right)k_z = n\pi\left[\left(\frac{u}{a}\right)^2 + \left(\frac{v}{b}\right)^2 + \left(\frac{w}{c}\right)^2\right]. \quad (2.13\text{-}8)$$

In a cubic lattice eqn (2.13-8) becomes:

$$uk_x + vk_y + wk_z = \frac{n\pi}{a}(u^2 + v^2 + w^2). \quad (2.13\text{-}9)$$

2.14 Brillouin Zones in a Square Lattice

(The reader is referred to L. Brillouin [2.9], p. 131 for a treatment of the three-dimensional case.)

As an example of the application of eqn (2.13-9) to determine Brillouin zones, we will examine a square lattice of constant a, where the equation reduces to

$$uk_x + vk_y = \frac{n\pi}{a}(u^2 + v^2). \quad (2.14\text{-}1)$$

It is important to realize that eqn (2.14-1) gives the outer contour of the appropriate zone, and the Brillouin zone is the area between this outer contour and the next one in. Table 2D gives the Miller indices of the lines forming the outer contours and the corresponding zones. The first seven zones are shown in fig. 2.14a(i).

It is important to note that one property of Brillouin zones is that they are all the same size for a given reciprocal lattice*, which must be so, as all the zones can be reduced to the first. Figure 2.14a(ii) shows that

---

Hence substituting for $\cos \alpha$, $\cos \beta$, and $\cos \gamma$, we get

$$\left(\frac{u}{a}\right)k_x + \left(\frac{v}{b}\right)k_y + \left(\frac{w}{c}\right)k_z = \frac{k_{uvw}}{d_{uvw}}.$$

Therefore, by means of eqns (2.13-5) and (7),

$$\left(\frac{u}{a}\right)k_x + \left(\frac{v}{b}\right)k_y + \left(\frac{w}{c}\right)k_z = n\pi\left[\left(\frac{u}{a}\right)^2 + \left(\frac{v}{b}\right)^2 + \left(\frac{w}{c}\right)^2\right].$$

* A reciprocal lattice is one where the distances along the axes are inversely proportional to the lattice constants [2.11].

Table 2D

Miller indices			Brillouin zone boundary
u	v	n	
± 1	0	$1 \big\}$	1st Zone
0	± 1	1	
± 1	± 1	1	2nd Zone
± 2	0	$1 \big\}$	3rd Zone (n.b. 1st zone boundary
0	± 2	1	extended to intercept)
± 2	± 1	$1 \big\}$	4th, 5th and 6th Zones
± 1	± 2	1	(moving out from centre)
0	± 3	$1 \Big\}$	
± 3	0	1	7th Zone
± 1	± 1	2	

this property is exhibited by the construction used to produce fig. 2.14a(i).

2.15 The Tightly Bound and Nearly Free Electron Approximations [2.11], [2.12], [2.13].

The square shape of the electron potential function adopted by Kronig and Penney gives, as we have seen in section 2.10, an exact solution for the variation of electron energy with electron momentum, but this potential distribution is obviously far from the true one. Two other approximations are worth brief consideration.

In the tightly bound electron approximation it is assumed that the orbital electrons in a particular atom are only slightly affected by the presence of the neighbouring atoms. Hence the approximation is only valid for electrons in the inner electronic shells, which are relatively far away from the other atoms. Here, in fact, atomic orbitals are combined to represent an electronic state extending through the crystal. The approximation is often referred to as the linear combination of atomic orbitals (LCAO). The method shows that if N similar atoms, each with the same set of electronic states, are brought together, so that the orbitals overlap, all the states split into N closely spaced states; fig. 2.15a. Hence,

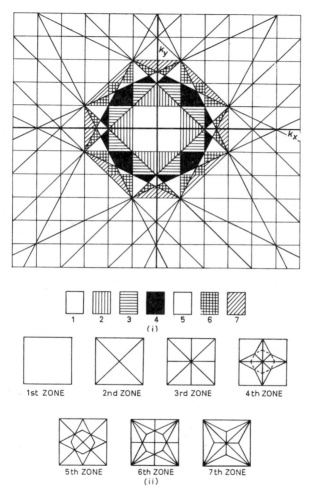

Figure 2.14a(i). Brillouin zones for a square lattice
(ii). The zones reduced to the first zone

the final function must be a combination of the individual atomic orbitals. One of the principal objections to this approximation is that in regions away from the atomic cores, the potential is fairly constant, and this method is therefore inapplicable. This is the case when the electron behaves as if it were nearly free.

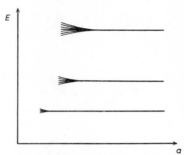

Figure 2.15a. Energy levels for single atoms broadening into bands as the atomic spacing *a* is decreased

Hence we are led to attack the problem by considering the electrons to be nearly free, a method called the nearly free electron (NFE) approximation. The energy E of a free electron is given by

$$E = \frac{1}{2m}(\hbar\mathbf{k})^2 = \frac{1}{2m}(\hbar k)^2 \qquad (2.15\text{-}1)$$

where $\mathbf{k}$ is the wave vector and k is the magnitude of the wave vector, and is proportional to the electron momentum. Therefore, for a free electron the E–k curve is parabolic. When the presence of the other atoms and electrons in the crystal are taken into account, discontinuities occur in the E–k curve at values of k equal to $(n\pi/a)$, fig. 2.10c, that is, at the Brillouin zone edges. The variation of energy with the wave vector is found by expressing the potential as a Fourier series, where the Fourier coefficients are now small compared with the average potential. In practice, it is apparent that this is only true at appreciable distances away from the atomic nuclei.

It is of interest to see the difference in the constant energy curves for the tight binding and nearly free electron approximations, but before showing this the shape of the curve near the corners of a square lattice can be found as follows.

Let E_0 be the energy at a corner of the Brillouin zone square, and E the energy of a wave vector distance δk_x and δk_y from the corner. Then, by Taylor's theorem, we have approximately

$$E - E_0 = \left(\frac{\partial E}{\partial k_x}\right)(\delta k_x) + \tfrac{1}{2}\left(\frac{\partial^2 E}{\partial k_x^2}\right)(\delta k_x)^2 + \tfrac{1}{2}\left(\frac{\partial^2 E}{\partial k_x \partial k_y}\right)(\delta k_x)(\delta k_y)$$
$$+ \left(\frac{\partial E}{\partial k_y}\right)(\delta k_y) + \tfrac{1}{2}\left(\frac{\partial^2 E}{\partial k_y^2}\right)(\delta k_y)^2 + \ldots \qquad (2.15\text{-}2)$$

where the partial derivatives are all taken at a corner. However, we have already found, in section 2.10, that in one-dimension (dE/dk) is zero at the edge of a band, so that, extended to two-dimensions, it is reasonable to assume that

$$\left(\frac{\partial E}{\partial k_x}\right) = \left(\frac{\partial E}{\partial k_y}\right) = 0 \qquad (2.15\text{-}3)$$

at the corner of a Brillouin zone. Hence eqn (2.15-2) becomes

$$E - E_0 = \tfrac{1}{2}\left(\frac{\partial^2 E}{\partial k_x^2}\right)(\delta k_x)^2 + \tfrac{1}{2}\left(\frac{\partial^2 E}{\partial k_y^2}\right)(\delta k_y)^2 + \ldots \qquad (2.15\text{-}4)$$

In a square lattice, the second derivatives of E with respect to k_x and k_y are equal, so eqn (2.15-4) reduces to

$$E - E_0 = \tfrac{1}{2}\left(\frac{\partial^2 E}{\partial k_x^2}\right)\{(\delta k_x)^2 + (\delta k_y)^2\} + \ldots \qquad (2.15\text{-}5)$$

Equation (2.15-5) shows that near the corners of a Brillouin zone square the constant energy contours are quadrants of a circle; this result is independent of the type of electron energy approximation used. Constant energy contours for the tight binding and nearly free electron are shown in fig. 2.15b.

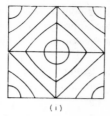 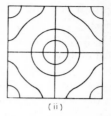

(i)　　　　　　　　　　　　　　(ii)

Figure 2.15b. Constant energy contours in the first Brillouin zone of a two-dimensional square lattice (i) on the tight binding approximation, and (ii) on the nearly free electron approximation

It is interesting to note that both approximations give similar contours at the centre and at the corners of a zone, and as semiconductors have nearly full bands or almost empty bands, the type of approximation used is unimportant. The type used is, in fact, only important when dealing with metals, as only these materials have appreciably filled bands, as will be mentioned in section 2.19.

2.16 The Density of States in Energy Bands

When we considered the maximum number of wave functions permitted in a band, we obtained the expression, eqn (2.11-5), that in one-dimension the allowed wave numbers are given by

$$k = \left(\frac{2\pi}{L} \right) n$$

where L is the length of the crystal, and n is an integer. If we consider a three-dimensional **k**-space, the allowed wave numbers will be spaced at intervals of $2\pi/L$ in the k_x, k_y, and k_z directions for a cube of crystal of side L. If the number of allowed waves in the three directions are n_1, n_2, and n_3, respectively, we have

$$k_x = \left(\frac{2\pi}{L} \right) n_1 \tag{2.16-1}$$

$$k_y = \left(\frac{2\pi}{L}\right) n_2 \qquad (2.16\text{-}2)$$

$$k_z = \left(\frac{2\pi}{L}\right) n_3 . \qquad (2.16\text{-}3)$$

These three relations must be satisfied for each point in **k**-space where there is an allowed wave number. Now, we can divide **k**-space into cubes of side $2\pi/L$; the co-ordinates of corners of the cubes will then satisfy the three equations, and it becomes apparent that, in fact, each cube contributes one allowed wave number, and, therefore, one energy state. Each cube has a volume of $8\pi^3/L^3$. Now, a sphere in **k**-space of radius k has a volume of $(4\pi/3)k^3$, and hence the number of states it can contain is $(L^3 k^3)/(6\pi^2)$, for a crystal of volume L^3. Therefore the density of allowed states up to a wave vector **k** is $k^3/6\pi^2$. From section 2.15, we have, where the constant energy contours are spherical,

$$k = \frac{2\pi(2mE)^{\frac{1}{2}}}{h} .$$

Hence the density of allowed states up to an energy E is $[4\pi(2mE)^{\frac{3}{2}}]/3h^3$. From this we obtain the density of allowed states in an energy range dE, which is written as $N(E)dE$, by differentiation, thus

$$N(E)dE = \frac{4\pi}{h^3}(2m)^{\frac{3}{2}} E^{\frac{1}{2}} dE , \qquad (2.16\text{-}4)$$

where allowance has been made for the doubling due to spin. This result will be obtained by a different method in chapter 3.

It is seen from eqn (2.16-4) that $N(E)$ increases as $E^{\frac{1}{2}}$, assuming that the mass of the electron is constant. However, for values of the wave vector greater than (π/a), the density decreases because the spherical constant energy surfaces are intersected by the Brillouin zone edges. In fact, in a cubic lattice the density falls to zero when the wave vector equals $(\pi/a\sqrt{3})$. The shape of the density of states curve for free electrons is shown in fig. 2.16a. Now, if the energy contours are not spherical, but are as shown in fig. 2.15b, the density of states curve is as in fig. 2.16a(ii). For values of the energy when the density is low the curve

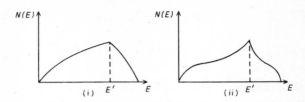

Figure 2.16a. Density of states for a cubic lattice (E' is energy at which $k = \pi/a$)

　　　(i) assuming spherical energy contours (free electrons)

　　　(ii) assuming partly bound electron energy contours

is of the $E^{\frac{1}{2}}$ shape, because both in the centre, and at the corners, the energy contours are spherical.

2.17 The Motion of Electrons in a One-Dimensional Model

It is reasonable to assume that an electron moves with the group velocity of its associated wave packet. If the equation of the wave is given by

$$\psi(x, t) = u_k(x) \exp\left[j(kx - \omega t)\right] \tag{2.17-1}$$

then the group velocity v can be shown to be [2.1]

$$v = \left(\frac{d\omega}{dk}\right). \tag{2.17-2}$$

Now, the energy E of an electron wave is given by

$$E = hv = \hbar\omega . \tag{2.17-3}$$

Hence, the group velocity,

$$v = \frac{1}{\hbar} \cdot \left(\frac{dE}{dk}\right). \tag{2.17-4}$$

If a force F is exerted on an electron in a Brillouin zone for a time dt, the increase in the energy dE of the electron will be

$$dE = Fv\,dt = \frac{F}{\hbar}\left(\frac{dE}{dk}\right)dt \tag{2.17-5}$$

but
$$dE = \left(\frac{dE}{dk}\right) dk \, . \qquad (2.17\text{-}6)$$

Hence
$$\left(\frac{dk}{dt}\right) = \left(\frac{F}{\hbar}\right) . \qquad (2.17\text{-}7)$$

Now the acceleration f of the electron is given by
$$f = \left(\frac{dv}{dt}\right) = \frac{1}{\hbar}\left(\frac{d^2 E}{dk^2}\right) \cdot \left(\frac{dk}{dt}\right) . \qquad (2.17\text{-}8)$$

Hence
$$f = \frac{F}{\hbar^2}\left(\frac{d^2 E}{dk^2}\right) . \qquad (2.17\text{-}9)$$

Now, the acceleration of a free electron of mass m by a force F is given by
$$f' = \left(\frac{F}{m}\right) . \qquad (2.17\text{-}10)$$

Comparison of the forms of eqns (2.17-9) and (10), leads to the result that an electron in a Brillouin zone behaves as if its mass were
$$\left[\frac{\hbar^2}{\left(\dfrac{d^2 E}{dk^2}\right)}\right] .$$

This is called the effective mass m^* of the electron. Hence
$$m^* = \left[\frac{\hbar^2}{\left(\dfrac{d^2 E}{dk^2}\right)}\right] . \qquad (2.17\text{-}11)$$

It is of interest to note that at the points of inflection on the E–k curve, the effective mass is infinite. The ratio of the true mass of the electron to its effective mass (m/m^*) is of considerable importance, and it is given the symbol f_K.
$$f_K = \left(\frac{m}{\hbar^2}\right)\left(\frac{d^2 E}{dk^2}\right) . \qquad (2.17\text{-}12)$$

If f_K is greater than unity, the electron behaves as if it were lighter than a free electron, and if f_K is less than unity, the electron behaves as if it were heavier than a free electron. The variation of v, m^* and f_K according to the Kronig-Penney model is shown in fig. 2.17a. It should be pointed out that the m^* and f_k curves of this figure have the same form whether E is a minimum or maximum at k equal to zero, (see fig. 2.10d).

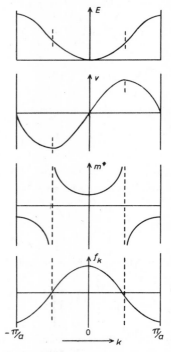

Figure 2.17a. Kronig-Penney curves for energy E, velicity v, effective mass m^* and f_k, as a function of k

2.18 The Effective Number of Conduction Electrons

We are now in a position to shed some light on the conductivity of materials, because the sum of the ratios f_K for each electron in a band tells us to how many free electrons the N in a band are equivalent.

For example, if the electrons are free, that is f_K is unity for each one, the sum will obviously give the total of electrons.

We have therefore, the effective number of electrons N_{eff} given by

$$N_{eff} = \Sigma f_K . \tag{2.18-1}$$

In a one-dimensional lattice of length L, the number of energy states in an interval dk is, see section 2.16, $(L.dk/2\pi)$, and therefore, allowing for

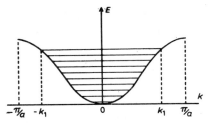

Figure 2.18a. Showing an energy band filled to k_1 on the Kronig-Penney model

electron spin, the number is $(L.dk/\pi)$. Hence, we see from fig. 2.18a, that

$$N_{eff} = \left(\frac{L}{\pi}\right)\int_{-k_1}^{k_1} f_k dk = \left(\frac{2Lm}{\pi\hbar^2}\right)\int_0^{k_1}\left(\frac{d^2 E}{dk^2}\right) dk$$

$$= \left(\frac{2Lm}{\pi\hbar^2}\right)\left(\frac{dE}{dk}\right)_{k=k_1}. \tag{2.18-2}$$

It is, therefore, immediately obvious that a full band does not contribute to conduction processes at all since $(dE/dk)_{(\pi/a)}$ is zero. On the Kronig-Penney model the maximum conductivity will occur for those materials in which the highest partly filled band is full to the point of inflection on the E–k curve. It should be emphasized that this only applies to the Kronig-Penney model, and in one-dimension. The three-dimensional case considerably complicates the situation, and in particular, what may appear to be an energy gap in one direction may not be in another direction.

2.19 The Difference Between Insulators, Metals and Semiconductors

We have already seen that if all the occupied energy bands in a material are full, there are no electrons available for conduction, and so the material is an insulator. If, however, the highest occupied band is not full, electrons are available for conduction processes, and so the material has metallic properties.

This is true at the absolute zero of temperature, as no account has, so far, been taken of the thermal energies of the electrons. However, if the temperature of the material is high enough for some electrons to have sufficient thermal energy to be excited from the highest full band to the next band up, conduction is possible, both by the excited electron, which is now said to be in the *conduction band*, and because the one time full band is now not full. The electrons in this band, known as the *valence band*, are now able to contribute to the conduction process. A material in which it is possible to excite an electron from a full band to an empty band is known as an *intrinsic semiconductor*. The size of the *forbidden gap* between the two bands is obviously of great importance in determining the temperature needed to make an insulator conduct. For instance diamond, with a forbidden gap of 7 eV, would need to be raised to about 2,000°K before appreciable semiconduction would occur, but germanium and silicon with gaps of 0·75 eV and 1·12 eV respectively, are semiconductors at room temperatures. Figure 2.19a shows diagrammatically the difference between the three types of material.

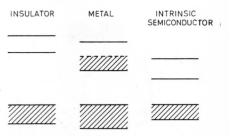

Figure 2.19a. The difference in electron energy distributions in insulators, metals, and intrinsic semiconductors, at the absolute zero of temperature

One very important difference between metals and semiconductors, which emphasizes the difference in the conduction processes in each, is concerned with the temperature coefficient of resistance. In metals, a rise in temperature increases the thermal agitation of the atoms and tends to increase the resistance, but there is no change in the density of the conduction electrons. Hence, metals have a positive temperature coefficient of resistance. However, in semiconductors, whilst there may be a small increase in the resistance due to thermal agitation as the temperature rises, there is also a large increase in the number of conduction electrons, so the temperature coefficient of resistance is negative.

2.20 The Hole

We have just seen that in a semiconductor at an elevated temperature some electrons from the full valence band will be excited to the conduction band. This leaves unoccupied energy levels in the valence band, and these are known as *positive holes*, or more often, simply as *holes*.

It is important to know both the charge and mass of a hole before discussing conduction processes, and this can be done by considering the case of a full band in which there will be no conduction electrons, and then removing one electron. We have, the current element $\mathbf{I}$ made up of the sum of the movements of all the i electrons of charge q moving with velocity $\mathbf{v}_i$. Hence,

$$\mathbf{I} = -\sum_i q\mathbf{v}_i = -q(\mathbf{v}_j + \sum_{i \neq j} \mathbf{v}_i) = 0 \qquad (2.20\text{-}1)$$

for a full band. Now, if the jth electron is removed from the band, leaving a hole, the current element $\mathbf{I}'$ is now

$$\mathbf{I}' = -q \sum_{i \neq j} \mathbf{v}_i = q\mathbf{v}_j . \qquad (2.20\text{-}2)$$

From this equation it is seen that the current is moving in the same direction as the absent charge, and so the hole has in effect a positive charge q. Now, if we apply an external force $\mathbf{F}$, we know from the three-dimensional form of eqn (2.17-10) that, for the hole the acceleration is

$$\mathbf{f}'_h = -\left(\frac{\mathbf{F}}{m_j^*}\right) \qquad (2.20\text{-}3)$$

since the hole charge is of opposite sign to the electronic charge.

But
$$\mathbf{f}'_h = \left(\frac{d\mathbf{v}_j}{dt}\right). \tag{2.20-4}$$

Hence
$$\frac{d\mathbf{v}_j}{dt} = -\left(\frac{\mathbf{F}}{m_j^*}\right). \tag{2.20-5}$$

Now, the holes will almost certainly be at the top of the valence band, where m_j^* is negative, see fig. 2.17a, and so the right-hand side of eqn (2.20-5) is positive. This means that the hole behaves as if it has a positive effective mass.

References

[2.1] See for example BORN, M. (1963), *Atomic physics*, pp. 92,348. Blackie.

[2.2] DAVISSON, C. and GERMER, L. H. (1927), 'Diffraction of electrons by a crystal of nickel', *Phys. Rev.*, **30**, 705–40.

[2.3] See for example: PIPES, L. A. (1946), *Applied mathematics for engineers and physicists*, pp. 353, and 331–2, McGraw-Hill.

[2.4] LOTHIAN, G. F. (1963), *Electrons in atoms*, pp. 89–104, and chapter 8, Butterworth.

[2.5] BLOCH, F. (1928), 'Quantum mechanics of electrons in crystal lattices', *Z. Physik*, **52**, 555–600.

[2.6] KRONIG, R. DE L. and PENNEY, W. G. (1930), 'Quantum mechanics of electrons in crystal lattices, *Proc. Roy. Soc.*, **A130**, 499–513.

[2.7] SHOCKLEY, W. (1950), *Electrons and holes in semiconductors*, p. 143, Van Nostrand.

[2.8] BRAGG, W. L. (1913), 'Diffraction of short electromagnetic waves by a crystal', *Proc. Camb. Phil. Soc.*, **17**, 43–51.

[2.9] BRILLOUIN, L. (1953), *Wave propagation in periodic structures*, Dover Publications.

[2.10] A more thorough study of crystallography will be found in BARRETT, C. S. (1952), *Structure of metals*, McGraw-Hill.

[2.11] ZIMAN, J. M. (1964), *Principles of the theory of solids*, Cambridge Univ. Press.

[2.12] DEKKER, A. J. (1962), *Solid state physics*, MacMillan.

[2.13] JONES, H. (1962), *Theory of brillouin zones and electronic states in crystals*, North-Holland.

CHAPTER 3

Statistical Mechanics

In this chapter it is proposed to deal only with those aspects of statistical mechanics relevant to the understanding of energy distributions of charge carriers in metals and semiconductors. Consequently the thermodynamic implications of statistical mechanics will not be dealt with in any detail. Some knowledge of elementary thermodynamics is required in order to understand the foundation of the theory.

3.1 Probability

The study of statistical mechanics enables us to calculate the energy distribution of current carriers in a system in thermodynamic equilibrium, but before we are in a position to do this we must first consider a term called the *thermodynamic probability*. The thermodynamic probability of finding a certain distribution is defined as the number of *favourable* cases or ways in which the final distribution can be realized, and is not to be confused with the mathematical definition of probability, which is the thermodynamic probability divided by the number of possible cases or ways in which the final distribution can be realized. When dealing with a large number of particles (charge carriers) the thermodynamic probability is a large number, whereas the mathematical probability has a maximum value of unity, which corresponds to certainty.

To obtain a mathematical statement of the thermodynamic probability let us consider, for example, the distribution of N distinguishable objects, one in each of N cells. In the first cell we can place any of the N objects, in the second any one of the $(N-1)$ objects, and so on. Hence the total number of distinguishable arrangements is $N(N-1)(N-2)\ldots$, that is $N!$

Now, if we have more objects than cells, say, for instance that some of the cells are combined, then the number of ways of obtaining the final arrangement is reduced. For instance, if two of the cells are amalgamated, before amalgamation interchange of the objects between the cells produced a new arrangement, but after amalgamation, the interchange has no significance that is the total number of different arrangements is halved. If now three of the cells are combined, interchange of the three particles in these cells, which originally could have been done in 3! ways only represents one final arrangement. Hence the number of distinguishable arrangements is $N!/3!$ Further if other cells are combined so that we have one cell formed from n_1 original cells, and one cell formed from n_2 original cells, *etc.*, or put another way, we have n_1 objects in one cell, n_2 objects in another cell, n_i objects in the ith cell, then the total number of distinguishable arrangements, that is the thermodynamic probability, is

$$W = \frac{N!}{n_1! \, n_2! \dots n_i! \dots}. \tag{3.1-1}$$

In this book the only *objects* we shall consider are electrons and holes, and we can only distinguish between them by reference to their positions and either velocities or momenta. An electron or hole can be described completely by three co-ordinates of position and three momentum components. Hence the object can be represented by a point in a six-dimensional space, called *phase space*. If, in phase space, the position co-ordinates are q_1, q_2 and q_3, and the momentum co-ordinates are p_1, p_2, and p_3 the cell in phase space is defined as that volume lying between q_1 and $q_1 + dq_1$ *etc.* and p_1 and $p_1 + dp_1$ *etc.*, that is, it has a volume $dq_1 \, dq_2 \, dq_3 \, dp_1, dp_2 \, dp_3$.

Returning to the definition of thermodynamic probability

$$W = \frac{N!}{n_1! \, n_2! \dots n_i! \dots}.$$

Then

$$\ln W = \ln N! - \sum_i \ln n_i! \tag{3.1-2}$$

A theorem due to to Stirling* states that, if n is large

$$\ln n! = n(\ln n - 1) . \tag{3.1-3}$$

Hence

$$\ln W = N(\ln N - 1) - \sum_i n_i(\ln n_i - 1) . \tag{3.1-4}$$

the total number of objects N is given by

$$N = \sum_i n_i . \tag{3.1-5}$$

Therefore

$$\ln W = N \ln N - \sum_i n_i \ln n_i . \tag{3.1-6}$$

It is reasonable to assume that the arrangement of particles in thermodynamic equilibrium in phase space is that arrangement with the maximum probability. That is the condition will be given by

$$\delta(\ln W) = 0 . \tag{3.1-7}$$

Hence, as N is constant for a particular system we get, in equilibrium

$$\delta(\ln W) = - \sum_i \ln n_i \delta n_i - \sum_i \delta n_i = 0 .$$

But

$$\sum_i n_i = N .$$

Therefore

$$\sum_i \delta n_i = 0 . \tag{3.1-8}$$

* Proof of Stirling's theorem for large numbers.

Now,

$$\ln n! = \ln 1 + \ln 2 + \ln 3 + \ldots \ln(n-1) + \ln n .$$

$$= \sum_1^n \ln x .$$

For large values of x the summation can be replaced by an integration. Therefore,

$$\sum \ln n! \simeq \int_1^n \ln x \, dx \quad \text{for large } n$$

$$\simeq n \ln n - n .$$

This gives $$\delta(\ln W) = -\sum_i \ln n_i \delta n_i = 0 \qquad (3.1\text{-}9)$$

as the condition for maximum probability, which is the equilibrium condition.

Using the method of the Lagrange Undetermined Coefficients*, and multiplying eqn (3.1-8) by λ, and subtracting eqn (3.1-9) gives

$$\sum(\ln n_i - \gamma)\delta n_i = 0 . \qquad (3.1\text{-}10)$$

The Lagrange method demands that every coefficient of δn_i is zero, hence

$$n_i = \exp(\lambda) . \qquad (3.1\text{-}11)$$

Therefore, we see that every cell has the same number of particles in the most probable distribution.

3.2 Energy Distribution

We will now consider a system of N particles, in phase space, distributed in M cells in such a way that all the particles n_i with momenta p_i are in the ith cell, and each particle has an energy E_i given by

$$E_i = \frac{p_i^2}{2m} \qquad (3.2\text{-}1)$$

where m is the mass of a particle, see fig. 3.2a.

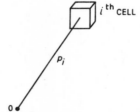

Figure 3.2a. A cell in phase space

---

* Equations (3.1-8), (3.1-9), and (3.2-4) show that all but two of the δn_i can be chosen to be independent variables. Suppose, for example, that δn_1 and δn_2 are the dependent variables, let λ and μ be chosen to make the coefficients of δn_1 and δn_2 in eqn (3.2-5) zero. Then, since the remaining δn_i are independent, eqn (3.2-5) implies that all the remaining coefficients are *zero*.

The probability is as before given by

$$W = \frac{N!}{n_1! \, n_2! \ldots n_i! \ldots n_M!}.$$ (3.2-2)

Now, the total energy U of the N particles is given by

$$U = \sum_i E_i n_i$$ (3.2-3)

If the energy of the system is constant, that is

$$\delta U = \sum E_i \delta n_i = 0$$ (3.2-4)

since δE_i equals zero for the ith cell.

This condition is a requirement additional to those already stated in eqns (3.1-8) and (3.1-9).

A single equation embodying eqns (3.1-8), (3.1-9), and (3.2-4) is obtained by using Lagrange's method of undetermined multipliers.* Hence, if we multiply eqn (3.1-8) by λ and (3.2-4) by μ we get

$$\sum_i (\ln n_i + \lambda + \mu E_i) \delta n_i = 0.$$ (3.2-5)

Since this equation must hold for every value of i, the condition becomes

$$\ln n_i + \lambda + \mu E_i = 0$$

or

$$n_i = \exp\left[-(\lambda + \mu E_i)\right].$$ (3.2-6)

Writing $\exp[-\lambda] = A$ we get

$$n_i = A \exp[-\mu E_i].$$ (3.2-7)

The multipliers A and μ must now be determined from other considerations.

3.3 Probability and Entropy

If a gas takes in an amount of heat dQ at a temperature T, its *entropy* is said to increase by an amount

$$dS = dQ/T.$$ (3.3-1)

The heat dQ may be produced by doing work on the gas, such as by

* See footnote on p. 60.

compressing it. Now the action of doing work can be considered as an orderly process; it is the product of a force in a particular direction and a motion of the point of application of the force also in a particular direction. However, the increase in heat of the gas is manifest by an increase in the random motion of the gas molecules, which is obviously an increase in the disorder of the gas. Hence an increase in entropy is equivalent to an increase in disorder. Further if we have two gases subjected to increases in entropy, the change of entropy of the two gases taken together will be the sum of the two separate increases in entropy. It can be seen that this principle can be extended in such a way that if S_1 and S_2 are the total entropies of the two gases, then the total entropy S of the system of the two gases is given by

$$S = S_1 + S_2. \tag{3.3-2}$$

Now, if the thermodynamic probabilities of the two gases are W_1 and W_2 the probability of the combination of the two systems W is

$$W = W_1 W_2 \tag{3.3-3}$$

as any particular arrangement of the gas molecules in one system can be taken with all the possible arrangements in the other system.

Both eqns (3.3-2) and (3) are only different ways of describing the states of the systems and therefore it is to be expected that there is some relationship between them and hence between entropy and probability. Further, this relationship must satisfy both equations.

We have from eqn (3.3-3):

$$\ln W = \ln W_1 + \ln W_2. \tag{3.3-4}$$

Comparison with eqn (3.3-2) leads to a relationship of the type

$$S = k \ln W. \tag{3.3-5}$$

This relationship is known as the Boltzmann-Planck equation. It was propounded by Boltzmann in 1872 and generalized in this form by Planck in 1932. The constant k is known as Boltzmann's constant $(k = 1.38 \times 10^{-23}$ joule deg$^{-1})$.

3.4 Determination of the Multiplier μ in the Energy Distribution Equation

Starting from eqn (3.3-5) and substituting for W from eqn (3.1-6), we get

$$S = kN \ln N - k \sum_i n_i \ln n_i . \qquad (3.4\text{-}1)$$

Hence, using eqn (3.2-7)

$$S = kN \ln N - k \sum_i n_i (\ln A - \mu E_i) .$$

By eqns (3.1-5) and (3.2-3)

$$S = kN \ln N - kN \ln A + \mu k U .$$

Therefore, as at constant volume N is constant, so

$$\delta S = - \frac{kN \delta A}{A} + \mu k \delta U + kU \delta\mu . \qquad (3.4\text{-}2)$$

Now, $$n_i = A \exp[-\mu E_i] .$$

Therefore

$$\delta n_i = - A E_i \exp[-\mu E_i] \delta\mu + \exp[-\mu E_i] \delta A \qquad (3.4\text{-}3)$$

as E_i is a constant for the ith cell.

Therefore, for the whole system, and using eqn (3.2-7)

$$\sum_i \delta n_i = - \sum_i n_i E_i \delta\mu + \sum_i \exp[-\mu E_i] \delta A . \qquad (3.4\text{-}4)$$

As the total number of particles is constant $\Sigma_i \delta n_i$ equals zero. Also μ and A are independent of the cell being considered, so we get

$$\delta A = \frac{AU}{N} \delta\mu \qquad (3.4\text{-}5)$$

which, when substituted in eqn (3.4-2) gives

$$\delta S = \mu k \delta U . \qquad (3.4\text{-}6)$$

This equation will be written in a partial derivative form, as a constant volume was considered, hence

$$\left(\frac{\partial S}{\partial U} \right)_V = \mu k . \qquad (3.4\text{-}7)$$

from the second law of thermodynamics, [3.1]

$$T \delta S = \delta U + p \delta V. \tag{3.4-8}$$

Now, as the entropy can be expressed as a function of U and V only, or

$$S = f(U, V)$$

$$\delta S = \left(\frac{\partial S}{\partial U}\right)_V \delta U + \left(\frac{\partial S}{\partial V}\right)_U \delta V. \tag{3.4-9}$$

Comparing eqns (3.4-8) and (3.4-9) we have

$$(\partial S / \partial U)_V = 1/T. \tag{3.4-10}$$

Therefore, from eqn (3.4-7)

$$\mu = 1/kT. \tag{3.4-11}$$

3.5 Determination of the Multiplier A in Energy Distribution Equation

The energy distribution eqn (3.2-7) can now be written

$$n_i = A \exp[-E_i/kT]. \tag{3.5-1}$$

Now, the constant A will be proportional to the total number N of particles, and also to the size of the cells. Let us, then, obtain the cells by subdivision of phase space, and also consider unit volume of the physical space so that $dq_1 . dq_2 . dq_3 = 1$. Hence the volume of the cell in phase space will be $dp_1 . dp_2 . dp_3$ and A will be proportional to this volume.

Let

$$A = BN \, dp_1 \, dp_2 \, dp_3 \tag{3.5-2}$$

where B is another constant.

The constant B can be obtained by using the relation

$$N = \sum_i n_i$$

$$= BN \sum_i \exp[-(E_i/kT)] \, dp_1 \, dp_2 \, dp_3. \tag{3.5-3}$$

Now
$$E_i = \frac{1}{2m}(p_1^2 + p_2^2 + p_3^2) .$$

We can make the size of the phase cell infinitesimally small and then replace the summation sign by a triple integral. Equation (3.5-3) then becomes

$$\frac{1}{B} = \iiint_{-\infty}^{+\infty} \exp[-(p_1^2 + p_2^2 + p_3^2)/2mkT]\, dp_1\, dp_2\, dp_3 . \quad (3.5\text{-}4)$$

Now the integral

$$\int_{-\infty}^{+\infty} \exp[-\alpha x^2]\, dx = \left(\frac{\pi}{\alpha}\right)^{\frac{1}{2}} . \quad [3.2]$$

Hence

$$B = (2\pi mkT)^{-\frac{3}{2}} . \quad (3.5\text{-}5)$$

The energy distribution equation can now be written

$$n_i = \frac{N \exp[-E_i/kT]\, dp_1\, dp_2\, dp_3}{(2\pi mkT)^{\frac{3}{2}}} . \quad (3.5\text{-}6)$$

It is usually more convenient to express the energy distribution equation either in terms of momentum or energy but not, as above, in both.

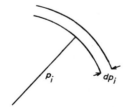

Figure 3.5a. A shell in phase space

This can be done by expressing the equation in polar co-ordinates taking as the ith cell in phase space a shell of radius $p_i = (2mE_i)^{\frac{1}{2}}$ and thickness dp_i where, see fig. 3.5a,

$$dp_1\, dp_2\, dp_3 = 4\pi p^2\, dp .$$

Then
$$\frac{n_i}{N} = \frac{4\pi p_i^2 \exp\left[-\dfrac{p_i^2}{2mkT}\right] dp_i}{(2\pi mkT)^{\frac{3}{2}}} . \tag{3.5-7}$$

If we now let n_i the number of particles in a phase cell of momentum range p to $(p+dp)$ equal dN_p, we get

$$\frac{dN_p}{N} = \frac{4\pi p^2 \exp\left[-\dfrac{p^2}{2mkT}\right] dp}{(2\pi mkT)^{\frac{3}{2}}} . \tag{3.5-8}$$

It is simple now to find the number dN_E of particle in the energy range E to $E+dE$ from eqn (3.5-8).

We have
$$p = (2mE)^{\frac{1}{2}} ,$$

therefore
$$dp = \frac{1}{2}\left(\frac{2m}{E}\right)^{\frac{1}{2}} dE .$$

Hence eqn (3.5-8) becomes

$$\frac{dN_E}{N} = \frac{2E^{\frac{1}{2}}}{\pi^{\frac{1}{2}}(kT)^{\frac{3}{2}}} \exp\left[-E/kT\right] dE . \tag{3.5-9}$$

This equation is known as the Maxwell-Boltzmann Energy Distribution equation.

We shall need, in section 5.2, to know the root mean square thermal velocity v_{T}, equal to $\sqrt{\langle v\rangle^2}$*, of electrons at a temperature T. This can be obtained by the relation

$$v_{\mathrm{T}}^2 = \int_0^\infty v^2 \left(\frac{dN}{N}\right)_v \tag{3.5-10}$$

where
$$\left(\frac{dN}{N}\right)_v = \frac{4m^{\frac{3}{2}} v^2 \exp\left[-\dfrac{mv^2}{2kT}\right] dv}{\pi^{\frac{1}{2}}(2kT)^{\frac{3}{2}}} \tag{3.5-11}$$

which is obtained by substituting v equal to p/m in eqn (3.5-8).

* In this book $\langle\ \rangle$ brackets indicate an average value.

Therefore
$$v_T^2 = \frac{4m^{\frac{3}{2}}}{\pi^{\frac{1}{2}}(2kT)^{\frac{3}{2}}} \int_0^\infty v^4 \exp\left[-\frac{mv^2}{2kT}\right] dv .$$ (3.5-12)

Now, see ref. [3.2],

$$\int_0^\infty v^4 \exp\left[-\frac{mv^2}{2kT}\right] dv = \frac{3}{8}\pi^{\frac{1}{2}}\left(\frac{2kT}{m}\right)^{\frac{5}{2}} .$$ (3.5-12)

Hence
$$v_T^2 = \frac{3kT}{m} .$$ (3.5-13)

Therefore the root mean square velocity

$$v_T = \left(\frac{3kT}{m}\right)^{\frac{1}{2}} .$$ (3.5-14)

3.6 The Failure of Classical Statistics

At the end of the nineteenth century there were a number of problems involving statistical mechanics the solutions of which were at variance with experiment.

For example the specific heat of solids per gram molecule is approximately

$$C = 3R$$

where R is the gas constant. This is consistent with Maxwell's Law of Equipartition for a system of linear oscillators with three degrees of freedom. Drude's theory of thermal and electrical conductivity showed that the free, that is conduction, electrons in a metal behave like a monatomic gas, and should, by the classical theory, contribute to the specific heat an amount $\frac{3}{2}ZR$, where Z is the valency of the element. No such contribution is found experimentally.

Inconsistencies were also found in connexion with the radiation laws and entropy. For a further account, see ref [3.3].

3.7 Classical Quantum Mechanics

In connexion with the problem of radiation Planck in 1900 advanced the hypothesis that a simple linear harmonic oscillator can absorb energy only in integral multiples of a minimum quantity of energy, and that this quantity is proportional to the frequency of the oscillator.

That is, the energy of the oscillator is given by

$$E = nh\nu \tag{3.7-1}$$

where n is an integer, h is Planck's constant ($h = 6 \cdot 6 \times 10^{-34}$ joule/sec.) and ν is the frequency.

One immediate effect of this is to put a condition on the cells in phase space, for there can no longer be equal probability for cells of equal size. There will only be points where the energy is exactly $nh\nu$. It is apparent that the space must be divided in a particular way.

Consider a particle behaving as a linear oscillator; its position in phase space can be represented by an ellipse called a phase orbit, see fig. 3.7a.

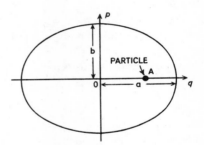

Figure 3.7a. The phase orbit

If we consider a particle at A, a distance q from its position of maximum velocity, and having a momentum p, and that it is executing simple harmonic motion, then the energy of the particle is given by

$$E = \tfrac{1}{2}fq^2 + \frac{1}{2m}p^2 \tag{3.7-2}$$

where f is a force constant, and m is the mass of the particle. The first term represents potential energy and the second term kinetic energy.

Planck proposed that this energy E is also equal to $nh\nu$.

Therefore

$$nh\nu = \tfrac{1}{2}fq^2 + \frac{1}{2m}p^2 \tag{3.7-3}$$

or

$$1 = \frac{q^2}{2nh\nu/f} + \frac{p^2}{2mnh\nu} \tag{3.7-4}$$

This is the equation of an ellipse the phase orbit, the major and minor axis of which are $a = (2nh\nu/f)^{\frac{1}{2}}$ and $b = (2mnh\nu)^{\frac{1}{2}}$.

Now, the area of an ellipse is given by πab, so the area of the n th phase orbit is $2\pi nh\nu \, . \, (m/f)^{\frac{1}{2}}$.

It can be shown that the frequency of an oscillator obeying eqn (3.7-2) is $1/2\pi(f/m)^{\frac{1}{2}}$, and this must be the frequency of the radiation ν. Hence the area of the phase orbit is nh, and the area between two adjacent orbits in phase space is h.

In fact Planck's hypothesis leads to the more general statement that only those states can occur for which the value of the phase integral over a closed path $\oint p\,dq$ is an integral multiple of h. The energy value ascribed to each orbit corresponds to the inner boundary, that is 0, $h\nu$, $2h\nu$, etc.

For a one-dimensional oscillator we have seen that the size of the cell is h, and so for a three-dimensional oscillator the volume becomes h^3. This therefore, is the smallest volume of a cell in phase which can accommodate a particle.*

This is the most important outcome of classical quantum mechanics, but it is also apparent that a summation sign can no longer be replaced by an integral sign except when n is large, in which case classical quantum mechanics tends to Maxwell-Boltzmann statistics.

To return to statistical mechanics, if we consider the i th cell containing n_i particles each with energy E_i equal to $ih\nu$, we have

$$N = \sum{}' n_i \, .$$

* It is interesting to note as an aside that the smallest linear cell of size $h = dp \, . \, dq$ is also directly connected with the accuracy of measurement of position and velocity in Heisenburg's Principle of Uncertainty. This Principle states that if a particle has a momentum p and is at a position q the error dq to which p can be measured multiplied by the error dq to which q can be measured, can under no circumstances be less than h, Planck's constant.

Equation (3.5-3) must now be modified to give

$$N = BNh^3 \sum_i \exp\left(-\frac{ihv}{kT}\right). \qquad (3.7\text{-}5)$$

Hence

$$\frac{1}{B} = h^3\left[1 + \exp\left(-\frac{hv}{kT}\right) + \exp\left(-\frac{2hv}{kT}\right) + \dots\right]. \qquad (3.7\text{-}6)$$

which is a geometrical progression.

Therefore
$$\frac{1}{B} = \frac{h^3}{1 - \exp\left(-\dfrac{hv}{kT}\right)} \qquad (3.7\text{-}7)$$

compared with $(2\pi m k T)^{\frac{3}{2}}$ in Maxwell-Boltzmann statistics.

3.8 Bose-Einstein Statistics

The main difference between these statistics produced by Bose and applied to gases by Einstein, and the Maxwell-Boltzmann statistics is that the particles are not now considered to be distinguishable. When molecules in a gas or electrons in a metal are considered, this condition of indistinguishability, which affects the calculation of the probability, is quite reasonable.

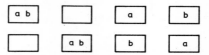

Figure 3.8a. Possible distributions of two particles between two boxes

This difference is illustrated simply by considering the distribution of two particles 'a' and 'b' between two boxes, as shown in fig. 3.8a. From this figure we see that on the Maxwell-Boltzmann theory we have four arrangements, but if the particles are identical, as for Bose-Einstein statistics, the last two arrangements are the same, that is only three arrangements are different.

As we cannot now distinguish between the particles, but only between the cells in phase space, we divide the space into cells as before, and find the number N_0 containing no particles, the number N_1 containing one particle, the number N_2 containing two particles, and so on. Then the probability W is defined as

$$W = \frac{N!}{N_0!\, N_1!\, N_2!\,\ldots} \tag{3.8-1}$$

where N is the total number of cells. This equation is similar to eqn (3.1-1), except that we are now dealing with cells and not particles. In addition we have the conditions that the total number of cells

$$N = \sum_i N_i \tag{3.8-2}$$

and the total number of particles

$$n = \sum_i i\, N_i \,. \tag{3.8-3}$$

The phase space is now divided into shells of constant particle energy, and if there are a total of N_s cells in the s shell, the probability W_s for that shell will be given by

$$W_s = \frac{N_s!}{N_{0s}!\, N_{1s}!\, N_{2s}!\,\ldots} \,. \tag{3.8-4}$$

The total number of particles n_s in the s shell is

$$n_s = \sum_i i\, N_{is} \,. \tag{3.8-5}$$

The whole of phase being considered is made up of a number of shells, and so the probability W for the whole space is, see section 3.3,

$$W = W_1 . W_2 . W_3 \ldots \tag{3.8-6}$$

or

$$\ln W = \sum_s \ln W_s \,. \tag{3.8-7}$$

From eqn (3.8-4)

$$\ln W = \sum_s \ln N_s! - \sum_s \sum_i \ln N_{is}! \,. \tag{3.8-8}$$

By Stirling's theorem the equation becomes

$$\ln W = \sum_s N_s(\ln N_s - 1) - \sum_s \sum_i N_{is}(\ln N_{is} - 1) . \qquad (3.8\text{-}9)$$

But

$$\sum_s \sum_i N_{is} = \sum_s N_s \qquad (3.8\text{-}10)$$

and this is constant for the whole space.

Therefore

$$\ln W = \sum_s N_s \ln N_s - \sum_s \sum_i N_{is} \ln N_{is} . \qquad (3.8\text{-}11)$$

At equilibrium the probability will be a maximum, hence

$$\delta(\ln W) = 0 .$$

From eqn (3.8-11)

$$\delta(\ln W) = \sum_s \delta N_s + \sum_s (\ln N_s)\delta N_s - \sum_s \sum_i \delta N_{is}$$

$$- \sum_s \sum_i (\ln N_{is})\delta N_{is} . \qquad (3.8\text{-}12)$$

The number of cells in a particular shell is fixed, as it depends on the geometry of the shell.

Hence

$$\sum_i N_{is} = N_s = \text{const} .$$

Therefore

$$\sum_i \delta N_{is} = \delta N_s = 0 \qquad (3.8\text{-}13)$$

and so the condition for maximum probability becomes

$$\delta(\ln W) = - \sum_s \sum_i (\ln N_{is})\delta N_{is} = 0 . \qquad (3.8\text{-}14)$$

The total number of particles n_s in the shell under equilibrium conditions will be constant. Therefore δn_s equals zero.

But from eqn (3.8-5)

$$n_s = \sum_i i N_{is}$$

and the total number of particles in the whole system, which is also constant is

$$\sum_s n_s = \sum_s \sum_i i N_{is} \, .$$

Therefore

$$\sum_s \delta n_s = \sum_s \sum_i N_{is} \delta i + \sum_s \sum_i i \, \delta N_{is} = 0 \, . \tag{3.8-15}$$

Since i is the number of particles in the N_{is} cell, and this is constant by definition, δi is zero.

Hence eqn (3.8-15) reduces to

$$\sum_s \delta n_s = \sum_s \sum_i i \, \delta N_{is} = 0 \, . \tag{3.8-16}$$

Also, eqn (3.8-10) gives

$$\sum_s \sum_i \delta N_{is} = \sum_s \delta N_s = 0 \, . \tag{3.8-17}$$

If the energy of the particles in the s shell is E_s, then the total energy of the system, from eqn (3.8-5) is

$$E = \sum_s \sum_i i \, E_s N_{is}$$

and this will be constant for the system in equilibrium. Therefore:

$$\delta E = \sum_s \sum_i i \, E_s \delta N_{is} + \sum_s \sum_i i \, N_{is} \delta E_s + \sum_s \sum_i E_s N_{is} \delta i = 0 \, . \tag{3.8-18}$$

But $$\delta E_s = \delta i = 0 \, , \quad \text{by definition}$$

Hence $$\delta E = \sum_s \sum_i i \, E_s \delta N_{is} = 0 \, . \tag{3.8-19}$$

Again, using Lagrange's method of undetermined multipliers, and multiplying eqn (3.8-14) by 1, eqn (3.8-16) by β, eqn (3.8-17) by α and eqn (3.8-19) by γ we get

$$\sum_s \sum_i (\ln N_{is} + \alpha + \beta i + \gamma i \, E_s) \delta N_{is} = 0 \, . \tag{3.8-20}$$

The Lagrange method demands that every coefficient of δN_{is} should be zero.

Therefore

$$N_{is} = \exp(-\alpha)\exp[-i(\beta+\gamma E_s)] \tag{3.8-21}$$

and the total number of cells in the shell

$$N_s = \sum_i N_{is} = \exp(-\alpha)\sum_i \exp[-i(\beta+\gamma E_s)] \tag{3.8-22}$$

which is a geometrical series.

Hence

$$N_s = \frac{\exp(-\alpha)}{1-\exp[-(\beta+\gamma E_s)]}. \tag{3.8-23}$$

The total number of particles in the s shell (eqn 3.8-5) is

$$n_s = \sum_i i N_{is}$$

and using eqn (3.8-21), this becomes

$$n_s = \sum_i i\exp(-\alpha)\exp[-i(\beta+\gamma E_s)]$$

$$= -\exp(-\alpha)\frac{\partial}{\partial(\beta+\gamma E_s)}\left\{\sum_i \exp[-i(\beta+\gamma E_s)]\right\}. \tag{3.8-24}$$

The series is a geometrical progression with a ratio $\exp[-(\beta+\gamma E_s]$ and so the sum is $1/\{1-\exp[-(\beta+\gamma E_s)]\}$.

Hence

$$n_s = -\exp(-\alpha)\frac{\partial}{\partial(\beta+\gamma E_s)}\left\{\frac{1}{1-\exp[-(\beta+\gamma E_s)]}\right\}$$

$$= \frac{\exp(-\alpha)\exp[-(\beta+\gamma E_s)]}{\{1-\exp[-(\beta+\gamma E_s)]\}^2}. \tag{3.8-25}$$

Substituting for $\exp(-\alpha)$ from eqn (3.8-23) gives

$$n_s = \frac{N_s}{\exp(\beta+\gamma E_s)-1}. \tag{3.8-26}$$

Following similar reasoning to that used in section 3.4 to determine μ in the Maxwell-Boltzmann equation, it can be shown that γ in the above equation is equal to $1/kT$. It is usual to replace $\exp \beta$ by B, so that the equation becomes

$$n_s = \frac{N_s}{B \exp(E_s/kT) - 1}.$$ (3.8-27)

Bose-Einstein statistics have not been used extensively, but they are relevant to the problem of the thermal and magnetic properties of materials [3.4], and also the Fermi-Dirac statistics are a development of Bose-Einstein statistics.

3.9 Fermi-Dirac Statistics

This form of the statistics accounts very well for the behaviour of electrons in a metal or semiconductor, and arises from the application of a condition first used in the quantum theory of the structure of the atom. From this theory it has been found that in a given atom each orbiting electron must have a different set of quantum numbers. This requirement, which is of such fundamental importance, is known as the *Pauli Exclusion Principle*, and has already been mentioned in section 2.5.

This means in the theory of statistics that a particular cell in phase space cannot be occupied by more than one particle.

From Bose-Einstein statistic we have (eqn 3.8-21)

$$N_{is} = \exp(-\alpha) \exp\left[-i(\beta + \gamma E_s)\right].$$

Now, by imposing the requirements of the Exclusion Principle, i can have the values of zero or one only, so that eqn (3.8-22) gives

$$N_s = \exp(-\alpha) \left\{1 + \exp\left[-(\beta + \gamma E_s)\right]\right\}.$$ (3.9-1)

The number of particles n_s in the s shell is $\Sigma_i i N_{is}$, which gives

$$n_s = 1 \cdot N_{1s} = \exp(-\alpha) \exp\left[-(\beta + \gamma E_s)\right]$$

$$= \frac{N_s \exp\left[-(\beta + \gamma E_s)\right]}{1 + \exp\left[-(\beta + \gamma E_s)\right]}$$

$$= \frac{N_s}{1 + B \exp(E_s/kT)}$$ (3.9-2)

writing, as before, $\exp(\beta) = B$ and $\gamma = 1/kT$.

Comparing this equation with the corresponding equation obtained from Bose-Einstein statistics in eqn (3.8-27), it is seen that the only difference is the sign of the 1 in the denominator. It will be shown later, in section 3.11, that B is a function of the density of the particles, and is small for high densities, such as one would find in a solid, and large for low densities as in a gas. It is apparent, therefore, that both Fermi-Dirac and Bose-Einstein statistics lead to equations of the Maxwell-Boltzmann type when applied to gases. This is quite understandable when it is realized that it is only at very high densities that there is appreciable interaction between the particles and so only then do the requirements of quantum statistics and the Exclusion Principle impose any practical restrictions on the statistics. We shall be particularly interested in the energy distributions of electrons in metals and semi-conductors, where the density is large. These electrons can be considered to be a gas which obeys Fermi-Dirac statistics. Such a gas, obeying Fermi-Dirac statistics rather than Maxwell-Boltzmann, is said to be *degenerate*. We shall also see, particularly in semiconductors, that there are many occasions when the electron density is low and consequently Maxwell-Boltzmann statistics apply.

3.10 Determination of the Number of Cells in a Shell

The calculation of N_s in eqn (3.9-1) is most simply achieved by adopting a similar approach to that in section 3.5 with the addition of the restrictions on the size of an individual cell imposed by quantum considerations discussed in section 3.7.

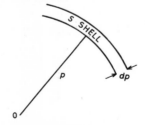

Figure 3.10a. s th shell in phase space

Consider a surface in phase space of constant energy E and therefore constant momentum. The surface will be a sphere of radius $p = (2mE)^{\frac{1}{2}}$, where m is the mass of the particle. If the energy range within the shell is to be dE, and the corresponding momentum range is dp, then

$$dp = \tfrac{1}{2}(2m/E)^{\frac{1}{2}} dE . \tag{3.10-1}$$

Now, the phase space is divided into cells the minimum size of which by the quantum requirements is h^3 and each cell can accommodate one particle. The volume of the spherical shell of radius p is $4\pi p^2 dp$, and the density of cells N_s in the shell is given by

$$\begin{aligned}
N_s &= \frac{4\pi p^2 dp}{h^3} \\
&= \frac{2\pi}{h^3} (2m)^{\frac{3}{2}} E^{\frac{1}{2}} dE .
\end{aligned} \tag{3.10-2}$$

3.11 Energy Distribution of Electrons

If the particles we are considering, which so far have been unspecified, are in fact electrons, the number of cells in a given shell is usually doubled. This is because the electron is considered to have a spin in a magnetic field, see section 2.6, and can rotate either clockwise or anticlockwise about the field direction. Since the applications to which we shall be putting our statistics are entirely connected with semiconductor theory, it is convenient here to drop the subscript s indicating the s shell.

We shall therefore modify eqn (3.10-2) to represent the maximum density of electrons that could be accommodated in a shell of width dE, and subsequently called the density of states, and write it as

$$N(E)dE = \frac{4\pi}{h^3} (2m)^{\frac{3}{2}} E^{\frac{1}{2}} dE . \tag{3.11-1}$$

This agrees with the result obtained in section 2.16, when it is remembered that allowance has again been made for the doubling of the density due to electron spin.

To obtain the density of electrons $n(E)dE$ with energies in the range dE, it is only necessary to substitute for N_s in eqn (3.9-2) the value for $N(E)dE$.

This gives

$$n(E)dE = \frac{4\pi(2m)^{\frac{3}{2}} E^{\frac{1}{2}} dE}{h^3 \{1 + B \exp [E/kT]\}}. \tag{3.11-2}$$

This we see is, in fact, the density of states multiplied by the probability of occupation of these states by a particle.

Hence the total density of electrons

$$n = \frac{4\pi}{h^3} (2m)^{\frac{3}{2}} \int_0^\infty \frac{E^{\frac{1}{2}} dE}{1 + B \exp [E/kT]} \tag{3.11-3}$$

The integral cannot be solved rigorously except at the absolute zero of temperature, and then only by further discussion of the nature of the constant B.

At the absolute zero of temperature it is reasonable to assume that all the cells, or states, will be filled up to a certain value of the energy, that is the value of $n(E)$ will fall abruptly to zero at this energy level. The level is called the Fermi level and is denoted by E_F. The abrupt fall in $n(E)$ must be brought about by the term $B \exp(E/kT)$ in the denominator of eqn (3.11-3). In fact this term must change from zero to infinity at E_F. Hence B must be of the form $\exp(-E_F/kT)$, so that the denominator becomes $\{1 + \exp[(E - E_F)/kT]\}$ which satisfies the requirement that at the absolute zero of temperature, as the energy is increased through E equals E_F the value of the exponential term changes discontinuously from zero to infinity. The full expression for the energy distribution of the electron gas in the metal is, therefore

$$n(E)dE = \frac{4\pi(2m)^{\frac{3}{2}} E^{\frac{1}{2}} dE}{h^3 \left\{1 + \exp\left[\dfrac{E - E_F}{kT}\right]\right\}} \tag{3.11-4}$$

The value of the constant E_F is obtained by evaluating the integral giving the electron density at the absolute zero of temperature, namely

$$n = \frac{4\pi(2m)^{\frac{3}{2}}}{h^3} \int_0^{E_F} E^{\frac{1}{2}} dE. \tag{3.11-5}$$

This gives a value for the energy at Fermi Level

$$E_F = \frac{h^2}{8m}\left(\frac{3n}{\pi}\right)^{\frac{2}{3}} . \qquad (3.11\text{-}6)$$

It is interesting to note that for silver, E_F is 5·5 eV, taking a value of n equal to $6 \times 10^{28}/\text{m}^3$ and the accepted values of h approx. equal to $6 \cdot 6 \times 10^{-34}$ joule/sec. and the electronic mass m as 9×10^{-31} kg.

As the temperature of the metal is raised, some of the electrons receive additional energy, as is shown by eqn (3.11-4), since the exponential term $\exp\left[(E-E_F)/kT\right]$ changes from zero to infinity progressively less abruptly. Curves showing the effect of temperature on the value of $n(E)$ are shown in fig. 3.11a.

It should be noted that as the area under the $n(E)$–E curve gives the total density of electrons, the two similar shaped areas in fig. 3.11a are equal.

The function which gives the probability that a state, or cell, at an

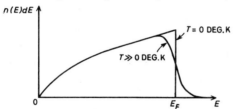

Figure 3.11a. The distribution of electron density with energy at zero degrees absolute, and at a high temperature

energy E is occupied is known as the Fermi function, and denoted by $F(E)$. It is readily seen from eqns (3.11-1) and (4) that

$$F(E) = \frac{1}{1+\exp\left[\dfrac{E-E_F}{kT}\right]} \qquad (3.11\text{-}7)$$

so that

$$n(E)dE = N(E)F(E)dE . \qquad (3.11\text{-}8)$$

The form of $F(E)$ shows that at values of E much less than E_F, $F(E)$ equals one, and at values of E much greater than E_F, $F(E)$ is zero. Further, it is readily shown from eqn (3.11-7) that $F(E)$ exceeds 0·9 if E is less than

E_F by more than approximately 2·3 kT, and that $F(E)$ is less than 0·1 provided E is greater than E_F by about 2·3 kT. The transition from 0·9 to 0·1 therefore occurs for an energy increase which is inversely proportional to T and which is about 0·12 eV at room temperatures. Curves of $F(E)$ against E are given in fig. 3.11b. It is interesting to note that the Fermi level E_F is the energy level at which the probability of occupation by an electron is one half.

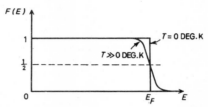

Figure 3.11b. The Fermi function at zero degrees absolute, and at a high temperature

Frequently it is required to know not the fraction of the states which are occupied, but the fraction which are *not* occupied.

The fraction unoccupied is given the symbol $\tilde{F}(E)$, which will be termed the inverse Fermi function, and is given as

$$\tilde{F}(E) = 1 - F(E) = \frac{1}{1 + \exp\left[-(E - E_F)/kT\right]}. \qquad (3.11\text{-}9)$$

Many applications of these equations will be found in the next chapters.*

* Although it is not relevant here to deal in detail with the fact that Fermi-Dirac statistics succeed where the classical statistics fail, it is worth mentioning at least that the specific heat contribution of the electron gas predicted by theory agrees with experiment, since it is apparent that if the temperature of the metal changes, only a small fraction of the electrons change their energies. Hence the specific heat contribution of the conduction electrons is very small, and much below the value of 3 $kT/2$ predicted by Maxwell-Boltzmann statistics.

3.12 Degeneracy of Electron Spin

In section 3.11 it was stated that the number of cells in a shell, as computed by dividing the phase space into volumes of sizes h^3, could be doubled without violating the Pauli Exclusion Principle. This was because of the two spin quantum numbers which could be associated with an electron. However if the electron spin is degenerate, that is if the two energy levels associated with the two spin directions become equal, only one cell in each pair can be occupied. This modifies the expression for the probability as it is no longer permissible to double N_s to obtain the total number of cells.

This case is most simply analysed starting from first principles. Let us now take the cells in pairs, each pair having a different energy, but as the spin is now degenerate, only one cell of each pair can be occupied by an electron, and so the probability eqn (3.8-1) for the s shell becomes

$$W_s = \frac{N_s!\, 2^{N_{1s}}}{N_{0s}!\, N_{1s}} \tag{3.12-1}$$

where N_s is the total number of pairs of cells in the s shell, N_{0s} is the number of empty cells in the s shell, and N_{1s} is the number of cells containing one electron. The term $2^{N_{1s}}$ represents the condition that an electron can be in either of a particular pair of cells, and so the probability is doubled for each *occupied* pair. Also we have, the total number of cells

$$N_s = N_{0s} + N_{1s} \tag{3.12-2}$$

and the number of electrons in the s shell

$$n_s = N_{1s}. \tag{3.12-3}$$

For the whole space we have the probability

$$W = W_1, W_2, W_3, \ldots, W_s \ldots$$

or

$$\ln W = \sum_s \ln W_s. \tag{3.12-4}$$

Hence by eqns (3.12-1) and (3.12-2) we have

$$\ln W = \sum_s \ln N_s! + \sum_s N_{1s} \ln 2 - \sum_s \ln(N_s - N_{1s})! - \sum_s \ln N_{1s}! \tag{3.12-5}$$

By Stirling's theorem we then get

$$\ln W = \sum_s N_s(\ln N_s - 1) + \sum_s N_{1s} \ln 2 - \sum_s (N_s - N_{1s})\{\ln(N_s - N_{1s}) - 1\}$$
$$- \sum_s N_{1s}(\ln N_{1s} - 1) . \qquad (3.12\text{-}6)$$

Differentiating eqn (3.12-6) with respect to N_{1s}, the only variable, and equating to zero for equilibrium gives

$$\delta(\ln W) = \sum_s \ln 2 \delta N_{1s} + \sum_s \ln(N_s - N_{1s})\delta N_{1s} - \sum_s \ln N_{1s}\delta N_{1s} = 0 .$$
$$(3.12\text{-}7)$$

Hence
$$\sum_s \left[\ln 2\left(\frac{N_s - N_{1s}}{N_{1s}}\right) \right] \cdot \delta N_{1s} = 0 . \qquad (3.12\text{-}8)$$

Also, we have the total number of electrons

$$n = \sum_s N_{1s} \qquad (3.12\text{-}9)$$

so that

$$\delta n = \sum_s \delta N_{1s} = 0 \qquad (3.12\text{-}10)$$

as the total number of electrons in the space is constant.

The total energy of the phase space is

$$E = \sum_s E_s . N_{1s} . \qquad (3.12\text{-}11)$$

Hence, in equilibrium

$$\sum_s E_s \delta N_{1s} = 0 . \qquad (3.12\text{-}12)$$

We can now use the method of Lagrange's undetermined multipliers, multiplying eqn (3.12-8) by 1, eqn (3.12-10) by β and eqn (3.12-12) by γ. This gives

$$\sum_s \left\{ \ln\left[2\left(\frac{N_s - N_{1s}}{N_{1s}}\right) \right] + \beta + \gamma E_s \right\} \delta N_{1s} = 0 . \qquad (3.12\text{-}13)$$

Hence
$$2N_s/N_{1s} - 2 = \exp[-\beta] \exp[-\gamma E_s] \qquad (3.12\text{-}14)$$

from which we get

$$\frac{N_{1s}}{N_s} = \frac{1}{1 + \frac{1}{2} \exp\left[-\beta\right] \exp\left[-\gamma E_s\right]} \qquad (3.12\text{-}15)$$

Therefore, the number of electrons in the s shell

$$n_s = \frac{N_s}{1 + \frac{1}{2} B \exp\left[-\gamma E_s\right]} \qquad (3.12\text{-}16)$$

where $B = \exp\left[-\beta\right]$.

Further, it can be shown that $B = \exp(-E_F/kT)$ and $\gamma = -1/kT$ so that

$$F(E) = \frac{n_s}{N_s} = \frac{1}{1 + \frac{1}{2} \exp\left[\dfrac{E_s - E_F}{kT}\right]}. \qquad (3.12\text{-}17)$$

Comparison with eqn (3.11-7) shows that the Fermi function is only modified by the factor $\frac{1}{2}$ in front of the exponential term.

The spin degeneracy factor is of importance in semiconductor theory as, in the case of an impurity doped material, whilst the impurity atoms are far enough apart not to interact, so that each atom has two closely spaced energy levels, one for each spin quantum number, only one level is occupied at a given time. This is because the electric field associated with the electron in the occupied level repels electrons from the second level, so that the probability of occupation of this level is negligible.

Considering the conduction band however, when the density of states is so large, compared with the density of electrons, the probability of occupation of both spin levels is negligible. In counting the number of levels available for occupation, the occupation of all levels is equally probable. Hence the density of states is doubled to allow for the spin degeneracy. When the density of occupation becomes comparable to the density of states, since all the levels are closely spaced, the electrostatic repulsion against an electron completing the occupation of a pair of spin levels is essentially the same as that opposing its occupation of any other level. Hence, once again, it is only necessary to double the density of states to allow for the spin levels. It will be seen later, in the simplification of eqn (4.2-3) to eqn (4.2-4) that whether the density of states is halved, or the spin degeneracy Fermi function is used, the result for low occupation densities is precisely the same.

The method used to obtain this result can equally well be applied to obtain the usual Fermi function, thus eliminating the need to base the Fermi-Dirac statistics on the results of the Bose-Einstein statistics.

Summary table of statistics

Type	Density of states (in range E to $E+dE$)	Occupation probability
M.B.	$\dfrac{2E^{\frac{1}{2}}\,dE}{\pi^2(kT)^{\frac{3}{2}}}$	$\exp\left[-E/kT\right]$
B.E.	$\dfrac{2\pi}{h^3}(2m)^{\frac{3}{2}}E^{\frac{1}{2}}\,dE$	$\dfrac{1}{B\exp\left[E/kT\right]-1}$
F.D.	$\dfrac{2\pi}{h^3}(2m)^{\frac{3}{2}}E^{\frac{1}{2}}\,dE$	$\dfrac{1}{\exp\left[(E-E_{\mathrm{F}})/kT\right]+1}$

References

[3.1] See for example, ZERMANSKY, M. W. (1957), *Heat and thermodynamics*, McGraw-Hill.

[3.2] JEANS, J. H. *Dynamical theory of gases*, 3rd edn. p. 435. Cambridge Univ. Press.

[3.3] DARROW, K. (1943), 'Memorial to the classical statistics', *Bell system tech. journ.*, pp. 108–135.

[3.4] ZIMAN, J. M. (1964), *Principles of the theory of solids*, pp. 42 and 316. Cambridge Univ. Press.

CHAPTER 4

Semiconductors in Thermodynamic Equilibrium

In general there are two types of semiconductors. Those in which electrons and holes are produced by thermal generation in pure germanium and silicon are called intrinsic semiconductors. In the other type the current carriers, holes or free electrons, are produced by the addition of small quantities of elements of Group III or V of the Periodic Table, and are known as extrinsic semiconductors. The elements added are called the impurities.

Having looked at the energy band structure of semiconductors and the expressions which give the energy distributions of electrons in materials, we are now in a position to calculate the densities of electrons and holes in the conductor and valence bands of semiconductors, and to find the position of the Fermi levels. The densities n and p, together with the mobilities, μ_n and μ_p, of the electrons and holes then enable us to determine the conductivity σ of the semiconductor from the relation

$$\sigma = q(n\mu_n + p\mu_p)$$

where q is the electronic charge. The electron and hole mobilities can be defined as the average drift velocities of the carriers in an electric field of unit intensity. The subject of mobility will be considered in Chapter 5.

4.1 The Number of Current Carriers

We have seen from the previous chapter, section 3.11, that the number of electrons $n(E)dE$ per unit volume in an energy range E to $E+dE$ in a substance in thermal equilibrium is given by

$$n(E)dE = N(E)F(E)dE . \tag{4.1-1}$$

It will be assumed through the remainder of this book that the electron spin energy levels are not degenerate, so that, from eqn (3.11-1)

$$N(E) = \frac{4\pi}{h^3} (2m)^{\frac{3}{2}} E^{\frac{1}{2}} \qquad (4.1\text{-}2)$$

and $F(E)$, the Fermi distribution function, eqn. (3.11-7) is given by

$$F(E) = \frac{1}{1 + \exp\left[\dfrac{E - E_F}{kT}\right]} . \qquad (4.1\text{-}3)$$

In metals the Fermi level E_F is the highest occupied energy level at the absolute zero of temperature, and the level remains constant as the temperature is raised. However this definition is inappropriate in the case of a semiconductor because at the absolute zero of temperature the valence band is full and the conduction band is empty, which would mean that in the above definition E_F would be at the top of the valence band, and would remain there as the temperature increased. For electrons to appear in the conduction band the 'tail' of the $F(E)$ curve would have to rise into this band, and this would create many more unoccupied levels in the valence band than electrons in the condition band. Clearly this is an impossible situation, and it is therefore apparent that E_F must be somewhere approximately mid-way between the valence and conduction bands, at least in the case of an intrinsic semiconductor such as pure germanium of silicon.

In general, the Fermi level can be determined with the aid of the relationship

$$\int n(E)\,dE = \int N(E) F(E)\,dE . \qquad (4.1\text{-}4)$$

The integral, the limits of which are the edges of a band, in fact represents the total number of electrons in the band.

4.2 The Insulator and the Intrinsic Semiconductor

We have already seen in section 2.19 that insulators and intrinsic semiconductors differ only in the size of the forbidden gap E_g in fig. 2.19a. The arrangement of the conduction and valence bands, together with the corresponding Fermi function $F(E)$ and resulting density of states $N(E)$ are shown in fig. 4.2a.

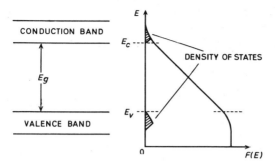

Figure 4.2a. Showing the Fermi function and density of states in an intrinsic semiconductor

The density n of electrons in the conduction band is given by

$$n = \int_{\text{bottom}}^{\text{top}} n(E) dE = \int_{\text{bottom}}^{\text{top}} N(E) F(E) dE . \qquad (4.2\text{-}1)$$

Now,

$$N(E) = \frac{4\pi}{h^3} (2m_n)^{\frac{3}{2}} (E - E_c)^{\frac{1}{2}} . \qquad (4.2\text{-}2)$$

The term $(E - E_c)$ replaces E in the previous formula for $N(E)$ as now the electron with the lowest energy to be transferred from the valence to the conduction band must have an energy equal to E_c, that is the equation for the number of possible states builds up from its zero at the bottom of the conduction band. The symbol m_n in the equation is the effective mass of an electron at the bottom of the conduction band. It will be assumed that the mass remains constant with position in the band as in practice the electrons do not penetrate very far up the band.

We now have

$$n = \frac{4\pi}{h^3} (2m_n)^{\frac{3}{2}} \int_{E_c}^{\infty} \frac{(E - E_c) dE}{1 + \exp\left[(E - E_F)/kT\right]} . \qquad (4.2\text{-}3)$$

Now, kT at room temperature is about 0.03 eV, and if the Fermi level is somewhere in the centre of the forbidden gap $(E - E_F)$ will be of the order of 0.3 eV at least. Hence $\exp[(E - E_F)/kT]$ is very much greater than unity.

The upper limit may be written as ∞ as the Fermi function becomes zero before the top of the band is reached.

Therefore eqn (4.2-3) can be simplified to

$$n = \frac{4\pi}{h^3}(2m_n)^{\frac{3}{2}} \int_{E_c}^{\infty} (E - E_c)^{\frac{1}{2}} \exp\left[-(E - E_F)/kT\right] dE . \quad (4.2-4)$$

Let $(E - E_c) = \varepsilon$. Then

$$n = \frac{4\pi}{h^3}(2m_n)^{\frac{3}{2}} \exp\left[(E_c - E_F)/kT\right] \int_0^{\infty} \varepsilon^{\frac{1}{2}} \exp-(\varepsilon/kT) d\varepsilon . \quad (4.2-5)$$

It is of interest to note that the distribution function is of the Maxwell-Boltzmann type, that is the electron density in the conduction band is low enough for the energy distribution to be non-degenerate.

Hence*

$$n = 2(2\pi m_n kT/h^2)^{\frac{3}{2}} \exp\left[-(E_c - E_F)/kT\right] . \quad (4.2-6)$$

* Evaluation of $I = \int_0^{\infty} \varepsilon^{\frac{1}{2}} \exp\left[-\varepsilon/kT\right] d\varepsilon$.
Let $\varepsilon = x^2$.

Therefore $\qquad\qquad I = 2\int x^2 \exp\left[-x^2/kT\right] dx$.

Now $\qquad\qquad \int_0^{\infty} \exp\left[-\alpha x^2\right] dx = \frac{1}{2}\left(\frac{\pi}{\alpha}\right)^{\frac{1}{2}}$.

Therefore

$$\left(\frac{\partial}{\partial\alpha}\right) \int_0^{\infty} \exp\left[-\alpha x^2\right] dx = -\int_0^{\infty} x^2 \exp\left[-\alpha x^2\right] dx = -\frac{1}{4}\left(\frac{\pi^{\frac{1}{2}}}{\alpha^{\frac{3}{2}}}\right)$$

(see *Dynamical theory of gases*, by J. H. Jeans, Camb. Univ. Press.).

The interchange of the order of differentiation and integration is allowable because the integral on the right-hand side is uniformly convergent with respect to α.

Hence $\qquad\qquad \int_0^{\infty} \varepsilon^{\frac{1}{2}} \exp\left[-\varepsilon/kT\right] d\varepsilon = \frac{1}{2}\pi^{\frac{1}{2}}(kT)^{\frac{3}{2}}$.

The term $2(2\pi m_n kT/h^2)^{\frac{3}{2}}$ is almost constant compared with the exponential, and so it is called a *pseudo-constant* and given the symbol N_c.

So finally, we have

$$n = N_c \exp\left[-(E_c - E_F)/kT\right] . \qquad (4.2\text{-}7)$$

The calculation of the Fermi level is most simply done by determining the number of holes in the valence band, and since we are dealing with an intrinsic semiconductor, equating the expressions for the numbers of electrons and holes.

As the presence of a hole can be regarded as the absence of an electron, the Fermi function for holes in the valence band is the inverse Fermi function $\tilde{F}(E)$ equal to $\{1 - F(E)\}$. The expressions for the number of holes p in the valence band is therefore given by

$$p = \int_{-\infty}^{E_v} N(E)\tilde{F}(E)dE . \qquad (4.2\text{-}8)$$

This time, by similar reasoning to that used for the possible states for the electrons in the conduction band

$$N(E) = \frac{4\pi}{h^3}(2m_p)^{\frac{3}{2}}(E_v - E)^{\frac{1}{2}} \qquad (4.2\text{-}9)$$

where m_p is the effective mass of the holes at the top of the valence band. The Fermi function is

$$\tilde{F}(E) = \frac{1}{1 + \exp\left[-(E - E_F)/kT\right]}. \qquad (4.2\text{-}10)$$

Therefore

$$p = \frac{4\pi}{h^3}(2m_p)^{\frac{3}{2}}\int_{-\infty}^{E_v}\frac{(E_v - E)^{\frac{1}{2}}dE}{1 + \exp\left[-(E - E_F)/kT\right]} \qquad (4.2\text{-}11)$$

Substituting $(E_v - E) = \varepsilon$ and assuming $(E_F - E)$ is much larger than kT leads to

$$p = \frac{4\pi}{h^3}(2m_p)^{\frac{3}{2}}\exp\left[-(E_F - E_v)/kT\right]\int_0^{\infty}\varepsilon^{\frac{1}{2}}\exp\left[-\varepsilon/kT\right]d\varepsilon . \qquad (4.2\text{-}12)$$

By using the value of this integral, obtained previously, we get

$$p = 2(2\pi m_p kT/h^2)^{\frac{3}{2}} \exp\left[-(E_F - E_v)/kT\right].\qquad(4.2\text{-}13)$$

Once again we have a *pseudo-constant*

$$N_v = 2(2\pi m_p kT/h^2)^{\frac{3}{2}}.$$

Therefore eqn (4.2-13) becomes

$$p = N_v \exp\left[-(E_F - E_v)/kT\right].\qquad(4.2\text{-}14)$$

Now, as we are dealing with an intrinsic material the density of electrons is equal to the density of holes.

Therefore

$$(m_n)^{\frac{3}{2}} \exp\left[-(E_c - E_F)/kT\right] = (m_p)^{\frac{3}{2}} \exp\left[-(E_F - E_v)/kT\right]\quad(4.2\text{-}15)$$

and so the Fermi level is given by

$$E_F = \tfrac{1}{2}(E_c + E_v) + \tfrac{3}{4}kT\,\ln(m_p/m_n).\qquad(4.2\text{-}16)$$

If it happens that m_p equals m_n then

$$E_F = \tfrac{1}{2}(E_c + E_v)\qquad(4.2\text{-}17)$$

that is, the Fermi level is mid-way between the valence band and conduction bands, but normally m_p is greater than m_n so E_F is just above the middle, and rises slightly with increasing temperature.

Equation (4.2-16) can be re-written in terms of the pseudo-constants, as it can be seen that

$$\frac{N_c}{N_v} = \left(\frac{m_n}{m_p}\right)^{\frac{3}{2}}.\qquad(4.2\text{-}18)$$

Therefore

$$E_F = \tfrac{1}{2}(E_c + E_v) + \frac{kT}{2}\ln\left(\frac{N_v}{N_c}\right).\qquad(4.2\text{-}19)$$

4.3 The Product of Holes and Electrons

If we take the product of the expressions for electrons and holes, eqns (4.2-6) and (13) we get

$$n \cdot p = 4 \left(\frac{2\pi kT}{h^2} \right)^3 (m_n m_p)^{\frac{3}{2}} \exp\left[-(E_c - E_v)/kT \right] . \qquad (4.3\text{-}1)$$

Now, $(E_c - E_v)$ equals E_g, the width of the forbidden gap. Therefore we can write

$$n \cdot p = 4 \left(\frac{2\pi kT}{h^2} \right)^3 (m_n m_p)^{\frac{3}{2}} \exp(-E_g/kT) \qquad (4.3\text{-}2)$$

or, alternatively, using the pseudo-constants,

$$n \cdot p = N_c N_v \exp(-E_g/kT) . \qquad (4.3\text{-}3)$$

It is important to observe that neither of these last two equations contains the Fermi level, and therefore they are general results, which, whilst they have been obtained by considering an intrinsic material, apply equally well to impurity doped, that is extrinsic, semiconductors, provided that the Fermi level is never within about $2kT$ of either forbidden band edge. In fact all that happens is that if an intrinsic material has impurities added so that the Fermi level rises, then n becomes greater than p, and if the Fermi level drops below the intrinsic level, p exceeds n. All the time, however, the product $n \cdot p$ is constant at constant temperature.

Returning to the case of the intrinsic semiconductor, the density of electrons equals the density of holes, and they are both called the *intrinsic density*, n_i, where

$$n_i = (n \cdot p)^{\frac{1}{2}} = (N_c N_v)^{\frac{1}{2}} \exp\left(-\frac{E_g}{2kT} \right) . \qquad (4.3\text{-}4)$$

The total density of carriers is, of course $2n_i$ and the equation for the conductivity

$$\sigma = q(n\mu_m + p\mu_p) \qquad (4.3\text{-}5)$$

becomes

$$\sigma = n_i q(\mu_n + \mu_p). \qquad (4.3\text{-}6)$$

If, as is the case in practice, the mobilities μ_n and μ_p and the pseudo-constants vary little with temperature, the value of the forbidden gap E_g can be obtained simply by a plot of the logarithm of the conductivity σ against $1/T$. The slope of this, which will be a straight line, will have a value of $(-E_g/2kT)$.

Further, we can find the incremental temperature ΔT, necessary to double the conductivity, or more accurately to double the number of carriers.

Using eqn (4.3-4) we have

$$n_i = (N_c N_v)^{\frac{1}{2}} \exp \left(- \frac{E_g}{2kT} \right) \qquad (4.3\text{-}7)$$

and at the higher temperature

$$2n_i = (N_c N_v)^{\frac{1}{2}} \exp \left[- \frac{E_g}{2k(T + \Delta T)} \right]. \qquad (4.3\text{-}8)$$

Hence

$$2 = \exp \left[\frac{E_g \cdot \Delta T}{2kT^2} \right] \qquad (4.3\text{-}9)$$

or

$$\frac{\Delta T}{T} = \frac{2kT \ln 2}{E_g}. \qquad (4.3\text{-}10)$$

For germanium with a gap of 0·75 eV* the conductivity at room temperature doubles in 15°C, and for silicon with a gap 1·12 eV, the conductivity doubles in 10°C. This, incidently, shows how sensitive these semiconductors are to temperature changes.

4.4 Impurity or Extrinsic Semiconductors

The electrical conductivity of a semiconductor is very dependent on purities and imperfections in the lattice. For instance the conductivity of silicon is increased a thousand times by the addition of 10 parts per million of boron. In this book, the study will be confined to the addition of impurities to germanium and silicon semiconductors.

First we will examine the crystal structure of germanium and silicon. They have the same structure as diamond, that is there is a tetrahedral

---

* For the purposes of this book the value of E_g for germanium will be taken as 0·75 eV and for silicon as 1·12 eV, but it is a complicated function of temperature, crystallographie orientation, and mode of electron excitation. For further discussion see, for example, J. R. Tillman and F. F. Roberts, *An introduction to the theory and practice of transistors*, pp. 42–44 (Pitman, 1961).

co-valent bonding between each atom and its four nearest neighbours, as shown in fig. 4.4a.

Intrinsic semiconduction arises from the breaking of one of the co-valent bonds, and it is seen, fig. 4.4b(i), that a hole-electron pair is

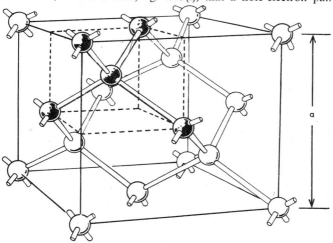

Figure 4.4a. The crystal structure of diamond, germanium, and silicon, showing the tetrahedral bond arrangement (After W. Shockley, *Electrons and Holes in Semiconductors.* Copyright 1950, D. Van Nostrand Company, Inc., Princeton, N.J.

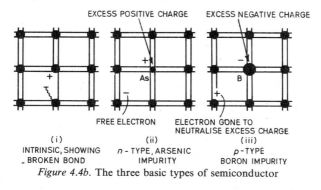

Figure 4.4b. The three basic types of semiconductor

produced. *Extrinsic* semiconduction arises by the replacement of a semiconductor atom by a different atom, called an impurity atom, and usually of group 3 or 5 of the Periodic Table. If the impurity atom is from group 5, this results in the co-valent bonds being completed with one electron left over [fig. 4.4b(ii)]. This electron can take part in conduction processes. The material is then said to be an *n-type* (negative current carrier) or *donor* semiconductor because the impurity donates electrons. On the other hand, if a semiconductor atom is replaced by an atom from group 3 of the Periodic Table, say boron, this impurity atom is unable to complete the co-valent bonding by itself, and so takes up an electron from another bond. This results in the net loss of an electron, that is, the formation of a hole, as shown in fig. 4.4b(iii). The semiconductor is then said to be a *p-type* (positive charge carrier) or an *acceptor* semiconductor, because the impurity accepts electrons from the intrinsic material.

4.5 The Bohr Theory Applied to Impurities in Semiconductors

We will consider the effect of introducing a group 5 atom to a semiconductor lattice, producing, as we have seen, an excess electron. This electron, however, is weakly bound to the impurity atom as the atom has only a small excess positive charge, and by applying Bohr's atomic theory already discussed in section 1.3, an evaluation of the ionization energy of this electron can be made. We now need to take into account the fact that the impurity atom is immersed in a material, the semiconductor, with a high relative permittivity. In the case of germanium the relative permittivity ε_r is 16 and for silicon ε_r is 12. But as the impurity atoms are normally well separated with a concentration similar to that of gas atoms, each atom can be considered as on its own, but in a medium of high relative permittivity. The analysis carried out in section 1.3 must therefore be modified. Eqn (1.3-3) becomes

$$m^* a\omega^2 = \frac{q^2}{4\pi\varepsilon_0\varepsilon_r a^2} \tag{4.5-1}$$

where not only the permittivity appears, which in eqn (1.3-3) was taken as ε_0, but also Z equals one, as only the *excess* positive nuclear charge exerts an attraction on the electron. The mass is now an effective mass m^*, approximately equal to m, in line with the findings of section 2.12. Eqn (1.3-7) therefore becomes

$$E = - \left(\frac{m^* q^4}{32 \pi^2 \varepsilon_0^2 \varepsilon_r^2 \hbar^2} \right) \left(\frac{1}{n^2} \right). \tag{4.5-2}$$

The ionization energy E of free hydrogen is 13·6 eV, a value given by eqn (4.5-2) with m^* equal to m and ε_r equal to 1. Hence the ionization energy of the electron attached to the arsenic atom is reduced by a factor $m^*/m\varepsilon_r^2$. Values obtained from this theory are considerably lower than experimental values, a fact which is largely due to the anisotropic behaviour of the effective mass, but the results are of the correct order. Also the use of the bulk relative permittivity is somewhat dubious on the atomic scale. The ionization energies of some impurities are given in Table 4A.

Table 4A. *Ionization energies in eV of trivalent and pentavalent impurities in silicon and germanium*

		Silicon	Germanium
Trivalent impurities	B	0·045	0·010
	Al	0·060	0·010
	Ga	0·070	0·011
	In	0·160	0·011
Pentavalent impurities	P	0·045	0·012
	A_0	0·053	0·013
	Sb	0·039	0·010

4.6 Impurity Energy Levels in Extrinsic Semiconductors

The previous section showed that only a small amount of energy, very much less than the size of the forbidden gap, is necessary to ionize the donor impurity atoms. Hence the energy level of the fifth electron, the conduction electron, must be just below the conduction band. Similar reasoning applied to acceptor materials leads to the conclusion that the acceptor energy level is only just above the valence band. A semiconductor containing both donors and acceptors therefore has energy levels as shown in fig. 4.6a. In addition to the energy levels, the amounts of impurities and the corresponding numbers ionized are of importance.

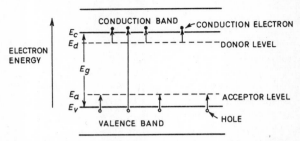

Figure 4.6a. Positions of donor and acceptor levels and the production of holes and conduction electrons

We will use the following symbols:

N_d = Density of donor atoms.

N_d^+ = Density of ionized donor atoms.

N_a = Density of acceptor atoms.

N_a^- = Density of ionized acceptor atoms.*

n = Density of electrons in the conduction band.

p = Density of holes in the valence band.

and n_i = Density of intrinsic holes and electrons.

The number of ionized donor atoms is equal to the number of electrons donated to the conduction band, and the number of ionized acceptor atoms is equal to the number of holes produced in the valence band by the addition of the acceptors.

When donors and acceptor atoms, which are electrically neutral initially, are added to an electrically neutral semiconductor the resulting material must, by the conservation of charge, be itself neutral.

Hence

$$n + N_a^- = p + N_d^+ \tag{4.6-1}$$

* Note that by ionization of acceptors is meant the removal of their holes, i.e. the impurity centres are occupied by electrons.

as in the intrinsic material n equals p and the addition of an ionized donor atom increases n by one, and similarly for acceptors.

We can apply Fermi statistics to determine the ratios N_a^-/N_a and N_d^+/N_d but throughout we shall assume that the spin-degenerate effect can be ignored, and hence each cell in phase space can accommodate two electrons.

Now, dealing with acceptors, holes are generated when electrons are raised from the valence band to the acceptor energy level. Therefore we have

$$\frac{N_a^-}{N_a} = F(E_a) = \frac{1}{1 + \exp\left[(E_a - E_F)/kT\right]} \tag{4.6-2}$$

where E_a is the acceptor energy level. It is assumed that the energy level E_a is not degenerate, so the factor $\frac{1}{2}$ does not appear before the exponential term. In the case of donors, one electron appears in the conduction band as a result of ionization, when the donor level E_d is *not* occupied by the electron. Hence we need here the inverse Fermi function $\tilde{F}(E)$. Therefore

$$\frac{N_d^+}{N_d} = \tilde{F}(E_d) = \frac{1}{1 + \exp\left[-(E_d - E_F)/kT\right]}. \tag{4.6-3}$$

Therefore substituting eqns (4.2-7), (4.2-14), (4.6-2) and (4.6-3) in eqn (4.6-1) we obtain the general relationship

$$N_c \exp\left[-(E_c - E_F)/kT\right] + \frac{N_a}{1 + \exp\left[(E_a - E_F)/kT\right]} =$$

$$N_v \exp\left[-(E_F - E_v)/kT\right] + \frac{N_d}{1 + \exp\left[-(E_d - E_F)/kT\right]}. \tag{4.6-4}$$

It is extremely difficult to solve this equation for E_F as it stands, and so a number of cases, which are common in practice, will be taken.

4.7 A Near Intrinsic or Near Compensated Crystal

Here we shall deal with the case where either the density of donors or acceptors is small compared with the density of intrinsic charge carriers, or the difference between the densities of donors and acceptors is small compared with the density of the intrinsic carriers, that is either

$$N_d \ll n_i \quad \text{and} \quad N_a \ll n_i$$

or

$$(N_d - N_a) \ll n_i \,.$$

We know, therefore, from the case of the intrinsic semiconductor that the Fermi level, E_F, will be somewhere near the middle of the forbidden gap.

Now, from eqn (4.6-2), and the knowledge that $(E_F - E_a)$ is much greater than kT we have

$$N_a^- \approx N_a \tag{4.7-1}$$

and from eqn (4.6-3) and knowing that $(E_d - E_F)$ is much greater than kT we obtain

$$N_d^+ \approx N_d \tag{4.7-2}$$

that is, all the donors and acceptors are ionized. Therefore our relationship for charge neutrality (eqn 4.6-1), becomes

$$n + N_a = p + N_d \,. \tag{4.7-3}$$

Now, eqn (4.2-7) gave

$$n = N_c \exp\left[-(E_c - E_F)/kT\right]$$

which can be written as

$$n = N_c \exp\left[(E_{Fi} - E_c)/kT\right] \exp\left[(E_F - E_{Fi})/kT\right] \tag{4.7-4}$$

where E_{Fi} is the Fermi level for the intrinsic semiconductor.

But eqn (4.2-7) also gives the density of intrinsic carriers as

$$n_i = N_c \exp\left[(E_{Fi} - E_c)/kT\right] \,. \tag{4.7-5}$$

Therefore eqn (4.7-4) becomes

$$n = n_i \exp\left[(E_F - E_{Fi})/kT\right] \,. \tag{4.7-6}$$

Also, as $n \,.\, p$ is n_i^2 we obtain

$$p = n_i \exp\left[-(E_F - E_{Fi})/kT\right] \,. \tag{4.7-7}$$

These two equations are very useful as they are true under all conditions when the Fermi level E_F is more than about $3kT$ from either band edge. Returning to eqn (4.7-3) we get

$$n_i \exp[(E_F - E_{Fi})/kT] + N_a = n_i \exp[-(E_F - E_{Fi})] + N_d . \quad (4.7-8)$$

This equation becomes

$$\sinh[(E_F - E_{Fi})/kT] = \frac{N_d - N_a}{2n_i}. \quad (4.7-9)$$

In the case under consideration $[(N_d - N_a)/2n_i]$ is small.

Therefore

$$E_F = E_{Fi} + \frac{kT}{2n_i}(N_d - N_a) . \quad (4.7-10)$$

Substituting this result back in eqns (4.7-6) and (4.7-7) gives

$$n = n_i \exp\left[\frac{N_d - N_a}{2n_i}\right] \approx n_i + \tfrac{1}{2}(N_d - N_a) \quad (4.7-11)$$

and

$$p = n_i \exp\left[-\left(\frac{N_d - N_a}{2n_i}\right)\right] \approx n_i - \tfrac{1}{2}(N_d - N_a) . \quad (4.7-12)$$

If the actual values of n and p are required, the value of n_i can be obtained, as before, from eqn (4.3-4).

4.8 An Extrinsic Semiconductor with a Large Donor Concentration

It will be assumed here that the material is at such a temperature that the intrinsic carrier density is low, and as $n.p$ is equal to n_i^2, then p is almost zero.

It will also be assumed that N_d is much less than n_i, that is, the donor doping is not excessively high, say of the order of one part in 10^7.

Now, we have already, eqn (4.6-3)

$$N_d^+ = \frac{N_d}{1 + \exp[-(E_d - E_F)/kT]}. \quad (4.6-3)$$

Now, as the density of states in the conduction band is very much greater than the density of donor atoms, and the ionisation energy of the impurities is comparable with the thermal energy of the electrons at room temperature, most of the donor atoms are ionised. The exponential term in the above equation will, therefore, be sufficiently small for only the first two terms of the binomial expansion to be required.

Therefore eqn (4.6-3) becomes

$$N_d^+ = N_d - N_d \exp\left[-(E_d - E_F)/kT\right] . \qquad (4.8\text{-}1)$$

As N_a is zero and n is much greater than p in the n-type material, the equation for charge neutrality reduces to

$$n = N_d^+ . \qquad (4.8\text{-}2)$$

But from eqn (4.2-7)

$$n = N_c \exp\left[-(E_c - E_F)/kT\right] .$$

Hence

$$N_c \exp\left[-(E_c - E_F)/kT\right] = N_d(1 - \exp\left[-(E_d - E_F)/kT\right]) . \qquad (4.8\text{-}3)$$

Therefore

$$\frac{N_c}{N_d} = \exp\left[(E_c - E_F)/kT\right] - \exp(E_c - E_d)/kT] \qquad (4.8\text{-}4)$$

from which

$$E_F = E_c - kT \ln\left\{\frac{N_c}{N_d} + \exp\left[(E_c - E_d)/kT\right]\right\} . \qquad (4.8\text{-}5)$$

In almost all practical cases the exponential term can be ignored in comparison with N_c/N_d, as N_c/N_d is usually of the order of 100 for normal doping. In germanium the exponential term is between one and two, if the semiconductor is at about room temperature, and obviously can then be neglected. In silicon, however, where the ionization energies of the impurities are between four and seven times those in germanium, as shown in Table 4A, the exponential term is sometimes significant. In both cases it becomes important at temperatures below about 150°K.

Substituting the above value for E_F in eqn (4.2-7) gives

$$n = \frac{N_c}{\dfrac{N_c}{N_d} + \exp\left[(E_c - E_d)/kT\right]}$$

$$= \frac{N_d}{1 + \dfrac{N_d}{N_c}\exp\left[(E_c - E_d)/kT\right]} . \qquad (4.8\text{-}6)$$

If the approximation cannot be applied, at least the binomial expansion can be used giving

$$n = N_d - \frac{N_d^2}{N_c}\exp\left[(E_c - E_d)/kT\right] . \qquad (4.8\text{-}7)$$

The hole concentration p, can as before, be obtained from

$$n . p = n_i^2 .$$

Similar reasoning applied to acceptor impurities leads to the conclusion that p is approximately equal to N_a.

4.9 A Donor Semiconductor at a Very Low Temperature

At a very low temperature, say of the order of 5°K, very few of the donor impurities will be ionized, and intrinsic carriers will be almost entirely absent. Hence we have N_a^- and p equal to zero. The charge neutrality equation becomes

$$n = N_d^+ \qquad (4.9\text{-}1)$$

and we have from eqns (4.6-3) and (4.2-7)

$$N_d^+ = \frac{N_d}{1 + \exp\left[(E_F - E_d)/kT\right]} \qquad (4.9\text{-}2)$$

and

$$n = N_c \exp\left[-(E_c - E_F)/kT\right] . \qquad (4.9\text{-}3)$$

Now, $(E_F - E_d)$ is much greater than kT as T is very small, so the exponential term in eqn (4.9-2) is very much greater than unity.

Equation (4.9-2) therefore becomes

$$N_d^+ = N_d \exp\left[-(E_F - E_d)/kT\right].\qquad(4.9\text{-}4)$$

Hence, using eqn (4.9-1) we get

$$N_c \exp\left[-(E_c - E_F)/kT\right] = N_d \exp\left[-(E_F - E_d)/kT\right].\qquad(4.9\text{-}5)$$

Therefore

$$E_c + E_d - 2E_F = kT\,\ln(N_c/N_d)\qquad(4.9\text{-}6)$$

and so

$$E_F = \tfrac{1}{2}(E_c + E_d) + \tfrac{1}{2}kT\,\ln(N_d/N_c).\qquad(4.9\text{-}7)$$

From this equation we see that as the temperature rises from absolute zero, the Fermi level falls.

Substituting the value of E_F in eqn (4.9-3) gives

$$\begin{aligned}
n &= N_c \exp\left[E_d - E_c)/2kT + \tfrac{1}{2}\ln N_d/N_c\right]\\
&= (N_c N_d)^{\frac{1}{2}} \exp\left[-(E_c - E_d)/2kT\right].
\end{aligned}\qquad(4.9\text{-}8)$$

$(E_c - E_d)$ is a positive quantity, so as would be expected, n increases as T is raised.

4.10 The Position of the Fermi Levels in a System of Two or More Semiconductors in Thermal Equilibrium

There is another very important reason for determining the positions of Fermi levels in addition to their use in calculating carrier densities. This occurs when two or more semiconductors of the same bulk material, but with different impurity content, are in intimate electrical contact. We will consider the situation depicted in fig. 4.10a.

Let us assume that semiconductor (1) has a density $n_1(E)dE$ of electrons in the conduction band in an energy range E to $(E + dE)$, that the density of states is $N_1(E)$, and the Fermi function is $F_1(E)$. The corresponding quantities for semiconductor (2) in the *same* energy range are $n_2(E)dE$, $N_2(E)$ and $F_2(E)$.

For electrons to flow, non-energetically, from (1) to (2) there must be empty states at an energy E in semiconductor (2), and it is reasonable

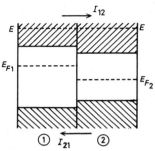

Figure 4.10a. Two similar semiconductors, with different amounts of doping, in contact

to assume that the current I_{12} will be proportional to the density of vacancies in (2) and the density of electrons in (1) at the energy E. That is

$$I_{12} \propto n_1(E)dE\{N_2(E) - n_2(E)\}dE . \qquad (4.10\text{-}1)$$

Similarly the current

$$I_{21} \propto n_2(E)dE\{N_1(E) - n_1(E)\}dE . \qquad (4.10\text{-}2)$$

In thermodynamic equilibrium for zero net current

$$I_{12} = I_{21} . \qquad (4.10\text{-}3)$$

Therefore

$$n_1(E)dE\{N_2(E) - n_2(E)\}dE = n_2(E)dE\{N_1(E) - n_1(E)\}dE . \qquad (4.10\text{-}4)$$

Hence

$$n_1(E) . N_2(E) = n_2(E)N_1(E) . \qquad (4.10\text{-}5)$$

But

$$n(E) = N(E)F(E) .$$

Therefore

$$N_1(E)F_1(E)N_2(E) = N_2(E)F_2(E)N_1(E) \qquad (4.10\text{-}6)$$

and so

$$F_1(E) = F_2(E) . \qquad (4.10\text{-}7)$$

This means, in particular, that

$$E_{\text{F1}} = E_{\text{F2}} \ . \tag{4.10-8}$$

Hence, the Fermi level through any number of semiconductors in thermodynamic equilibrium is a constant. Conversely, if the materials in contact have the same Fermi level, then they must be in thermodynamic equilibrium. This is a most important result.

4.11 The Electrostatic Potential of a Semiconductor
The potential at a point is defined as the work done in moving a positive unit charge from infinity to that point.

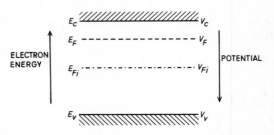

Figure 4.11a. Electron energies and corresponding potentials in a semiconductor

If we let the potentials of the top of the valence band, intrinsic Fermi level, Fermi level and bottom of the conduction band be V_{v}, V_{Fi}, V_{F}, and V_{c} respectively, fig. 4.11a, so that we get the relationships

$$V_{\text{v}} = -E_{\text{v}}/q + C \tag{4.11-1}$$

$$V_{\text{Fi}} = -E_{\text{Fi}}/q + C \tag{4.11-2}$$

$$V_{\text{F}} = -E_{\text{F}}/q + C \tag{4.11-3}$$

$$V_{\text{c}} = -E_{\text{c}}/q + C \tag{4.11-4}$$

where q is the electronic charge, and C is a constant. Since we are only interested in differences of potential C can be made zero.

In defining the potential of a piece of semiconductor it is necessary to choose some energy level which is a property of the bulk semiconductor rather than of the doped material, as there is no reason to suppose that adding a small quantity of an impurity would change the potential of the semiconductor. In practice the potential of the intrinsic Fermi level is commonly called the potential of the semiconductor. However, it would be more correct to use $\frac{1}{2}(V_v + V_c)$ which may be slightly different, at temperatures other than the absolute zero, as V_{Fi} may vary slightly with temperature.

CHAPTER 5

Current Flow in Semiconductors

5.1 Introduction

Current flow in a semiconductor arises from the motion of charge carriers in both the conduction and valence bands. As explained in chapter 4, the mobile charges in the conduction band are electrons and those in the valence band are holes. The current is in general made up of two components, drift current and diffusion current, although in certain instances one or other of these two components may predominate. Drift current occurs in the presence of an electric field which, as a result of the force it causes to act on each charge carrier, produces a net motion of positively charged carriers in the same sense as the field, and negatively charged carriers in the opposite sense.

A diffusion current arises whenever there is a spatial variation in density of mobile charge carriers. The random thermal motion of the carriers causes a net flow from regions of high density to regions of low density; thus the diffusion current at any point is opposite in sense to the density gradient at that point.

For this and subsequent chapters of the book, the carriers in both the conduction and valence bands are assumed to be corpuscular in nature, with effective masses, see section 2.12, which are in general different from the free electron mass. Each carrier is assumed to have a charge $-q$, for electrons in the conduction band, or $+q$, for holes in the valence band, where q is the magnitude of the electronic charge. The motion of the carriers is then given by the usual Newtonian laws of dynamics. In electric and magnetic fields, they are subject to forces as predicted by classical electrodynamics.

Among other simplifications, it will be assumed that all electrons in the conduction band have the same effective mass, namely, that corresponding to the bottom of the band. Similarly, it will be assumed that all holes in the valence band have the same effective mass, namely that corresponding to the top of the band. Experiment [5.1], [5.2] shows that both electrons and holes in a semiconductor are present with more than one value of effective mass, but that one value usually predominates. Further, the effective masses are functions of the direction in the crystal. The assumption of a single effective mass for each type of carrier does not lead to qualitatively incorrect results and since, in the work that follows, effective masses appear only as factors in quantities which are normally determined experimentally, any quantitative error is relatively unimportant.

In section 4.2, it was explained that the electron and hole densities in the conduction and valence bands respectively, are normally non-degenerate for a semiconductor. By this is meant that the density of electrons in any small energy range of the conduction band is small compared with the density of available energy levels in the same range. Because the energy levels in the band are very closely spaced in energy, an electron in the band has many adjacent levels to which it may move. A similar consideration applies to the motion of holes in the valence band. There is, therefore, no impediment to the motion of carriers, and each carrier in the conduction or valence band may be considered to contribute fully to any conduction process. This is contrary to the case of a conductor, where the electron density in the conduction band is degenerate and where, near the bottom of the band, all the available energy levels are full thus making it difficult for electrons to move.

It was also shown in section 4.2 that when the density is non-degenerate, the electrons have a Maxwell-Boltzmann distribution in energy, referred to the bottom of the conduction band. This is also true of the holes in the valence band, the energy being measured down from the top of the band. For the corpuscular picture of the electrons in the conduction band and holes in the valence band, the energy measured from the edge of the band is taken as the kinetic energy of motion of the carrier. It is thus possible to associate with each carrier, at any instant, a velocity analogous to the thermal velocity of a gas molecule.

Accordingly, the velocity distribution amongst the electrons and holes is assumed to be Maxwellian.

For the non-degenerate densities which carriers have in semiconductors, mutual interaction between carriers is negligible. The carriers will, however, suffer collisions with the lattice ions. The mean free path between such collisions is several orders larger than the separation of adjacent lattice ions [5.3]. The exact nature of carrier lattice collisions is rather complex; fortunately, a crude picture of the process as an elastic collision between a light particle and a heavy, elastically constrained, particle is adequate for a simple understanding of conduction processes in semiconductors.

In terms of the band theory, developed in chapter 2, it would be expected that an electron in the conduction band, or hole in the valence band, should be free to move without collision throughout the crystal. This is because only a small fraction of the closely spaced energy levels are occupied by carriers. The carriers should be able to move easily from level to level, suffering collisions only at the boundaries of the crystal. However, the band theory picture presented in chapter 2 is incomplete in one important feature. It does not allow for the vibrational energy states of the crystal lattice. The vibration of the crystal lattice is quantized in that only certain modes of oscillation are allowed. The situation is similar to that of a vibrating string fastened rigidly at its two ends, for which any vibration can be thought of as the superposition of the fundamental and overtone modes of oscillation. As in the quantum theory of electrons, see chapter 1, the lattice interaction with charge carriers can therefore only change its energy by discrete amounts. These discrete amounts are termed *phonons* and are the counterpart of *quanta* for electrons and *photons* for electromagnetic radiation. The theory of phonon interaction is not discussed in the present volume. For an account of this topic the reader is referred elsewhere [5.4]. The effect of the thermal vibration [5.5] of the lattice is to cause the edges of the energy bands to oscillate slightly about their normal energies. This oscillation is largely random in both amplitude and position in the crystal and is on a microscopic scale. Electrons and holes near the band edges may now be unable to move to adjacent energy levels, but may be reflected by the oscillating band edges. Because nearly all the electrons in the conduction band are near the bottom of the band, and holes in the valence band near the top, appreciable scattering and restriction of the motion of the carriers may be caused by the vibration of the lattice. This phenomenon is termed *lattice* scattering. The vibration of the lattice becomes more pronounced with increasing temperature; as a consequence, the lattice scattering and the electrical resistance* of the material also increase with temperature.

Another type of collision in which a carrier can be involved is that of ionized impurity scattering [5.6], [5.7]. Because a donor or acceptor impurity is normally ionized at room temperature, it gives rise to a localized electronic charge in the lattice. Mobile charge carriers moving near such an impurity centre, are deflected from their normal paths because of the electrostatic force existing between the carrier and the centre. This type of scattering is insignificant in relatively pure, that is near intrinsic, material. It is more significant for semiconductors with appreciable donor or acceptor impurity content.

In many ways, the electrons in the conduction band, or holes in the valence band, resemble the molecules of a gas, the density of which is sufficiently low that mutual interaction between the molecules is negligible. Some simplifying assumptions of the elementary kinetic theory of gases are useful in explaining the phenomena of drift and diffusion currents in semiconductors. These simplifying assumptions lead to substantially correct forms of expression relating the physical variables of a gas, but such expressions usually have numerical constants as much as thirty per cent in error. In a similar way, the analogous use of the simplifying concepts of kinetic theory leads to substantially correct results for semiconductors. The correct forms of expression for the drift and diffusion currents in a semiconductor are obtained. In any event, the numerical constants must be determined by experiment because the complexity of the system makes it difficult, if not impossible, to predict such constants theoretically.

---

* On the assumption that the carrier density is independent of temperature, which may or may not be true according to material and conditions.

In the sections which follow, expressions for the drift and diffusion current densities in a semiconductor will be obtained.

5.2 Drift Phenomena in a Semiconductor

A carrier, having a charge q', in an electric field of intensity $\mathbf{E}$ will experience a force $\mathbf{F}$ given by

$$\mathbf{F} = q'\mathbf{E} . \tag{5.2-1}$$

If the carrier is a hole in the valence band, the charge q' which it carries will be the electronic charge q. If it is an electron in the conduction band it will carry a charge $-q$. The carrier will be accelerated by the electric field according to the equation:

$$m\ddot{\mathbf{r}} = \mathbf{F} \tag{5.2-2}$$

where m is the mass of the carrier and $\mathbf{r}$ its position vector measured from some origin. This equation may be integrated with respect to time t to give:

$$m\dot{\mathbf{r}} = m\dot{\mathbf{r}}_0 + \mathbf{F}t \tag{5.2-3}$$

where $\dot{\mathbf{r}}_0$ is the carrier velocity immediately following a lattice collision, and the time t is measured from this instant. For this integration to be valid, $\mathbf{E}$, and hence $\mathbf{F}$, must not change appreciably during the time t. In section 4.2 it was shown that in the absence of electric fields, and at the non-degenerate densities found in most semiconductors, the carriers have a Maxwell-Boltzmann distribution of energies, and hence velocities, when considered as particles within the conduction and valence bands. The root-mean-square velocity v_T of such a distribution was shown in section 3.5 to be given by

$$v_T = \sqrt{\left(\frac{3kT}{m}\right)} \tag{5.2-4}$$

where T is the temperature of the crystal, m is the effective mass of the carriers and k is Boltzmann's constant. Using the free electron mass, which is of the same order as the effective mass of the carriers, and taking the temperature as 27°C, eqn (5.2-4) indicates a value of v_T of approximately 10^5 ms^{-1}. The distance travelled by carriers between lattice collisions is usually much less than 10 μ, that is 10^{-5} m [5.3], and so the time of flight of a carrier between lattice collisions is usually much less than 10^{-10} s.

In this estimation it is implied that the electric field does not (during their times of flight between collisions) accelerate the carriers to velocities which are orders of magnitude greater than the thermal velocities. This assumption is valid except for high electric field intensities. Keeping in mind the fact the number of carriers with velocity magnitudes appreciably less than v_T is very small, the integration of eqn (5.2-2) to give eqn (5.2-3) is valid provided the electric intensity $\mathbf{E}$ does not change appreciably in 10^{-10} s. The time t is, of course, restricted to the times of flight of carriers between collisions.

It may be concluded that the integration is valid, provided that the highest harmonic component of $\mathbf{E}$ has a frequency below 10^{10} s^{-1}. A similar conclusion may be drawn with regard to any subsequent integration. The velocities $\dot{\mathbf{r}}_0$ with which carriers leave collisions are assumed to have a Maxwellian distribution appropriate to the temperature of the crystal. Further the directions in which carriers leave collisions are assumed to be randomly orientated in space. It follows that the average $\langle \dot{\mathbf{r}}_0 \rangle$ of the velocities $\dot{\mathbf{r}}_0$ over a large number of collisions is zero. Because the density of carriers is in excess of 10^{20} m^{-3}, the averaging over a sufficiently large number of carriers can still be carried out in a time during which $\mathbf{F}$ may be assumed constant, say in less than 10^{-10} s.

The assumptions concerning the distribution in magnitude and direction of the velocities of carriers leaving collisions are plausible, provided that the additional energy acquired by a carrier, from the electric field in flights between collisions, is small compared with its thermal energy. The upper limit to the mean distance between collisions is of the order of 1 μ, that is 10^{-6} m; thus the mean energy a carrier acquires between collisions from an electric intensity of 3×10^4 Vm^{-1} is less than 0·03 eV. This is approximately the mean thermal energy of the carriers at room temperatures, and so the assumption of the last paragraph should be valid for electric intensities below 3×10^4 Vm^{-1}.

Equation (5.2-3) may be integrated again with respect to time to give:

$$\mathbf{r} = \mathbf{r}_0 + \dot{\mathbf{r}}_0 t + \left(\frac{1}{2m}\right)\mathbf{F}t^2 \qquad (5.2\text{-}5)$$

where $\mathbf{r}_0$ is the position vector of the collision from which the time t is measured. The vector displacement of the carrier from this collision to its next collision, at a point with position vector $\mathbf{r}_1$, is:

$$\mathbf{r}_1 - \mathbf{r}_0 = \dot{\mathbf{r}}_0 \tau + \left(\frac{1}{2m}\right)\mathbf{F}\tau^2 \qquad (5.2\text{-}6)$$

where τ is the time between the collisions. Averaging this displacement over a large number of collisions, but keeping the time for the averaging process less than 10^{-10} s, the mean displacement of the carriers between collisions is:

$$\langle\mathbf{r}_1 - \mathbf{r}_0\rangle = \langle\dot{\mathbf{r}}_0 \tau\rangle + \left(\frac{1}{2m}\right)\mathbf{F}\langle\tau^2\rangle . \qquad (5.2\text{-}7)$$

Provided the additional energy acquired from the electric field in flights between collisions is small compared with the thermal energies of the carriers, as has already been assumed, the time of flight τ is independent of the randomly orientated initial velocity $\dot{\mathbf{r}}_0$. As a consequence, the average value of $\dot{\mathbf{r}}_0 \tau$, over a very large number of collisions, vanishes just as the average value of $\dot{\mathbf{r}}_0$ vanished. The first term on the right hand side of eqn (5.2-7) is therefore zero and the mean displacement is thus in the direction of the force $\mathbf{F}$.

If the mean displacement is divided by the mean time of flight $\langle\tau\rangle$, the mean *drift* velocity $\mathbf{u}$, in the direction of $\mathbf{F}$, is obtained:

$$\mathbf{u} = \frac{\langle\mathbf{r}_1 - \mathbf{r}_0\rangle}{\langle\tau\rangle} = \left(\frac{1}{2m}\right)\mathbf{F}\left(\frac{\langle\tau^2\rangle}{\langle\tau\rangle}\right). \qquad (5.2\text{-}8)$$

Using eqn (5.2-1):

$$\mathbf{u} = \left(\frac{q'}{2m}\right)\left(\frac{\langle\tau^2\rangle}{\langle\tau\rangle}\right)\mathbf{E} = \mu\mathbf{E} . \qquad (5.2\text{-}9)$$

The quantity μ is called the *mobility* of the carriers. For electrons in the conduction band and holes in the valence band, eqn (5.2-9) becomes respectively:

$$\mathbf{u}_n = -\left(\frac{q}{2m_n}\right)\left(\frac{\langle\tau_n^2\rangle}{\langle\tau_n\rangle}\right)\mathbf{E} = -\mu_n\mathbf{E} \qquad (5.2\text{-}10)$$

$$\mathbf{u}_p = \left(\frac{q}{2m_p}\right)\left(\frac{\langle\tau_p^2\rangle}{\langle\tau_p\rangle}\right)\mathbf{E} = \mu_p\mathbf{E} . \qquad (5.2\text{-}11)$$

In these equations, m_n and τ_n are the effective mass and mean time between collisions respectively for electrons in the conduction band and m_p and τ_p are similarly defined for holes in the valence band. The quantities μ_n and μ_p are the electron and hole mobilities respectively. By convention, μ_n, the electron mobility, is defined as a positive quantity; this gives rise to the minus sign in eqn (5.2-10).

The carrier mobilities are determined experimentally [5.8], [5.9], [5.10]. Typical values* for intrinsic germanium and silicon at 300°K are given in table 5A.

Table 5A

		Germanium	Silicon
Electron mobility	μ_n	0·38	0·15
Hole mobility	μ_p	0·18	0·05

Units $m^2 V^{-1} s^{-1}$

These mobilities are independent of the electric field for intensities below about $3 \times 10^4 Vm^{-1}$ as estimated previously.

A reasonable postulate concerning collisions between carriers and the lattice, is that the probability of a carrier having a lattice collision in a small time interval Δt, is proportional to the displacement Δr of the carriers in the interval. Thus the probability of a collision in the interval Δt is:

$$P(\Delta t) = K . \Delta r = K|\dot{\mathbf{r}}|\Delta t \qquad (5.2\text{-}12)$$

* Mobilities vary with temperature, electric field and the impurity content of the semiconductor. These dependencies are discussed in sections 5.3 and 5.4. The experimental values also depend on the method of measurement. For further details, the reader should consult the references cited in sections 5.3 and 5.4.

where K is a constant of proportionality. Once again, let it be assumed that the additional energy acquired by a carrier, from the electric field in a flight between collisions, is small compared to its thermal energy. The velocity magnitude $|\dot{\mathbf{r}}|$ of a carrier, at any time, is then not greatly different from its initial value $|\dot{\mathbf{r}}_0|$ immediately after a collision. Eqn (5.2-12) is then:

$$P(\Delta t) = K|\dot{\mathbf{r}}_0|\,\Delta t \ . \tag{5.2-13}$$

The probability is thus a function of the thermal velocity of the carrier which is given by the Maxwellian distribution.

From eqn (3.5-11) of a total of n carriers, a number dn given by:

$$dn = \frac{4n}{\sqrt{\pi}}\left(\frac{m}{2kT}\right)^{\frac{3}{2}} v^2 \exp\left(\frac{-mv^2}{2kT}\right) dv \tag{5.2-14}$$

have velocity magnitudes in the range v to $(v+dv)$. Eqns (5.2-13) and (14) then predict the number of carriers, with velocities in the specified range, which will have lattice collisions in the interval Δt. This number is:

$$P(\Delta t).\,dn = Kv.\,\Delta t.\,dn$$

$$= \frac{4Kn}{\sqrt{\pi}}\left(\frac{m}{2kT}\right)^{\frac{3}{2}} \Delta t.\,v^3 \exp\left(\frac{-mv^2}{2kT}\right) dv \ . \tag{5.2-15}$$

Of the total of n carriers, the number having lattice collisions in the time interval Δt, can be obtained by integration of eqn (5.2-15), with respect to v, between the limits zero and infinity. Thus the total number n of carriers, of all velocities, having collisions in the time interval Δt is given by:

$$\Delta n = \frac{4Kn}{\sqrt{\pi}}\left(\frac{m}{2kT}\right)^{\frac{3}{2}}.\,\Delta t\,.\int_0^\infty x^3 \exp\left(\frac{-mx^2}{2kT}\right) dx \ . \tag{5.2-16}$$

Consider the integral:

$$\int_0^\infty x \exp(-\lambda x^2)dx = \frac{1}{2\lambda} \tag{5.2-17}$$

a result which is readily established.

Differentiation under the integral sign with respect to λ yields:

$$\int_0^\infty x^3 \exp(-\lambda x^2)dx = \frac{1}{2\lambda^2}. \qquad (5.2\text{-}18)$$

Equation (5.2-16) may then be written:

$$\Delta n = \left(\frac{n}{\tau'}\right)\Delta t \qquad (5.2\text{-}19)$$

where

$$\tau' = \frac{1}{K}\sqrt{\left(\frac{\pi m}{8kT}\right)}. \qquad (5.2\text{-}20)$$

For the purpose of calculation of the mean time of flight $\langle\tau\rangle$ of carriers between collisions, and also the mean square time $\langle\tau^2\rangle$, both of which quantities appear in eqn (5.2-8), consider a number n_0 of carriers at time zero. Suppose that after a time t, a number n of these have yet to have a lattice collision. During the interval t to $(t+\Delta t)$, of these n carriers, a number Δn given by eqn (5.2-19) will have lattice collisions. This latter equation can then be integrated to give:

$$n = n_0 \exp\left(-\frac{t}{\tau'}\right). \qquad (5.2\text{-}21)$$

Now the Δn carriers, which have collisions in the interval t to $(t+\Delta t)$, will have had a total life without collision of $t.\Delta n$. Equation (5.2-19) then gives:

$$t.\Delta n = \left(\frac{n}{\tau'}\right)t.\Delta t \qquad (5.2\text{-}22)$$

where n is given by eqn (5.2-21). The mean time between collisions is obtained by integration of eqn (5.2-22) with respect to t, from zero to infinity and subsequent division by n_0. This gives:

$$\langle\tau\rangle = \frac{1}{\tau'}\int_0^\infty t \exp\left(-\frac{t}{\tau'}\right)dt = \tau'. \qquad (5.2\text{-}23)$$

This identifies the time constant τ' of eqn (5.2-21) with the mean time $\langle\tau\rangle$. Similarly:

$$\langle \tau^2 \rangle = \frac{1}{\langle \tau \rangle} \int_0^\infty t^2 \exp\left(-\frac{t}{\tau'}\right) dt = 2\langle \tau \rangle^2 . \qquad (5.2\text{-}24)$$

It follows from eqns (5.2-9) and (24) that the mobility can be expressed as:

$$\mu = \left(\frac{q'}{2m}\right)\left(\frac{\langle \tau^2 \rangle}{\langle \tau \rangle}\right) = \left(\frac{q'}{m}\right)\langle \tau \rangle . \qquad (5.2\text{-}25)$$

5.3 Dependence of Mobility on Temperature and the Nature of the Collisions

From eqns (5.2-20), (23) and (25), it is seen that the mobility can be expressed as:

$$\mu = \frac{q'}{K} \bigg/ \sqrt{\left(\frac{\pi}{8mkT}\right)} . \qquad (5.3\text{-}1)$$

This equation shows that the mobility, as derived, is independent of the electric intensity and inversely proportional to the square root of the absolute temperature. However, this assumes that both m and K are independent of temperature. In order to investigate the temperature dependence of the latter of these two quantities, introduced as a constant of proportionality in eqn (5.2-12), it is necessary to distinguish between the types of collision in which a carrier may take part. As explained in section 5.1, collisions may be of either the *lattice scattered* or of the *impurity scattered* type.

It has been shown theoretically that the constant K ought to be inversely proportional to the absolute temperature, for the former type of collision [5.11], and ought to vary directly with the square of the absolute temperature for the latter type of collision [5.7]. If it is then assumed that the effective mass is independent of temperature, the mobility should vary inversely as the three-halves power of the temperature for lattice scattering and directly as the three-halves power for impurity scattering.

The inverse three-halves power is confirmed experimentally [5.9], [5.10] for electron mobilities, but hole mobilities vary inversely with a higher power of the temperature than three-halves. Experimental results on the temperature dependence of impurity scattering are more diverse and the three halves law cannot be considered confirmed.

Impurity centres are relatively few among normal lattice ions except for the more heavily doped semiconductors. In this circumstance most collisions are due to lattice scattering. Thus, for near intrinsic and lightly doped semiconductors, the effective mobilities are substantially those due to lattice collisions and are independent of the degree of doping. This is experimentally confirmed [5.9] for impurity densities up to about 10^{22} atoms m^{-3}. At higher doping densities, impurity scattering contributes appreciably to the mobilities and these quantities are no longer independent of the degree of doping.

5.4 Field Dependence of Mobility

As the electric intensity is increased above about $3 \times 10^4 \, Vm^{-1}$, the additional energy acquired by a carrier in flights between collisions is no longer small compared with the thermal energy of the carrier. The magnitudes of the velocities of carriers leaving collisions are not now distributed according to the Maxwell law, nor are the directions of the velocities randomly orientated in space. The derivations of eqns (5.2-9) and (23) are no longer viable and the carrier mobilities are no longer independent of the electric field. Experimentally [5.12] it has been shown that the mobilities of both electrons and holes in germanium and silicon are field independent for electric intensities up to a critical value, of the order of $10^5 \, Vm^{-1}$, roughly in agreement with the estimate of 3×10^4 Vm^{-1} made previously.

Above this value, the mobilities vary approximately as the inverse square-root of the electric intensity up to intensities of the order of $10^6 \, Vm^{-1}$. For still larger fields, they vary inversely as the intensity, and the drift velocity saturates to a constant value independent of the electric intensity.

Eventually, as the electric intensity is further increased, avalanche or Zener breakdown occurs, and the current rises independently of the intensity. These latter effects will be briefly discussed in another context in chapter 7.

5.5 Drift Current Density

In this section an expression will be obtained for the drift current density in terms of the carrier mobility, carrier density and the electric intensity. From this is deduced the electrical conductivity of the semiconductor.

With reference to fig. 5.5a, consider an imaginary cylinder of unit cross-section and length $|\mathbf{u}|$, with its axis parallel to the direction of $\mathbf{E}$. The average displacement per carrier in the direction of $\mathbf{E}$ in an interval of one second is $|\mathbf{u}|$, and hence every carrier in the imaginary cylinder

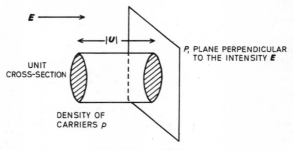

Figure 5.5a. Calculation of drift current density

at time t can be said to cross the plane P in the next second. The drift velocity is superimposed upon the random thermal velocities, and so it follows that carriers in the cylinder do not necessarily cross the base of the cylinder in the plane P. However, other carriers, outside the cylinder at time t, will cross the base of the cylinder and thereby compensate for those in the cylinder which do not. The net effect is as if the carriers had zero thermal velocity and as if all moved with simply the drift velocity in the direction of the electric intensity $\mathbf{E}$.

Thus, the total charge of the mobile carriers within the cylinder, or its equivalent, crosses the unit area base in one second. This, by definition, is the current density in the plane P. The charge within the cylinder is the product of the volume of the cylinder, the carrier density and the charge per carrier. Thus the current densities for electrons and holes are respectively:

$$\mathbf{J}_n = -qn \cdot \mathbf{u}_n = qn\mu_n \cdot \mathbf{E} \tag{5.5-1}$$

and

$$\mathbf{J}_p = qp\mathbf{u}_p = qp\mu_p \cdot \mathbf{E} \tag{5.5-2}$$

where n and p are the electron and hole densities respectively. Equations (5.2-10) and (11) have been used to express the drift velocities in terms of the mobilities and the electric intensity.

The use of a time interval of one second in the above derivation might be objected to on the grounds that $\mathbf{E}$ is not necessarily constant for this interval. This objection is readily avoided by using a time interval Δt instead of one second. The length of the cylinder would then be taken as $|\mathbf{u}| \cdot \Delta t$. However, the same reasoning leads again to eqns (5.5-1) and (2), the interval Δt cancelling out. It is only necessary that Δt be chosen large enough, so that the cylinder contains a sufficient number of carriers for the mobilities to be defined adequately with regard to the averaging processes of section 5.2. The use of a Δt of the order of 10^{-10} s, as in section 5.2, is satisfactory on all counts.

The two current densities of eqns (5.5-1) and (2) are in the same sense and the total current density is their sum, namely:

$$\mathbf{J} = \mathbf{J}_n + \mathbf{J}_p = q(n\mu_n + p\mu_p) \cdot \mathbf{E} . \tag{5.5-3}$$

The constant of proportionality between the current density $\mathbf{J}$ and the electric intensity $\mathbf{E}$ is the conductivity σ of the semiconductor. That is:

$$\sigma = q(n\mu_n + p\mu_p) . \tag{5.5-4}$$

Often one type of carrier, electron or hole, predominates and since μ_n and μ_p are of the same order, the contribution to σ of the carrier of lower density is negligible. The mobilities μ_n and μ_p are independent of the electric intensity, except for the cases discussed in section 5.4. It follows then, from eqn (5.5-4), that the conductivity σ is also independent of $\mathbf{E}$ and hence the semiconductor obeys Ohm's law in so far as drift current is concerned. As discussed in section 5.4, at high electric intensities, the mobilities become field dependent and eqn (5.5-4) then implies that the conductivity has the same field dependence as the mobilities*. For this

* At the very highest intensities, n and p may also become field dependent. This case will be excluded.

reason, experimental determinations of the current voltage characteristics of semiconductors are used [5·12] to investigate the field dependence of mobility.

5.6 Temperature Dependence of Conductivity

The conductivity σ, given by eqn (5.5-4), depends on the temperature of the semiconductor through the carrier densities and through the mobilities. The temperature dependence of the carrier densities is given by the equations which were obtained in chapter 4. The temperature dependence of the mobilities was discussed in section 5.3. The carrier densities are often exponentially dependent on temperature. This tends to swamp any dependence of the mobility on a small power of the temperature.

By way of example, consider an n-type semiconductor. At low temperatures, the electron density in the conduction band is given by eqns (4.2-6) and (4.9-8) as:

$$n = \left(\frac{2\pi k m_n}{h^2}\right)^{\frac{3}{4}} (2N_d)^{\frac{1}{2}} T^{\frac{3}{4}} \exp\left(-\frac{\Delta E}{2kT}\right) \tag{5.6-1}$$

where N_d is the donor density and ΔE is the depth of the donor levels below the bottom of the conduction band. The temperature dependence of the exponential term swamps the three-quarter power term, and also any power term in the mobility when eqn (5.6-1) is used in eqn (5.5-4) for the conductivity σ. For low temperatures, a plot of $\ln \sigma$ against T^{-1} yields an approximately straight line of slope $(-\Delta E/2k)$, from which ΔE can be deduced. If the terms in $\ln T$ are subtracted from $\ln \sigma$ in making this plot, an exact straight line should result. However, the magnitudes of these $\ln T$ terms are often negligible compared with $\ln \sigma$, or at least the magnitude of their changes are negligible compared with that of $\ln \sigma$.

At higher temperatures, an appreciable fraction of the donors become ionized and eqn (5.6-1) is no longer valid. The electron density becomes less dependent on an exponential function of the temperature until, for temperatures above which virtually all the donors are ionized, it becomes temperature independent. The density of electrons is then simply equal to the density of donors. In this range of temperatures, the temperature dependence of the conductivity is that of the mobilities.

For room temperatures and above, thermal generation of hole-electron pairs by the intrinsic process, breaking of covalent-bonds, begins to contribute to the carrier densities. At sufficiently high temperatures, intrinsically generated electrons may greatly predominate over the electrons from the donor centres. In this circumstance, by eqn (4.3-2), both electron and hole densities become:

$$n_i = 2 \left(\frac{2\pi k}{h^2} \right)^{\frac{3}{2}} (m_n m_p)^{\frac{3}{4}} T^{\frac{3}{2}} \exp \left(- \frac{E_g}{2kT} \right) \qquad (5.6\text{-}2)$$

where E_g is the energy gap of the semiconductor. Again, the three-halves power term in T, and any power term in the mobility, is swamped by the exponentially temperature dependent term. A plot of $\ln \sigma$ against T^{-1}, now gives a substantially straight line of slope $(-E_g/2k)$ from which the energy gap E_g can be deduced.

At still higher temperatures, the electron and hole densities become degenerate. This means that the freedom of movement of carriers, particularly those near the bottom of the conduction band or top of the valence band, is impaired owing to the large number of adjacent levels which are occupied by others carriers. The number of carriers which can take part in the conduction process is effectively limited. The temperature dependence of the conductivity is then largely that of the lattice scattering process. The semiconductor has, under this condition, essentially metallic conduction properties. In a heavily doped semiconductor, this limit to the increase in conductivity might manifest itself before all the donors have become ionized.

To summarize briefly, semiconductors usually have positive temperature coefficients of conductivity while metals have negative temperature coefficients.

5.7 Diffusion Current in Semiconductors

In the introductory section 5.1 of this chapter, it was explained that diffusion current arises whenever there is a spatial variation of carrier concentration in the semiconductor. This flow of carriers from regions of high concentration, to those of low concentration, is a direct consequence of the random thermal motion of the carriers. The diffusion current is independent* of any electric field in the semiconductor, although such a field will give rise to a drift current as outlined in previous sections. The net current density at any point is the vector sum of the diffusion and drift current densities at the point. Because the diffusion current depends on differences of carrier concentration, its magnitude and direction at any point, depend on the concentration gradient at the point. In the next section, it will be shown that, under diffusion, the flux of carriers Φ, that is the number of carriers crossing unit area per unit time, is given by:

$$\Phi = -D \ \nabla d \qquad (5.7\text{-}1)$$

where d is the density of the carriers and D is called the diffusion constant. This means that the diffusion current density is proportional to the magnitude of the concentration gradient and is directed in opposite sense to it. Equation (5.7-1) is known as *Fick's* Law of Diffusion.

If the carriers are holes, each carries a charge q. The diffusion current density of holes is then:

$$J_p = -qD_p\nabla p \qquad (5.7\text{-}2)$$

where p is the hole density and D_p is the hole diffusion constant. For electrons, however, the charge carried is $-q$, and so the diffusion current density of electrons is:

$$J_n = qD_n\nabla n . \qquad (5.7\text{-}3)$$

Because the diffusion process depends on the random thermal motion of carriers, the diffusion constant D depends on the nature of the collisions which the carriers make with the lattice. Since the mobility also depends on the nature of these collisions, there must be some functional relationship between the diffusion constant and the mobility. This will become apparent in the next section.

---

* Subject to certain reservations which will be considered later.

5.8 Fick's Law and the Einstein Relation

Consider a piece of p-type semiconductor which has a non-uniform density of acceptor impurities. This will give rise to a non-uniform hole density throughout the crystal. For simplicity, it will be assumed that the forbidden energy gap E_g is sufficiently large for the electron density in the conduction band to be considered negligible at the temperature concerned. This implies a semiconductor of very low intrinsic carrier density at the given temperature. It will also be assumed that the acceptor impurity density is low enough for the hole density in the valence band to be non-degenerate.

In general, at any point in the crystal there will be a concentration gradient of holes. It follows, that at such a point, there will be a diffusion current density $\mathbf{J}_{\text{diff}}$. If the crystal is isolated, the net current flow at any point in the crystal must be zero and hence a drift current density, $\mathbf{J}_{\text{drift}}$, must exist at each point such that:

$$\mathbf{J}_{\text{diff}} = -\mathbf{J}_{\text{drift}} . \tag{5.8-1}$$

The existence of this drift current implies the setting up of an internal electric field, of correct magnitude and direction, at each point of the crystal such as to support the drift current density at that point. Using eqn (5.5-2), the diffusion current density may thus be written as:

$$\mathbf{J}_{\text{diff}} = -qp\mu_p \mathbf{E} . \tag{5.8-2}$$

The electric intensity $\mathbf{E}$ may be expressed in terms of the electrostatic potential V in the crystal by:

$$\mathbf{E} = -\nabla V \tag{5.8-3}$$

and it has been shown, eqn (4.11-2), that:

$$V = -\frac{1}{q} E_{\text{Fi}} \tag{5.8-4}$$

where E_{Fi} is the intrinsic Fermi level at the point of interest. Combining eqns (5.8-2), and (4):

$$\mathbf{J}_{\text{diff}} = -p\mu_p \nabla E_{\text{Fi}} . \tag{5.8-5}$$

The hole density at any point is, by eqn (4.7-7):

$$p = n_i \exp\left(\frac{E_{Fi} - E_F}{kT}\right) \tag{5.8-6}$$

whence:

$$E_{Fi} = E_F + kT \ln\left(\frac{p}{n_i}\right). \tag{5.8-7}$$

Now ∇E_F is zero for a semiconductor in thermodynamic equilibrium, in particular, for an isolated crystal; and so, taking the gradient of eqn (5.8-7):

$$\nabla E_{Fi} = kT \nabla \ln\left(\frac{p}{n_i}\right) = kT\left(\frac{1}{p}\right)\nabla p. \tag{5.8-8}$$

Substituting (eqn 5.8-8) into eqn (5.8-5):

$$\mathbf{J}_{diff} = -(kT\mu_p)\nabla p. \tag{5.8-9}$$

This equation is the same as eqn (5.7-2), provided the diffusion constant for holes is assumed to be given by:

$$D_p = \left(\frac{kT}{q}\right)\mu_p. \tag{5.8-10}$$

Fick's law is thus established.

Equation (5.8-10) is known as *Einstein's relation* and shows that the diffusion constant has the same field independence, or dependence in the case of high electric intensities, as the mobility. It also shows that the diffusion constant and mobility vary in the same way with lattice properties, in particular, impurity distribution, and further it predicts the temperature dependence of the diffusion constant in terms of that for the mobility.

An exactly similar relation, namely:

$$D_n = \left(\frac{kT}{q}\right)\mu_n \tag{5.8-11}$$

connects the diffusion constant for electrons to the electron mobility.

The units of diffusion constant are readily deduced from the Einstein relation, they are $m^2 s^{-1}$ since those of mobility are $m^2 V^{-1} s^{-1}$ and (kT/q) is a voltage.

5.9 The Total Current Density

When a semiconductor is not in thermodynamic equilibrium, the net current density at any point is not necessarily zero. It is given by the vector sum of the drift and diffusion current densities. With two types of carrier present, electrons and holes, there are four components to the total current density. These are electron drift, electron diffusion, hole drift and hole diffusion. The electron current and hole current densities are, respectively:

$$\mathbf{J}_n = qn\mu_n\mathbf{E} + qD_n\nabla n \qquad (5.9\text{-}1)$$

$$\mathbf{J}_p = qp\mu_p\mathbf{E} - qD_p\nabla p \qquad (5.9\text{-}2)$$

and the total current density is the sum of these.

5.10 The Uniform Base Transistor: An Example where Diffusion Current Predominates

Although the minority carrier transistor will be discussed in chapter 8, it is convenient to study certain aspects of the device as illustrations of semiconductor theory prior to a complete account. The diffusion of minority carriers across the base of a transistor will be considered here although, being an example of a semiconductor in non-thermodynamic equilibrium, strictly this work belongs in the next chapter.

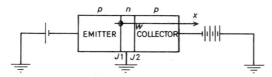

Figure 5.10a. One-dimensional minority carrier transistor

With reference to fig. 5.10a, a one-dimensional transistor is one in which the current flow is assumed to be planar. The direction normal to the planar flow will be described by an x-axis. The junction J1 between the p-type emitter region and the n-type base is forward biased by an external battery. Holes are thereby injected from the emitter into the base and electrons from the base are injected into the emitter. The exact nature of the junction, and the relation between the bias voltage and the density of carriers injected, will be considered in chapter 7, the details being unimportant in the present context. It suffices to say that a hole density p_0 is maintained by the bias just inside the base region.

The junction J2, between the base and p-type collector region, is reverse biased, so that holes reaching this latter junction are swept across into the collector region. This has the effect of maintaining zero hole density on the base side of the junction. Thus a concentration gradient of holes exists across the base region and holes diffuse from J1 towards J2.

In practical transistors, the base region is very narrow and is made of high resistivity material compared with that of the emitter and collector regions. As a consequence of this high resistivity, the majority carrier density in the base is low compared with that in the other regions. This, together with the narrowness of the base region, ensures that virtually all the injected holes diffuse right across the base to the collector junction without recombining with majority carrier electrons. In this example, it will be assumed that such recombination is negligible, and hence that the hole current density at any point across the base is a constant.

Again, because the majority carrier density in the base is much less than that in the emitter, virtually all the current across the forward biased emitter junction is due to holes flowing from emitter to base, and very little is due to electrons flowing from base to emitter. The ratio of the hole current to the total current, across this junction, is called the emitter injection efficiency γ, and will be considered in chapter 8. In practice its value is usually closer to unity than 0·995 and for the purpose of the present example it will be taken as unity.

On the other hand, the collector junction is reverse biased for majority carriers and so there is no electron flow from base to collector*.

* There is, as will be discussed in chapter 7, a very small electron flow from collector to base; this is negligible as far as the present example is concerned.

There is thus no appreciable majority carrier flow in the base. If the base is of uniform resistivity, that is the electron density is constant across the base*, there can be no electric field in the base. Thus, in the absence of an electric field, the constant hole current across the base is a diffusion current. By eqn (5.7-2), the diffusion current density is:

$$J_p = -qD_p\left(\frac{dp}{dx}\right)$$ (5.10-1)

and because this is constant, (dp/dx) is constant.

Integrating and using the boundary conditions:

$$\left. \begin{array}{ll} p = p_0 \; ; & \text{at} \quad x = 0 \\ p = 0 \; ; & \text{at} \quad x = W \end{array} \right\}$$ (5.10-2)

the hole density across the base is found to be:

$$p = p_0\left(1 - \left(\frac{x}{W}\right)\right).$$ (5.10-3)

This distribution is shown in fig. 5.10b.

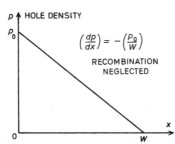

Figure 5.10b. Hole density distribution across the base

The gradient (dp/dx) is equal to $-(p_0/W)$ and so from eqn (5.10-1):

$$J_p = qD_p\left(\frac{p_0}{W}\right).$$ (5.10-4)

* Again this is not quite true; space charge equilibrium demands a small field, as will be explained in chapters 6 and 7.

A transistor of this kind, having a base of uniform resistivity, is called a *diffusion* transistor, or more strictly a *minority-carrier-diffusion* transistor, since the current across the base is carried predominantly by the diffusion process. If the transistor has a base region with a non-uniform resistivity, an electric field exists in the base. This arises in a similar manner to that in the piece of semiconductor considered in section 5.8, where the Einstein relation was obtained. In this case, the current flow across the base is not exclusively due to diffusion but is increased by a drift component. Such transistors are called *drift* transistors, or more strictly, *minority-carrier-drift* transistors. The hole distribution across the base of such a transistor will be considered in chapter 6.

A NOTE ON TERMINOLOGY

A certain amount of confusion exists concerning the terminology of transistor types. As an aid to the reader the distinctions between the main classes are listed below.

(I) *Minority carrier transistors*
These are devices whose transistor action is dependent on the injection into the base of carriers of opposite type to those normally present. In their simplest form these transistors have a base material of *uniform resistivity* and the mode of transfer of carriers across the base is by *diffusion*. Consequently they are termed *Uniform Base* or *Diffusion* transistors.

In their more advanced form the *resistivity* of the base is *graded* from emitter to collector and the mode of transfer of carriers across the base is both by diffusion and drift. They are accordingly termed *Graded Base* or *Drift* transistors.

Confusion in terminology often arises because this latter type is manufactured by the *thermal diffusion* of impurities into the semiconductor.

(II) *Majority carrier transistors*

These differ from minority carrier transistors in that their action depends exclusively on carriers of the same type as those normally present in the semiconductor. (See Chapter 9).

References

[5.1] DRESSELHAUS, G., KIP, A. F. and KITTEL, C. (1955), 'Cyclotron reso-nance of electrons and holes in silicon and germanium crystals', *Phys. Rev.*, **98**, 368–384.

[5.2] DEXTER, R. N., ZEIGER, H. J. and LAX, B. (1956), 'Cyclotron resonance experiments in silicon and germanium', *Phys. Rev.*, **104**, 637–644.

[5.3] TILLMAN, J. R. and ROBERTS, F. F. (1961), *Theory and practice of transistors*, p. 33, Pitman.

[5.4] ZIMAN, J. M. (1964), *Principles of the theory of solids*, chapter 2, Cambridge Univ. Press.

[5.5] SHOCKLEY, W. (1950), *Electrons and holes in semiconductors*, sections 11.3, 12.8 and 17.2, Van Nostrand.

[5.6] CONWELL, E. M. and WEISSKOPF, V. F. (1950), 'Theory of impurity scattering in semiconductors', *Phys. Rev.*, **70**, 388–390.

[5.7] CONWELL, E. M. (1952), 'Properties of silicon and germanium', *Proc. I.R.E.*, **40**, 1327–1337.

[5.8] SHOCKLEY, W., PEARSON, G. L. and HAYNES, J. R. (1949), 'Hole injection in germanium: quantitative studies and filamentary transis-tors, *Bell Syst. Tech. Journ.*, **28**, 344–366.

[5.9] PRINCE, M. B. (1953 and 1954), Drift mobilities in semiconductors. I. 'Germanium', *Phys. Rev.*, **92**, 681–687; II. 'Silicon', *Phys. Rev.*, **93**, 1204–1206.

[5.10] MORIN, F. J. and MAITA, J. P. (1954), 'Conductivity and Hall effect in the intrinsic range of germanium, *Phys. Rev.*, **94**, 1525–1529 and 'Electric properties of silicon containing arsenic and boron', *Phys. Rev.*, **96**, 28–35.

[5.11] WILSON, A. H. (1954), *The Theory of metals*, pp. 251–266, Cambridge Univ. Press.

[5.12] RYDER, E. J. (1953), 'Mobility of holes and electrons in high electric fields', *Phys. Rev.*, **90**, 766–769.

CHAPTER 6

Semiconductors in Non-Equilibrium Conditions

6.1 Introduction

In the last chapter, drift and diffusion currents in a semiconductor were considered. Drift current results from the action of an electric field on the mobile carriers. Diffusion current occurs when there is a spatial variation in the density of the mobile carriers. For example, in section 5.8, a piece of semiconductor was used to establish Fick's law and the Einstein relation. The spatial variation in the carrier density was brought about by allowing a spatial variation of acceptor impurities. However, the net current at any point was zero, because the piece of semiconductor was electrically isolated from any external circuit and hence was in thermodynamic equilibrium.

In general, the semiconductor is connected with some external circuit and a net current flows at each point of the material. Very often, the density of impurities is uniform throughout a region of the semiconductor, yet there may still be a spatial variation in the density of mobile carriers. This may occur, for example, because of injection of additional minority carriers across a depletion layer into the region. Depletion layers, and injection across them, will be considered in chapters 7 and 8. The injection of extra carriers in this way, upsets the thermodynamic equilibrium of the semiconductor. The carrier densities are then no longer given by the equations of chapter 4.

For brevity, in the remainder of this book, the word thermodynamic will be omitted, and a semiconductor will be said to be in equilibrium or non-equilibrium.

6.2 Imrefs: Pseudo or Quasi Fermi Levels

When a semiconductor is in non-equilibrium, the concept of the Fermi level, introduced in chapter 4, loses its meaning. From the work of chapter 4 it is apparent that the position of the Fermi level determines the density of both the electrons in the conduction band and holes in the valence band. The Fermi level is used as a constant in the Fermi function $F(E)$. This function gives the probability of occupation of the energy levels and hence, if the density of states is known, the densities of carriers in the bands. If the Fermi level is moved up, the density of electrons in the conduction band increases and that of holes in the valence band decreases. This information is contained in eqns (4.7-6) and (7), namely:

$$n = n_i \exp \left(\frac{E_F - E_{Fi}}{kT} \right) \qquad (6.2\text{-}1)$$

$$p = n_i \exp \left(\frac{E_{Fi} - E_F}{kT} \right) \qquad (6.2\text{-}2)$$

where E_{Fi} is the intrinsic Fermi level, E_F the Fermi level, n_i the intrinsic carrier density and n and p are the electron density in the conduction band and hole density in the valence band, respectively.

If the semiconductor is in non-equilibrium, it is not possible to use the single Fermi level as a reference for the prediction of both the electron and the hole densities. It is necessary to introduce separate reference levels, for use in $F(E)$ and the *inverse* Fermi function $\tilde{F}(E)$, for the electrons and holes respectively.

Suppose some additional holes are injected into a region of an n-type semiconductor. In this region, the hole density may be increased appreciably by the injection process. It is therefore necessary for E_F to move down, towards the top of the valence band, in order to predict correctly the new density of holes in the valence band. This follows from eqn (6.2-2), where p increases when E_F is decreased. It will be shown in the next chapter that, excepting depletion regions where for example the semiconductor changes from n to p-type, any region of a semiconductor is always electrically neutral. Thus when the extra holes are injected

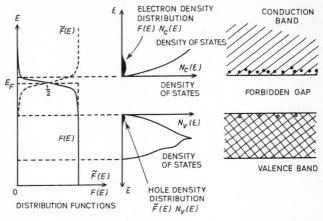

Figure 6.2a. Fermi and inverse Fermi functions for an *n*-type semiconductor in equilibrium

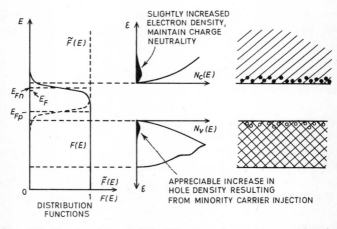

Figure 6.2b. Fermi and inverse Fermi functions for an *n*-type semiconductor in non-equilibrium. (Note that E_{Fp} has dropped appreciably below E_F, while E_{Fn} has increased only slightly above it)

into the n-type semiconductor, an equal number of majority carrier electrons will also be drawn into the region in order to maintain electrical neutrality. For the electron density to increase in this way, it is necessary for E_F to move up, towards the bottom of the conduction band. This follows from eqn (6.2-1), where an increase in E_F is accompanied by an increase in n.

Thus, to explain the increase in hole density, E_F must move down, while to explain the increase in electron density, E_F must move up. This difficulty can be resolved by introducing separate Fermi levels for electrons and holes. These Fermi levels are known as *Imrefs*, *Pseudo* Fermi levels, *Quasi* Fermi levels, or simply as electron or hole Fermi levels. They are denoted by the symbols E_{Fn} and E_{Fp} respectively.

Under non-equilibrium conditions, the electron and hole densities are expressed by the following modifications of eqns (6.2-1) and (2) respectively:

$$n = n_i \exp\left(\frac{E_{Fn} - E_{Fi}}{kT}\right) \tag{6.2-3}$$

$$p = n_i \exp\left(\frac{E_{Fi} - E_{Fp}}{kT}\right). \tag{6.2-4}$$

These equations can be interpreted as definitions of the Imrefs, for by re-arrangement they become respectively:

$$E_{Fn} = E_{Fi} + kT \ln\left(\frac{n}{n_i}\right) \tag{6.2-5}$$

$$E_{Fp} = E_{Fi} - kT \ln\left(\frac{p}{n_i}\right). \tag{6.2-6}$$

The distinction between the different Fermi levels is depicted in figs 6.2a and 6.2b, which are for an n-type semiconductor. In the first of these two figures, the semiconductor is in equilibrium. The single level E_F is used as a reference for both the *electron* Fermi function $F(E)$ and the *hole* fermi function $\tilde{F}(E)$. In the second figure, the hole density has been appreciably increased by some injection process. The hole Imref E_{Fp} is used as a reference for the function $\tilde{F}(E)$ and is appreciably below the Fermi level E_F of fig 6.2a. The fractional increase in the electron density, necessary to maintain charge neutrality, is much less than that for the holes. This is because the equilibrium hole density is much less than the equilibrium electron density. Consequently, the electron Imref E_{Fn}, which is now used as the reference level of $F(E)$, is lifted but slightly above the position of the equilibrium Fermi level E_F. (See fig 6.2b.)

One of the basic distinctions between the Fermi level and the Imrefs is that while the former depends only on the temperature, and the degree of doping of the semiconductor, the Imrefs depend also on factors external to the semiconductor. For example, they depend on the voltage which is being used to inject the minority carriers into the semiconductor. However, the example of fig. 6.2b, shows that, provided the majority carrier density remains an order or so greater than the minority carrier density, the injection of minority carriers does not significantly shift the majority carrier Imref from the position of the equilibrium Fermi level. When this is so, a valid approximation is to take this Imref coincident with the Fermi level. The minority carrier density may, however, be increased by many orders, and so its Imref can depart appreciably from the position of the equilibrium Fermi level. This is known as the *low-level-injection* approximation.

6.3 Excess Carrier Densities

It now becomes necessary to distinguish notationally between equilibrium and non-equilibrium densities. The equilibrium densities will be denoted by n_e and p_e for electrons and holes respectively. Equations (6.2-1) and (2) give these densities. The symbols n and p are retained for the electron and hole densities in general; these are given by eqns (6.2-3) and (4). It is often necessary to refer to the excess density over and above the equilibrium density of carriers. These excess densities, or densities of *excess carriers* as they are often called, will be denoted by N and P for electrons and holes respectively. They are related to the other quantities by:

$$n = N + n_e \qquad (6.3\text{-}1)$$

$$p = P + p_e . \qquad (6.3\text{-}2)$$

The excess densities may be negative quantities if minority carriers are abstracted from the semiconductor instead of being injected into it. As will be shown in chapter 7, the edge of a depletion layer acts as a *sink* for minority carriers and, at such a layer, the minority carrier density is zero. The excess density is therefore the negative of the equilibrium minority carrier density.

Outside depletion layers, charge neutrality is maintained; excess minority carriers will always be balanced by an equal number of excess majority carriers; that is:

$$P = N . \tag{6.3-3}$$

In much of the work of the later chapters, two types of semiconductor are present, one n-type and the other p-type, on either side of a depletion layer. The symbols n_e and p_e are then replaced by n_n and p_n for the n-type material and n_p and p_p for the p-type material. That is, when the symbol and its suffix coincide, it refers to a majority carrier density, otherwise to a minority carrier density.

Carrier densities in general may be expressed in terms of the equilibrium densities and the displacement of the Imrefs from the equilibrium Fermi level. Thus from eqn (6.2-3):

$$n = n_i \exp\left(\frac{E_{Fn} - E_{Fi}}{kT}\right)$$

$$= n_i \exp\left(\frac{E_F - E_{Fi}}{kT}\right) . \exp\left(\frac{E_{Fn} - E_F}{kT}\right)$$

$$= n_e \exp\left(\frac{E_{Fn} - E_F}{kT}\right) \tag{6.3-4}$$

where eqn (6.2-1) has been used. A similar expression for the hole density is:

$$p = p_e \exp\left(\frac{E_F - E_{Fp}}{kT}\right) . \tag{6.3-5}$$

Also the product of eqns (6.3-4) and (5) gives:

$$np = n_i^2 \exp\left(\frac{E_{Fn} - E_{Fp}}{kT}\right) \tag{6.3-6}$$

which of course reduces to np equals n_i^2, (eqn 4.3-4), for equilibrium conditions. Equations (6.3-1) and (4) give the excess electron density as:

$$N = n_e \left\{ \exp\left(\frac{E_{Fn} - E_F}{kT} \right) - 1 \right\}. \tag{6.3-7}$$

Similarly:

$$P = p_e \left\{ \exp\left(\frac{E_F - E_{Fp}}{kT} \right) - 1 \right\}. \tag{6.3-8}$$

It might be noted in passing, that the charge equilibrium condition expressed by eqn (6.3-3), namely the equality of N and P, imposes a relation between E_F, E_{Fn} and E_{Fp} through eqns (6.3-7) and (8). This relation does not find much application.

Equations (6.3-4) and (5) can be re-arranged to give respectively:

$$E_{Fn} = E_F + kT \ln(n/n_e) \tag{6.3-9}$$

$$E_{Fp} = E_F - kT \ln(p/p_e). \tag{6.3-10}$$

These two equations are equivalent to eqns (6.2-5) and (6) respectively, but are somewhat more useful than the former equations. This is because they give the displacement of the Imrefs, from E_F, in terms of the carrier densities and the equilibrium values of the latter. They are also useful in estimating the validity of the low-level-injection approximation. For example, if n_e is a thousand times greater than p_e, and if injection is such that p is a hundred times greater than p_e, eqns (6.3-9) and (10) show that $(E_{Fn} - E_F)$ is approximately $0.1kT$ and $(E_F - E_{Fp})$ is approximately $4.6kT$. At room temperatures these quantities are about 0.003 eV and 0.14 eV respectively. The low-level-injection approximation is indeed justified for this example.

6.4 The Current Density Expressed in Terms of the Imref

In section 5.9, expressions were obtained for the electron and hole current densities. Each of these current densities comprised two terms, a drift current component and a diffusion current component. It will now be shown that these two components can be combined into a single expression for the current density. Equation (5.9-2) is:

$$\mathbf{J}_p = (qp\mu_p)\mathbf{E} - qD_p\nabla p . \qquad (6.4\text{-}1)$$

In section 5.8, it was shown that $\mathbf{E}$ could be replaced by $(1/q)\nabla E_{\mathrm{Fi}}$, and in addition by eqn (5.8-10):

$$D_p = \left(\frac{kT}{q}\right)\mu_p . \qquad (6.4\text{-}2)$$

Substitution of these results into eqn (6.4-1) yields:

$$\mathbf{J}_p = q\mu_p\left[p\left(\frac{1}{q}\right)\nabla E_{\mathrm{Fi}} - \left(\frac{kT}{q}\right)\nabla p\right]. \qquad (6.4\text{-}3)$$

From eqn (6.2-4) is obtained:

$$\nabla p = \left(\frac{n_i}{kT}\right)\exp\left(\frac{E_{\mathrm{Fi}}-E_{\mathrm{F}p}}{kT}\right) . \ (\nabla E_{\mathrm{Fi}} - \nabla E_{\mathrm{F}p})$$

$$= \left(\frac{1}{kT}\right)p\ (\nabla E_{\mathrm{Fi}} - \nabla E_{\mathrm{F}p}) . \qquad (6.4\text{-}4)$$

Putting this last result into eqn (6.4-3):

$$\mathbf{J}_p = (qp\mu_p)\left(\frac{1}{q}\right)\nabla E_{\mathrm{F}p} . \qquad (6.4\text{-}5)$$

It is thus possible to express the total hole current, that is both drift and diffusion components, in a compact form as if it were simply a drift current in an electric intensity $(1/q)\nabla E_{\mathrm{F}p}$, or equivalently, in an electrostatic potential of $-(E_{\mathrm{F}p}/q)$. Similarly, the total electron current density is: ·

$$\mathbf{J}_n = (qn\mu_n)\left(\frac{1}{q}\right)\nabla E_{\mathrm{F}n} . \qquad (6.4\text{-}6)$$

6.5 A Relation Between the Electron and Hole Current Densities

A rearrangement of eqn (6.4-3) yields:

$$\nabla E_{\mathrm{Fi}} = kT\left(\frac{1}{p}\right)\nabla p + \left(\frac{1}{\mu_p p}\right)\mathbf{J}_p . \qquad (6.5\text{-}1)$$

The analogous equation to eqn (6.4-3) giving the electron current density is:

$$\mathbf{J}_n = q\mu_n \left[n\left(\frac{1}{q}\right)\nabla E_{\text{Fi}} + \left(\frac{kT}{q}\right)\nabla n \right]. \tag{6.5-2}$$

Elimination of ∇E_{Fi} by substitution of eqn (6.5-1) into eqn (6.5-2) gives:

$$\mathbf{J}_n = \left(\frac{n\mu_n}{p\mu_p}\right)\mathbf{J}_p + kT\mu_n\left[\left(\frac{n}{p}\right)\nabla p + \nabla n\right]$$

$$= \left(\frac{n\mu_n}{p\mu_p}\right)\mathbf{J}_p + \left(\frac{qD_n}{p}\right)\nabla(pn), \tag{6.5-3}$$

where the Einstein relation eqn (6.4-2) has been used to replace μ_n in terms of D_n. Transposition of eqn (6.5-3) and the use of the Einstein relation, leads to the analogous form for $\mathbf{J}_p$ in terms of $\mathbf{J}_n$, namely:

$$\mathbf{J}_p = \left(\frac{p\mu_p}{n\mu_n}\right)\mathbf{J}_n - \left(\frac{qD_p}{n}\right)\nabla(pn). \tag{6.5-4}$$

These equations are equivalent to those deduced by Van Roosbroeck [6.1].

When there is no spatial variation of carrier densities, the gradient density product vanishes and only drift current flows. Equations (6.5-3) and (4) then express the fact that both electrons and holes experience the same electrostatic field; a basic assumption of the particle approximation to conduction processes.* In certain cases, one or other of the current densities may be approximately zero throughout a region. In this case, the other current density is given by an expression somewhat similar to Fick's law; thus if $\mathbf{J}_n$ is zero, eqn (6.5-4) is:

$$\mathbf{J}_p = -\left(\frac{qD_p}{n}\right)\nabla(pn). \tag{6.5-5}$$

For low-level-injection, the electron density n does not increase greatly above the equilibrium density n_e. Equation (6.5-5) then becomes:

* It is probably true that the macroscopic average field is the same for carriers in the conduction and valence bands, but it is certainly not valid microscopically.

$$\mathbf{J}_p = -\left(\frac{qD_p}{n_e}\right) \nabla(pn_e) \qquad (6.5\text{-}6)$$

or:*

$$\mathbf{J}_p = -\left(\frac{qD_p}{n_e}\right) \nabla(Pn_e). \qquad (6.5\text{-}7)$$

The last equation follows from eqn (6.5-6) because the product:

$$p_e n_e = n_i^2 \qquad (6.5\text{-}8)$$

is dependent only on the nature of the semiconductor and its temperature. The product is independent of impurity distribution, accordingly its gradient is zero. This expression for the hole current density will be used in section (6.7) in connection with the *drift* transistor.

Although the electron current is assumed to be zero, the hole current is not necessarily predominantly caused by diffusion. There may be an appreciable electric field *built into* the semiconductor resulting from the spatial variation of donor density. The gradient of the majority carrier density is then non-zero and eqns (6.5-6) and (7), for the hole current, include both diffusion and drift components. They are valid provided the drift and diffusion components of electron current annul each other.

In the special case when the semiconductor material is uniform, ∇n_n is zero and hence eqn (6.5-5) reduces to:

$$\mathbf{J}_p = -qD_p\nabla p \qquad (6.5\text{-}9)$$

the normal expression for a diffusion current density.

In the next two sections, examples of the use of some of the equations of this and previous sections will be given.

6.6 The Uniform-Base Transistor

In the last chapter, section 5.10, the uniform-base, or diffusion, transistor was introduced. The picture of the transistor there presented will now be considered in more detail. It will be recalled (fig. 5.10b), that the

* The significance of these expressions for the current density in terms of the gradient of the product of the densities, or excess density product, was first pointed out by our colleague G. G. Bloodworth.

holes injected from the emitter into the base, give rise to a constant hole density gradient across the base. The equilibrium minority carrier density in the base is disturbed, being raised from p_e to p_0 at the junction J1 and being reduced from p_e to zero at the junction J2. In order to maintain charge neutrality, it follows that the majority carrier density in the base must readjust, drawing in extra electrons from the base metallic contact if necessary. The state of affairs is depicted in fig. 6.6a. In this figure it is seen that the hole density is everywhere balanced by adjustment of the electron density. The gradient of the latter is the same as that for the holes. It follows that electrons must diffuse, under this concentration gradient, in the same sense as the holes. However, with the assumption of unity emitter-injection-efficiency for J1, and remem-

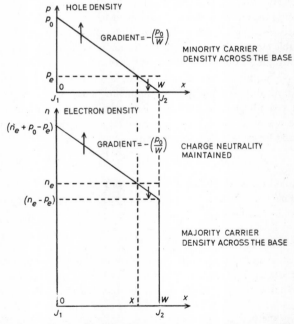

Figure 6.6a. Carrier densities across the base of a diffusion transistor

bering that J2 is reverse biased, the net electron current across the base is zero. The diffusion of electrons in the base must therefore be balanced by a drift current of electrons in the opposite sense. To support this drift, a small electric field must be set up in the base.

The total electron current density is given by eqn (6.5-2). By equating this to zero, an expression for the electric intensity in the base can be obtained:

$$\nabla E_{Fi} = -kT\left(\frac{1}{n}\right)\nabla n \ . \tag{6.6-1}$$

For the one-dimensional transistor under consideration, fig. 6.6a shows that ∇n is $-(p_0/W)$ and so:

$$\left(\frac{dE_{Fi}}{dx}\right) = \left(\frac{kT}{W}\right)\left(\frac{p_0}{n}\right) \ . \tag{6.6-2}$$

This usually represents a very small electric intensity for low-level-injection. Then, to a first approximation; n can be replaced by n_e. Integration of eqn (6.6-2) then gives the change of intrinsic Fermi level across the base:

$$\Delta E_{Fi} = kT\left(\frac{p_0}{n_e}\right) \ . \tag{6.6-3}$$

Thus, at room temperatures, ΔE_{Fi} is a small fraction of 0·03 eV. This represents an almost negligible electric field in the base of the transistor. Only for high-level-injection does the electric field become appreciable.

The presence of the electric field causes a hole drift current, which is small compared with the electron drift current. This is because the hole density in the base is small compared with the electron density.

It is instructive to compare the hole drift and diffusion components of current density in the base. Thus, from eqns (6.4-3) and (6.6-2), and the fact that (dp/dx) is $-(p_0/W)$:

$$\frac{J_{p(\text{drift})}}{J_{p(\text{diffusion})}} = -\frac{p(dE_{Fi}/dx)}{kT(dp/dx)} = \left(\frac{p}{n}\right) \ . \tag{6.6-4}$$

This ratio varies from approximately (p_0/n_e), for low-level-injection, at J1 to zero at J2. The ratio shows that the drift component of the hole current density is small compared with the diffusion component; thus justifying the term *diffusion* transistor for this particular type of transistor.

An alternative approach commences from eqn (6.4-6). This gives the electron current density in terms of the electron Imref. Because the electron current in the base is assumed to be zero, the equation gives:

$$\left(\frac{dE_{Fn}}{dx}\right) = 0 \ . \tag{6.6-5}$$

The electron Imref is thus constant across the base. Equation (6.2-5) relates E_{Fn} to the intrinsic Fermi level E_{Fi} and the electron density. Differentiation of this equation with respect to x, treating n_i as a constant, yields:

$$\left(\frac{dE_{Fn}}{dx}\right) = \left(\frac{dE_{Fi}}{dx}\right) + \left(\frac{kT}{n}\right)\left(\frac{dn}{dx}\right) \ . \tag{6.6-6}$$

Using eqn (6.6-5) and putting (dn/dx) equal to $-(p_0/W)$:

$$\left(\frac{dE_{Fi}}{dx}\right) = \left(\frac{kT}{W}\right)\left(\frac{p_0}{n}\right) \tag{6.6-7}$$

which is eqn (6.6-2) again. Equation (6.2-5) is the integrated form of this last equation. It gives the position of E_{Fi} relative to the constant E_{Fn}. For the diffusion transistor under consideration, where E_F is parallel to E_{Fi}, the equivalent eqn (6.3-9) is somewhat more useful. This is because E_{Fn} coincides with E_F when n is equal to n_e; this is shown as point X in fig. 6.6b. The linear distribution of electron density across the base, see fig. 6.6a, is:

$$n = (n_e - p_e + p_0) - p_0\left(\frac{x}{W}\right) \ . \tag{6.6-8}$$

Substitution of eqn (6.6-8) into eqn (6.3-9) gives:

$$E_F = E_{Fn} - kT \ln\left[\frac{(n_e - p_e + p_0) - p_0\left(\dfrac{x}{W}\right)}{n_e}\right] \ . \tag{6.6-9}$$

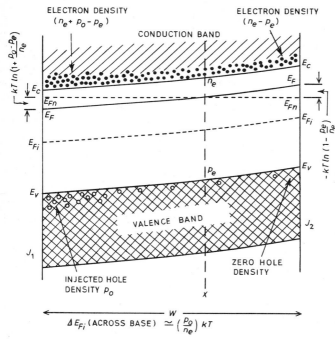

Figure 6.6b. Energy level diagram across the base of a diffusion transistor

The variation of E_F, and hence E_{Fi}, across the base is sketched from eqn (6.6-9) in fig. 6.6b. The variation is somewhat exaggerated in the figure for purposes of clarity. The total change of E_{Fi} across the base may be deduced readily from eqn (6.6-9) and is approximately $kT(p_0/n_e)$, in agreement with eqn (6.6-3). Even at injection levels for which p_0 approaches n_e, ΔE_{Fi} is only of the order of 0·03 eV at room temperatures. However, such fields should not be neglected without careful consideration for, according to eqn (6.6-4), injection levels this high imply a hole drift component of similar magnitude to the diffusion component. Neglect of the drift component might be considered allowable, see eqn (6.6-4), provided p_0 is less than say three per cent of n_e.

6.7 The Graded-Base Transistor

In section 5.10, the graded-base, or drift, transistor was briefly mentioned. Because of the graded base, even in the absence of minority carrier injection, there exists an electric field across the base region. Under conditions of minority carrier injection, the electric field is modified somewhat for reasons similar to those considered in the last section on the diffusion transistor. In section 5.10, the diffusion transistor was considered subject to the condition of low-level-injection and the injection dependent field in the base was neglected. In this section, the drift tranistor will be investigated subject to the same restriction. The electric field in the base will be assumed to be due, solely, to the variation in donor impurity density and to be independent of the injection level.

As previously, the emitter-injection-efficiency will be taken as unity, and the collector junction will be reverse biased. Carrier recombination in the narrow base region will be neglected. The electron current in the base is then everywhere zero. The conditions for the validity of eqn (6.5-6) are thus satisfied and, for the one-dimensional transistor under consideration:

$$J_p = - \left(\frac{qD_p}{n_e} \right) \frac{d}{dx} (pn_e). \tag{6.7-1}$$

Further, since recombination in the base is being neglected, J_p is a constant. Re-arrangement of eqn (6.7-1) and integration yields:

$$pn_e(x) \Big|_{x=0}^{x=W} = - \left(\frac{J_p}{qD_p} \right) \int_0^W n_e(x) dx \tag{6.7-2}$$

where $n_e(x)$ is the majority carrier density at any point x. Now, p is p_0 at the junction J1 and zero at J2 and so:

$$J_p = qD_p p_0 \left(\frac{n_e(0)}{\int_0^W n_e(x) dx} \right). \tag{6.7-3}$$

For uniform-base resistivity, the equation shows that J_p is $(qD_p p_0/W)$, as expected for a diffusion transistor.

In practical drift transistors, the impurity density, and hence $n_e(x)$,

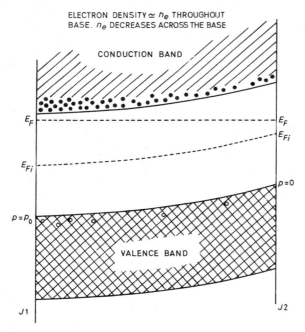

Figure 6.7a. Energy level diagram across the base of a drift transistor: low-level-injection

is made to decrease with increasing x; that is the resistivity of the base is increased from emitter to collector. A field is produced, fig. 6.7a, which causes the holes to drift from emitter to collector. This gives rise to a greater current density, for a given injection density p_0, than is obtained in the diffusion transistor. This is apparent also from eqn (6.7-3), for since $n_e(x)$ decreases monotonically with increasing x:

$$\int_0^W n_e(x).dx = \chi n_e(0) W \qquad (6.7\text{-}4)$$

where χ is a fraction in the range zero to unity. Equation (6.7-3) then gives:

$$J_p = \left(\frac{qD_p}{\chi}\right)\left(\frac{p_0}{W}\right) > qD_p\left(\frac{p_0}{W}\right). \qquad (6.7\text{-}5)$$

The right-hand side of this inequality is the current density of the diffusion transistor.

Alternatively, the same current density can be obtained, as in the diffusion transistor, but with a lower p_0 and consequently with a lower injected charge in the base. This is a direct consequence of the smaller transit time of a hole crossing the base. In chapter 8, it will be shown that higher frequencies of operation of transistors are possible if the charge, required to support a given current, can be reduced. Thus drift transistors are superior to diffusion transistors in this respect.

If the lower limit of integration in eqn (6.7-2) is taken as x instead of zero, the hole density as a function of x is obtained:

$$p(x) = \left(\frac{1}{\chi}\right)\left(\frac{p_0}{W}\right)\left(\frac{\int_x^W n_e(x')dx'}{n_e(x)}\right). \qquad (6.7\text{-}6)$$

The exact form of $p(x)$ will of course depend on the form of $n_e(x)$, but for any monotonically decreasing function $n_e(x)$, the form of $p(x)$ will be convex away from the x-axis, and will equal p_0 at x equal to zero, and zero at x equal to W. The general shape of this expression is shown in fig. 6.7b.

To investigate the behaviour of the drift transistor, at other than

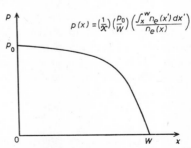

Figure 6.7b. Hole density distribution across the base of a drift transistor

low-level-injection, eqn (6.5-5) for J_p would have to be used in place of the more restricted eqn (6.5-6). The value of $n(x)$ to be used in the equation would, for a first approximation, be obtained by modifying the function $n_e(x)$ to maintain charge equilibrium in the base. The modification to the function would be deduced by reference to fig. 6.7b; for the majority carrier density must have the same profile, to a close approximation, as the minority carrier density. However, this problem is beyond the scope of the present text.

6.8 Elementary Theory of Carrier Lifetime

The manner in which carrier densities are affected by recombination of minority carriers with majority carriers will now be considered.

In the first instance, an oversimplified treatment will be adopted. This leads to an expression for the excess carrier lifetime which is a constant, and which is adequate for much of the remaining material in this and subsequent chapters. In section 6.16, a more sophisticated account of recombination phenomena will be presented and the consequences of using the more elementary concepts of this section noted.

Minority carriers are continually recombining with majority carriers either by what is known as the *direct-photon-radiative* mechanism or by a mechanism involving electron and hole *traps*. These traps are defects, or other peculiarities of the crystal lattice, which give rise to energy levels within the forbidden gap of the semiconductor. The former of these processes is readily understood by reference to the energy level diagrams of chapter 4. If an electron in the conductor, and a hole in the valence band, come to the same position in the lattice, they may recombine*, the electron dropping through the forbidden gap into the hole. A photon of radiation, corresponding to the loss of energy of the electron is emitted.

The mechanism involving traps is similar, but in this case the electron

* This is an oversimplification. Recombination is only possible if the net momentum of the two carriers is zero, an unlikely situation. It is believed that having met, they move through the lattice as a pair, termed an *exciton*, until they can give up their net momentum to the lattice in some way; possibly one of the particles is trapped. The electron is then able to drop down into the hole.

from the conduction band first drops into the trap level and subsequently drops into a hole in the valence band. Since the electron in the conduction band and the hole in the valence band do not need to coincide at the trap at the same instant of time, the trapping mechanism should predominate whenever there is any appreciable density of traps present. In any single recombination of an electron-hole pair, two small energy steps are involved instead of the comparatively large one of the direct-photon-radiative process. These small energy steps usually manifest themselves by the emission of *phonons* of lattice vibration, that is, the energy of recombination is given up to the lattice as vibrational energy.

Normally, the generation of electron-hole pairs is due to the inverse of the trapping recombination process; that is the absorption of phonons of lattice vibration energy, causes electrons from the valence band to be transferred to the intermediary traps, and thence to the conduction band. The inverse of the direct-photon-radiative process may also occur. For example, photons, of energy greater than that of the forbidden gap, may be absorbed from light irradiating the semiconductor. Alternatively, the absorption of an exceptionally large phonon of lattice vibration energy, may cause direct transfer of an electron from the valence to conduction band. The rate of transfer by this latter process will be negligible compared with that involving traps, unless the trap density is exceptionally small.

There is, however, a basic difference between the recombination and generation processes. As will be shown subsequently, recombination rates are essentially functions of the carrier densities; albeit, functions of the temperature and the nature of the lattice as well. On the other hand, thermal generation rates, that is generation by capture of lattice phonons, are functions of the lattice temperature, the nature of the lattice, its impurities and defects, and the density of *electrons* in the valence band, this latter quantity being the number of electrons available for transfer to the conduction band. The thermal generation rate is thus *independent* of the carrier densities, in particular the hole density, for this density is negligible compared with the density of electrons in the valence band. The thermal generation rate is also dependent on the density of *holes* in the conduction band, but this density is virtually constant, for the density of electrons in the conduction band is negligible compared with the density of states. Only when the carrier densities become degenerate will the generation rate become dependent on the carrier densities. For a given crystal therefore, the thermal generation rate in any region is simply a function of the temperature of that region. Similar considerations apply to generation by optical irradiation. In this case, the generation rate is a function of the nature of the lattice, its impurities and defects, its temperature and the rate of energy absorption from the irradiating beam.

Thermal equilibrium results when the carrier recombination process is just balanced by the thermal generation process. Thus if R_e is the equilibrium recombination rate, and G_e the thermal generation rate, both per unit volume, then:

$$R_e = G_e . \tag{6.8-1}$$

When the recombination rate R and generation rate G are made to differ, the minority carrier density will increase at a rate $(G-R)$. It is to be noted that the recombination and generation processes produce or annihilate electron-hole pairs, and so the rates are the same* for both minority and majority carriers. In particular, charge neutrality is preserved. The increase, or decrease, in carrier density is the same for both minority and majority carriers, although the fractional density changes are different because the equilibrium densities are not equal.

An expression for the recombination rate can be obtained using a simplified picture of the recombination processes. Here it is assumed that the probability of a minority carrier recombining with a majority carrier, is proportional to its probability of meeting a majority carrier in the lattice. This in turn is proportional to the majority carrier density. The number of minority carriers in the lattice is proportional to the minority carrier density, and so it follows that the recombination rate is proportional to the product of the carrier densities. That is:

$$R = Cpn \tag{6.8-2}$$

* This is usually true. However, it is not valid when the occupation density of the traps is changing. See section 6.16.

where C is a constant of proportionality. At equilibrium, the recombination rate equals the thermal generation rate, eqn (6.8-1), and so by eqn (6.8-2):

$$G_e = R_e = Cp_e n_e = Cn_i^2 . \qquad (6.8\text{-}3)$$

When equilibrium densities are disturbed, for example, following a light pulse incident on the semiconductor or following the injection of minority carriers, the recombination rate will change from its equilibrium value, to a value given by eqn (6.8-2). The thermal generation rate will remain unchanged, when the densities are disturbed, provided the crystal temperature remains constant. Thus, from eqns (6.8-2) and (3), the rates of change of carrier densities are:

$$\left(\frac{dn}{dt}\right) = \left(\frac{dp}{dt}\right) = G_e - R = C(p_e n_e - pn) . \qquad (6.8\text{-}4)$$

For low-level-injection, in an n-type semiconductor, n remains approximately equal to n_e. Equation (6.8-4) then approximates to:

$$\left(\frac{dn}{dt}\right) = \left(\frac{dp}{dt}\right) = -Cn_e(p - p_e) = -\left(\frac{P}{\tau}\right) \qquad (6.8\text{-}5)$$

where P is the excess hole density and τ, equal to $(1/Cn_e)$, is a constant for a given temperature, at a given point in the crystal. At a constant temperature and given position, p_e is independent of t and hence, part of eqn (6.8-5) can be written

$$\left(\frac{dP}{dt}\right) = -\left(\frac{P}{\tau}\right) . \qquad (6.8\text{-}6)$$

This equation integrates to give the excess hole density at any instant t, in terms of the initial value of this quantity. Thus:

$$P(t) = P(0) \exp\left(-\frac{t}{\tau}\right) \qquad (6.8\text{-}7)$$

which shows that the excess density decays to zero exponentially with time constant τ. By charge neutrality, it follows that the majority carrier excess density behaves in an exactly similar fashion. Equation (6.8-7) is

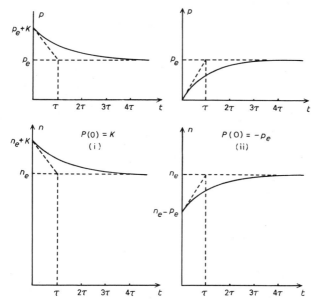

Figure 6.8a. Decay of excess carrier densities with time:
(*i*) Initial excess density equal to K
(*ii*) Initial excess density equal to $-p_e$

plotted in fig. 6.8a(i), for an initial hole density K and in fig. 6.8a(ii) for an initial excess hole density $-p_e$, that is zero hole density.

The time constant τ can be identified with the *mean lifetime*, or simply *lifetime*, of the excess carriers*. The justification of this statement follows exactly the argument used in section 5.2, eqns (5.2-21) to (5.2-23), to show that the mean time of flight $\langle \tau \rangle$ could be identified with the time constant τ'. The quantity τ of section 5.2 should not however be confused with the τ of the present section.

* More commonly it is known as the minority carrier lifetime: and strictly should be distinguished from the majority carrier lifetime. However, these lifetimes are the same for the simple treatment presented here.

That the lifetime was a constant, for a given temperature and position, was a consequence of the low-level-injection assumption. For high-level-injection, the density n cannot be taken as n_e and so τ is no longer a constant. The lifetime τ is then defined by:

$$\tau = -\frac{P}{(dP/dt)}. \tag{6.8-8}$$

Except where explicitly stated, carrier lifetimes independent of the excess densities will be assumed throughout the remainder of the book.

6.9 Charge Conservation or Continuity Equations

Let an arbitrary volume V of a semiconductor, bounded by a surface S, as illustrated in fig. 6.9a, be considered. Carriers of either type are removed from such a volume, both by recombination and by current

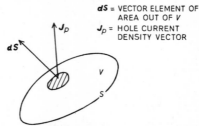

Figure 6.9a. An arbitrary volume V of a semiconductor bounded by a surface S.

flow out across the surface of the region. The conservation of the total charge carried by holes in the volume V will first be investigated. This total charge is:

$$Q_p = q \int_V p\, dV \tag{6.9-1}$$

where the integration is performed over the whole volume V. Differentiation with respect to t gives the rate of decrease of Q_p, where the volume remains constant, as:

$$-\left(\frac{dQ_p}{dt}\right) = -q \int_V \left(\frac{\partial p}{\partial t}\right) dV. \tag{6.9-2}$$

The hole recombination rate per unit volume at any point is (P/τ), eqn (6.8-6), and so the rate of decrease of Q_p resulting from recombination is:

$$- \left(\frac{dQ_p}{dt}\right)(\text{recomb}) = q \int_V \left(\frac{P}{\tau}\right) dV. \qquad (6.9\text{-}3)$$

The total *hole* charge per unit time removed from V across all its surface S is the integral of $\mathbf{J}_p . d\mathbf{S}$ over the surface. This surface integral may be transformed by the Gauss integral transformation theorem, to a volume integral. Thus, the rate of decrease of Q_p resulting from current flow out over the surface is:

$$- \left(\frac{dQ_p}{dt}\right)(\text{current flow}) = \int_S \mathbf{J}_p . d\mathbf{S} = \int_V \nabla . \mathbf{J}_p \, dV. \qquad (6.9\text{-}4)$$

By conservation of hole charge:

$$\left(\frac{dQ_p}{dt}\right) = \left(\frac{dQ_p}{dt}\right)(\text{recomb.}) + \left(\frac{dQ_p}{dt}\right)(\text{current flow}). \qquad (6.9\text{-}5)$$

Using eqns (6.9-2), (3) and (4), this becomes:

$$\int_V \left[\left(\frac{1}{q}\right)\nabla . \mathbf{J}_p + \left(\frac{P}{\tau}\right) + \left(\frac{\partial p}{\partial t}\right)\right] dV = 0. \qquad (6.9\text{-}6)$$

Because the volume of integration can be chosen arbitrarily, the integrand in the last equation must be everywhere zero. This follows, for if at some point it is not zero, it is possible to change the integral to a non-zero value, in contradiction to eqn (6.9-6), by including or excluding such a point in the arbitrary volume V. Hence:

$$\left(\frac{1}{q}\right)\nabla . \dot{\mathbf{J}}_p + \left(\frac{P}{\tau}\right) + \left(\frac{\partial p}{\partial t}\right) = 0. \qquad (6.9\text{-}7)$$

This is the *continuity equation* for holes.

A similar equation can be obtained for electrons:

$$- \left(\frac{1}{q}\right)\nabla . \mathbf{J}_n + \left(\frac{N}{\tau}\right) + \left(\frac{\partial n}{\partial t}\right) = 0 \qquad (6.9\text{-}8)$$

where it has been assumed that N is equal to P, (eqn 6.3-3).

Subtraction of eqns (6.9-7) and (8) gives:

$$\nabla . (\mathbf{J}_p + \mathbf{J}_n) = \nabla . \mathbf{J} = 0 . \qquad (6.9\text{-}9)$$

This is the current continuity equation, for zero space charge, of electromagnetic theory.

When charge neutrality is not valid, there is a residual space charge density ρ. The current continuity equation becomes:

$$\nabla . \mathbf{J} + \left(\frac{\partial \rho}{\partial t}\right) = 0 . \qquad (6.9\text{-}10)$$

This equation can be established directly, using a figure like 6.9a, by considering the total charge conservation in a volume V. The derivation is then very similar to that leading to eqn (6.9-7).

6.10 Continuity Equation for the Diffusion of Minority Carriers

When the drift component of minority carrier current is negligible compared with the diffusion component, a useful form of the continuity equation can be obtained. This condition is largely satisfied in the base of a diffusion transistor operated under low-level-injection conditions, and in certain other special cases. Assuming that the material is n-type, and that the hole drift current is negligible, the hole diffusion current density is:

$$\mathbf{J}_p = -qD_p \nabla p . \qquad (6.10\text{-}1)$$

Substitution of $\mathbf{J}_p$ into eqn (6.9-7) yields:

$$\nabla^2 p - \left(\frac{P}{D_p \tau}\right) - \frac{1}{D_p}\left(\frac{\partial p}{\partial t}\right) = 0 . \qquad (6.10\text{-}2)$$

The quantity $D_p \tau$ appearing in this continuity equation, has the dimensions of a length squared and is denoted by L_p^2. The length L_p is called the *diffusion length*. The physical significance of L_p will be explained in a later section. Equation (6.10-2) is amenable to exact solution in a number of special cases. In the following sections, a number of one-dimensional solutions of the equation will be considered.

6.11 Diffusion with Recombination: Semi-Infinite Bar

Figure 6.11a (*i*) shows a semi-infinite bar of uniform *n*-type semiconductor. Holes are injected so as to maintain a steady hole density p_0 at the free end of the bar. It will be assumed that recombination occurs only in

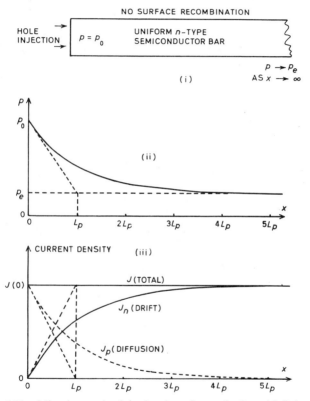

Figure 6.11a. Minority carrier injection into free end of semi-infinite bar:
(i) The semiconductor bar
(ii) Hole density distribution along the bar
(iii) Transfer of current from the diffusion process to the drift process with increasing distance from the injection contact

the bulk of the bar, that is surface recombination will be neglected*. Consequently, the direction of current flow will be that of the x-axis and hence the problem is one-dimensional. The continuity equation for the diffusion of minority carriers, eqn (6.10-2), will be used to determine the steady-state distribution of hole density and current flow along the bar. In the first instance it will be assumed that the electric field, and hence the hole drift current, is zero. In the steady state $(\partial p/\partial t)$ is zero, and so, for one-dimension, eqn (6.10-2) becomes:

$$\left(\frac{d^2 p}{dx^2}\right) - \left(\frac{P}{L_p^2}\right) = 0 . \tag{6.11-1}$$

For a uniform bar p_e is independent of x and so eqn (6.11-1) can be written:

$$\left(\frac{d^2 P}{dx^2}\right) - \left(\frac{P}{L_p^2}\right) = 0 . \tag{6.11-2}$$

The general solution of this equation is:

$$P = A \exp\left(-\frac{x}{L_p}\right) + B \exp\left(\frac{x}{L_p}\right) \tag{6.11-3}$$

where A and B are arbitrary constants. Because of recombination along the bar, the excess hole density P must tend to zero as x tends to infinity. It follows that B must be zero. At the free end of the bar, the excess hole density is P_0, that is $(p_0 - p_e)$, and so the constant A must equal P_0. Equation (6.11-3) is thus

$$P = P_0 \exp\left(-\frac{x}{L_p}\right) \tag{6.11-4}$$

or:

$$p = p_e + (p_0 - p_e) \exp\left(-\frac{x}{L_p}\right). \tag{6.11-5}$$

This equation is sketched in fig. 6.11a (ii). The diffusion length L_p is the distance from the free end of the bar over which the excess hole density

* In practice, surface recombination will contribute appreciably to the total recombination; this topic will be considered in section 7.11.

decays to $(1/e)$ of its initial value P_0. By analogy with the concept of mean excess lifetime τ of section 6.8, L_p is the mean distance a minority carrier diffuses between injection and recombination with a majority carrier.

Beyond a distance five times L_p into the bar, the excess density is below one per cent of its initial value and the hole density can be assumed to be equal to the equilibrium value.

The hole diffusion current density is:

$$J_p(x) = -qD_p\left(\frac{dp}{dx}\right) = \left(\frac{qD_p}{L_p}\right)P(x) \qquad (6.11\text{-}6)$$

where eqns (6.11-4) and (5) have been used. It follows that the hole diffusion current decays in the same way as the excess hole density. This decay is shown in fig. 6.11a(ii).

The total current density, that is the sum of hole and electron components, must however, be a constant independent of x. This follows from the intuitive concept of circuit theory, namely that the current at any point along a conductor has the same value at the same instant of time. In the present case, the statement is a direct consequence of eqn (6.9-9), which integrates to give:

$$J(x) = J_p(x) + J_n(x) = J(0) . \qquad (6.11\text{-}7)$$

Because the hole diffusion current decays with increasing x, the electron current must increase to maintain constancy of the total current. After approximately five diffusion lengths, the diffusion current is virtually zero. Furthermore, the carrier densities are then virtually the same as the equilibrium densities, and so beyond this point the current must result from carrier drift in an electric field. Because the semiconductor is n-type, this drift current is predominantly due to electrons.

For the sake of simplicity, it will be assumed that the hole emitter has unity injection-efficiency; that is the electron current at the injection contact is zero. Also any hole drift current will be assumed negligible compared with the corresponding electron drift current. This latter assumption implies that p is always negligible compared with n. Then all the current flow at the injection contact results from hole diffusion, while at distances of at least five diffusion lengths from the contact, all the current is due to electron drift. There is a gradual transfer from diffusion current to drift current through these five diffusion lengths. This situation is depicted in fig. 6.11a(iii).

The magnitude of the electric field, in the more remote parts of the bar, can be found by equating the hole diffusion current at the free end, to the electron drift current in the remote parts. Thus, from eqn (6.11-6):

$$J_p(0) = \left(\frac{qD_p}{L_p}\right) P_0 = \left(\frac{kT}{L_p}\right)\mu_p P_0 \qquad (6.11\text{-}8)$$

where the Einstein relation has been used. The drift current in the remote parts of the bar is:

$$J_n = qn_e\mu_n E \qquad (6.11\text{-}9)$$

where E is the electric intensity. Equating the right-hand sides of eqns (6.11-8) and (9):

$$E = \left(\frac{kT}{q}\right)\left(\frac{1}{L_p}\right)\left(\frac{\mu_p}{\mu_n}\right)\left(\frac{P_0}{n_e}\right). \qquad (6.11\text{-}10)$$

The value of (kT/q) is about 0·03 V at room temperatures; the mobilities μ_n and μ_p are of the same order. The electric intensity is thus less than 0·03 V per diffusion length for P_0 less than n_e, that is for low-level-injection. It should be noted that the electric intensity is proportional to the excess carrier density at the injection point.

Maintenance of charge equilibrium requires that the majority carrier electron density should increase in the neighbourhood of the injection contact to neutralize the charge of the injected holes. The spatial variation of electron density is thus the same as that for the holes, the difference in the densities being everywhere $(n_e - p_e)$. The gradient of the electron density is therefore everywhere the same as that of the hole density. Such a gradient gives rise to a diffusion component of electron current, which is just neutralized by a drift current component at the free end of the bar. This follows because the net electron current at this end of the bar is zero. The situation is very similar to that discussed in section 6.6, where these components cancelled out at the emitter junction.

The magnitude of the electric intensity at the free end of the bar will now be obtained. By analogy with eqn (6.11-8), the diffusion component electron current density is:

$$J_{n(\text{diff})} = -\left(\frac{qD_nP_0}{L_p}\right) = -\left(\frac{kT}{L_p}\right)\mu_n P_0 . \qquad (6.11\text{-}11)$$

Note that the electron density gradient is (P_0/L_p) as required by charge neutrality and not (P_0/L_n). The drift current density at the free end of the bar is:

$$J_{n(\text{drift})} = qn\mu_n E(0) = q(n_e + P_0)\mu_n E(0) \qquad (6.11\text{-}12)$$

where $E(0)$ is the electric intensity at the free end. Adding these last two equations and equating to zero:

$$E(0) = \left(\frac{kT}{q}\right)\left(\frac{1}{L_p}\right)\left(\frac{P_0}{n_e + P_0}\right). \qquad (6.11\text{-}13)$$

This value of $E(0)$ is different from the value of E in the remote parts

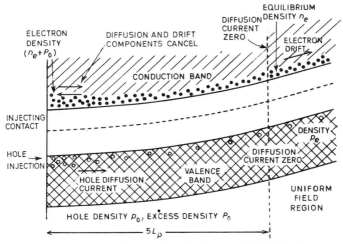

Figure 6.11b. Energy level diagram for minority carrier injection into a semi-infinite bar

of the bar, eqn (6.11-10), although these two intensities have similar orders of magnitude. Alternatively, these intensities can be expressed in terms of (dE_{Fi}/dx) as was done in section 6.6. Figure (6.11b) shows the energy level diagram along the bar. The carrier densities are depicted pictorially in this figure.

It will be shown, section 7.2, that a necessary and sufficient condition for charge neutrality is a constant electric intensity. In the example under consideration, the electric intensity is not constant and so the assumption of charge neutrality is not really justified. The magnitude of the residual charge density will be considered in section 7.3. It is sufficient to state here that, unless the current densities become very large, the charge equilibrium condition is approximately valid. In particular the approximation is very good when the excess carrier density is small compared with the majority carrier density.

6.12 A Technique for Solving the Continuity Equation

The example of the last section has illustrated an important technique for obtaining a solution to the continuity equation. In the first instance minority carrier diffusion only was considered. The principles of charge neutrality and vanishing divergence of the total current were then invoked to determine the drift currents and the diffusion component of the majority carrier current.

The original assumptions involved in the case of the restricted, diffusion only, continuity equation are thus revoked. The original solution for the density of minority carriers should then be corrected to allow for the presence of the drift components. However, such corrections, as in the example of the previous section, are often negligible.

This apparently circular procedure is adopted to avoid solving the general continuity equations, solutions for which are known only for a few special and often unimportant cases. On the other hand, the continuity equation for the diffusion of minority carriers is capable of analytical solution for a number of interesting cases. It is also amenable to known techniques of numerical analysis for cases where analytical solutions do not exist.

6.13 Uniform-Base Transistor with Bulk Recombination

In sections 5.10 and 6.6, the one-dimensional uniform-base, or diffusion, transistor was considered. In both cases recombination of minority carriers in the base was neglected. In the present section, the effect of base bulk recombination on the hole density profile, and on the diffusion current, will be investigated. For simplicity the small injection level dependent drift field in the base, as discussed in section 6.6, will be neglected. For moderate injection levels, the effects of recombination and drift field on the hole density profile are independent. Consequently the effect of the latter can be allowed for by adding the modifications of section 6.6 to those to be obtained in the present section.

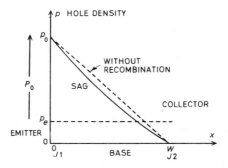

Figure 6.13a. Hole density distribution across the base of a diffusion transistor with recombination in the base

As in sections 5.10 and 6.6, the emitter junction J1 is forward biased in such a way that a constant hole density p_0 is maintained just inside the base region. The collector junction J2 is reverse biased and keeps the hole density zero at this side of the base. This is shown in fig. 6.13a, which should be compared with fig. 5.10b where, as explained earlier, hole recombination has been neglected. For the present case, the diffusion continuity equation, (eqn 6.10-2) becomes:

$$\left(\frac{d^2 P}{dx^2}\right) - \left(\frac{P}{L_p^2}\right) = 0 \qquad (6.13\text{-}1)$$

and is identical with eqn (6.11-2). As before, eqn (6.11-3) the general solution of this equation is:

$$P = A \exp\left(\frac{x}{L_p}\right) + B \exp\left(-\frac{x}{L_p}\right). \tag{6.13-2}$$

The constants of integration A and B are evaluated by reference to the boundary conditions:

$$\begin{array}{llll} p = p_0 \; ; & \text{i.e.} \; P = P_0 = p_0 - p_e \; ; & \text{at} \; x = 0 \\ p = 0 \; ; & \text{i.e.} \; P = -p_e \; ; & \text{at} \; x = W \end{array} \Bigg\} . \tag{6.13-3}$$

Substitution of these conditions into eqn (6.13-2) leads to:

$$\begin{aligned} A &= -\tfrac{1}{2} \operatorname{cosech}\left(\frac{W}{L_p}\right)\left[p_e + (p_0 - p_e)\exp\left(-\frac{W}{L_p}\right)\right] \\ B &= \tfrac{1}{2} \operatorname{cosech}\left(\frac{W}{L_p}\right)\left[p_e + (p_0 - p_e)\exp\left(\frac{W}{L_p}\right)\right] \end{aligned} . \tag{6.13-4}$$

The hole density at any point in the base is then:

$$p = p_e + \operatorname{cosech}\left(\frac{W}{L_p}\right)\left[(p_0 - p_e)\sinh\left(\frac{W-x}{L_p}\right) - p_e \sinh\left(\frac{x}{L_p}\right)\right]. \tag{6.13-5}$$

In any practical transistor, the base width W is made small compared with the hole diffusion length L_p. This is done to minimize base recombination. A first approximation to eqn (6.13-5) is:

$$p = p_0\left[1 - \left(\frac{x}{W}\right)\right] \tag{6.13-6}$$

when power terms higher than the first in $[(W-x)/L_p]$, (W/L_p) and (x/L_p) are neglected. This is, of course, the linear distribution of section 5.10, where recombination was neglected. This linear distribution is shown by the broken line in fig. 6.13a. The actual distribution given by eqn (6.13-5), sags somewhat from this straight line and is shown by the full line in the figure, for a typical case. The sag becomes greater as W becomes a larger fraction of L_p.

The diffusion current density at any point across the base is, from eqn (6.13-2):

$$J(x) = -qD_p\left(\frac{dP(x)}{dx}\right) = -\left(\frac{qD_p}{L_p}\right)\left[A\exp\left(\frac{x}{L_p}\right) - B\exp\left(-\frac{x}{L_p}\right)\right].$$
(6.13-7)

This current density has the value J_E at the emitter junction J1, which from eqns (6.13-4) and (7) has the value:

$$J_E = J(0) = \left(\frac{qD_p}{L_p}\right)\operatorname{cosech}\left(\frac{W}{L_p}\right)\left[p_e + (p_0 - p_e)\cosh\left(\frac{W}{L_p}\right)\right]. \quad (6.13-8)$$

The value* $-J_C$ of $J(x)$ at the collector junction J2 is similarly obtained as:

$$-J_C = J(W) = \left(\frac{qD_p}{L_p}\right)\operatorname{cosech}\left(\frac{W}{L_p}\right)\left[p_e\cosh\left(\frac{W}{L_p}\right) + (p_0 - p_e)\right]. \quad (6.13-9)$$

A relation exists between J_C and J_E; it can be obtained by multiplying eqn (6.13-8) by $\operatorname{sech}(W/L_p)$; a quantity which will be denoted by the symbol α. Thus:

$$\alpha J_E = \left(\frac{qD_p}{L_p}\right)\operatorname{cosech}\left(\frac{W}{L_p}\right)\left[p_e\operatorname{sech}\left(\frac{W}{L_p}\right) + (p_0 - p_e)\right]$$

$$= \left(\frac{qD_p}{L_p}\right)\operatorname{cosech}\left(\frac{W}{L_p}\right)\left[p_e\cosh\left(\frac{W}{L_p}\right) + (p_0 - p_e)\right]$$

$$+ \left(\frac{qD_p}{L_p}\right)\operatorname{cosech}\left(\frac{W}{L_p}\right)p_e\left[\operatorname{sech}\left(\frac{W}{L_p}\right) - \cosh\left(\frac{W}{L_p}\right)\right]. \quad (6.13-10)$$

The first term on the right-hand side of this last equation is $-J_C$, eqn (6.13-9), while the second term, which can be simplified, see eqn (6.13-12) below, is denoted by $-J_{CB0}$. Equation (6.13-10) can therefore be written:

$$-J_C = \alpha J_E + J_{CB0} \quad (6.13-11)$$

where
$$J_{CB0} = \left(\frac{qD_p p_e}{L_p}\right)\tanh\left(\frac{W}{L_p}\right) \quad (6.13-12)$$

---

* By convention, currents flowing into the base are counted positive; since $J(W)$ flows from base to collector, it is negative.

and
$$\alpha = \text{sech}\left(\frac{W}{L_p}\right). \qquad (6.13\text{-}13)$$

J_{CB0} is the current density across the junction J2, from base to collector*, when the emitter is open circuit, that is when J_E is zero. It is called the collector-base leakage current density. The symbol** α is called the current gain of the transistor; it is the fraction of the hole current across the junction J1 which reaches the junction J2, and so becomes collector current. A fraction $(1 - \alpha)$ of the current density J_E is lost as recombination current in the base. In the absence of recombination, α would of course be unity. The situation for this model transistor is shown in fig. 6.13b, wherein total currents I are indicated instead of current densities.

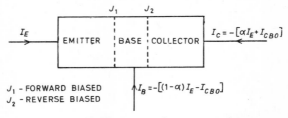

Figure 6.13b. The currents in a *pnp* transistor

In practical transistors, W is small compared with L_p; valid approximations may therefore be made for J_{CB0} and α. When W is very small compared with L_p, eqns (6.13-12) and (13) give J_{CB0} and α as zero and unity respectively. This is the case of negligible recombination in the base. A more accurate approximation retains the terms in (W/L_p) and its square. The equations then give:

---

* J_{CB0} is a B.S.I. symbol and is interpreted as follows: the suffix C refers to the collector, B refers to the base and 0 indicates that the remaining terminal, emitter, is open circuit. J_{CB0} is therefore the collector to base current density with the emitter open circuit. By eqn (6.13-11), J_{CB0} flows from base to collector and hence strictly should be denoted by J_{BC0}. However, J_{CB0} is used universally for this symbol.

** Strictly α is called the common-base current gain; an alternative B.S.I. symbol for this quantity is $-h_{\text{FB}}$, but the origin of this symbol cannot readily be made clear in the present context.

$$J_{CB0} \simeq \left(\frac{q D_p p_e W}{L_p^2} \right) \tag{6.13-14}$$

and

$$\alpha \simeq 1 - \tfrac{1}{2} \left(\frac{W}{L_p} \right)^2 . \tag{6.13-15}$$

These approximations are adequate for all purposes since for any useful transistor α would exceed 0·95, thereby indicating a negligible error in neglecting higher order terms.

It would have been possible, with great simplification, to have made this approximation in the initial expression for the excess hole density, namely eqn (6.13-2). However, since exact expressions could be obtained, it was worth while to present the full analysis.

6.14 A.C. Current Density: Uniform-Base Transistor

Up to the present section, only steady-state solutions of the continuity equation, for the diffusion of minority carriers, have been considered. In this section an example which includes the time dependent term is discussed. Again, the one-dimensional diffusion transistor will be used for the example. For simplicity, the injection dependent drift field and

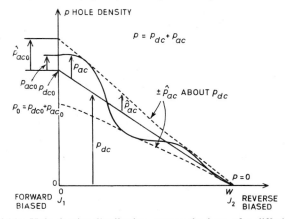

Figure 6.14a. Hole density distribution, across the base of a diffusion transistor, with small signal a.c. component

recombination in the base are neglected. The omission from consideration of the latter factor causes only second order effects in the results to be obtained, as does also that of the first factor for moderate injection levels.

As before, the junction J2 is reverse biased, thereby maintaining the hole density zero at this edge of the base, fig. 6.14a. The junction J1 is forward biased to give a hole density p_0 just inside the base. This density is to have a d.c. component p_{dco} and an alternating component p_{aco} of angular frequency ω. The hole density p, at any point across the base, will therefore have a d.c. component p_{dc} and an a.c. component p_{ac}:

$$p = p_{dc} + p_{ac} . \tag{6.14-1}$$

Substitution into the continuity equation, (eqn 6.10-2), gives for one-dimension, and with the omission of the recombination term:

$$\left(\frac{d^2 p_{dc}}{dx^2}\right) + \left[\left(\frac{\partial^2 p_{ac}}{\partial x^2}\right) - \frac{1}{D_p}\left(\frac{\partial p_{ac}}{\partial t}\right)\right] = 0 . \tag{6.14-2}$$

Now p_{dc} and p_{ac} must be considered independent, for different values of p_{ac} can be obtained for different values of the p_{aco} component at the junction J1, without affecting the p_{dc} component. This is a consequence of the linearity of the continuity equation. Equation (6.14-2) thereby reduces to two independent equations:

$$\left(\frac{d^2 p_{dc}}{dx^2}\right) = 0 \tag{6.14-3}$$

and:

$$\left(\frac{\partial^2 p_{ac}}{\partial x^2}\right) - \frac{1}{D_p}\left(\frac{\partial p_{ac}}{\partial t}\right) = 0 . \tag{6.14-4}$$

The first of these equations integrates immediately to give a linear fall of the d.c. component of p from p_{dco} to zero across the base. This is shown in fig. 6.14a and is identical to the steady-state solution of section 5.10. The d.c. component of current density across the base is therefore:

$$J_{dc} = \left(\frac{q D_p p_{dco}}{W}\right) . \tag{6.14-5}$$

To deal with the second equation, it is first noted that p_{ac} will have the same angular frequency as p_{aco}; again this is ensured by the linearity of the equation. The a.c. component of hole density may thus be written:

$$p_{ac} = \hat{p}_{ac} \exp(j\omega t) \qquad (6.14\text{-}6)$$

where $\hat{p}_{ac}$ is the amplitude, or peak value, of p_{ac}. Substitution into eqn (6.14-4) yields:

$$\left(\frac{d^2\hat{p}_{ac}}{dx^2}\right) - \left(\frac{j\omega}{D_p}\right)\hat{p}_{ac} = 0 . \qquad (6.14\text{-}7)$$

The general solution of this equation is:

$$\hat{p}_{ac} = A \exp(\theta x) + B \exp(-\theta x) \qquad (6.14\text{-}8)$$

where*

$$\theta = \left(\sqrt{\frac{\omega}{2D_p}}\right)(1+j) . \qquad (6.14\text{-}9)$$

The constants A and B are evaluated with reference to the boundary conditions:

$$\left.\begin{array}{ll} \hat{p}_{ac} = \hat{p}_{aco} , & \text{at} \quad x = 0 \\ \hat{p}_{ac} = 0 , & \text{at} \quad x = W. \end{array}\right\} \qquad (6.14\text{-}10)$$

Substitution of these equations into eqn (6.14-8) leads to:

$$\left.\begin{array}{l} A = -\tfrac{1}{2}\operatorname{cosech}(\theta W).\exp(-\theta W)\hat{p}_{aco} \\ B = \tfrac{1}{2}\operatorname{cosech}(\theta W).\exp(\theta W)\hat{p}_{aco} \end{array}\right\} \qquad (6.14\text{-}11)$$

In fig. 6.14a, is shown a sketch of how p_{ac} might vary across the base at any instant of time. The broken curves show the amplitude limits of p_{ac} as they might be given by eqns (6.14-8) and (11). The exact form of these curves is of course an involved function of the angular frequency ω.

The a.c. component of current density at any point across the base is given by, using eqn (6.14-8):

* Note: $\sqrt{(j)} = \dfrac{1}{\sqrt{2}}(1+j).$

$$J_{ac}(x) = -qD_p \left(\frac{dp_{ac}}{dx}\right) =$$

$$= -qD_p \theta [A \exp(\theta x) - B \exp(-\theta x)] \exp(j\omega t). \quad (6.14\text{-}12)$$

In particular, at the emitter junction this becomes, with the aid of eqn (6.14-11):

$$J_{ac}(0) = qD_p \theta \hat{p}_{aco} . \coth(\theta W) . \exp(j\omega t). \quad (6.14\text{-}13)$$

The current density $J_{ac}(0)$ is a complex quantity, because θ is complex, eqn (6.14-9). It has a component in phase with $\hat{p}_{aco}$, the conductive component, and a component in quadrature to $\hat{p}_{aco}$, the susceptive component. The conductive and susceptive components are complicated functions of ω, and cannot be represented by the current flow into a parallel combination of a constant conductance and a constant capacitance. If however the magnitude of the angular frequency is restricted such that

$$\omega \ll \left(\frac{2D_p}{W^2}\right) \quad (6.14\text{-}14)$$

that is:

$$\left(\sqrt{\frac{\omega}{2D_p}}\right) W \ll 1 \quad (6.14\text{-}15)$$

then the magnitude of (θW) is small compared with unity. A simple approximation for $\coth(\theta W)$ can then be made. Thus retaining terms of the order of $(\theta W)^2$ and lower, eqn (6.14-13) approximates to:

$$J_{ac}(0) = J_{dc}\left(\frac{\hat{p}_{aco}}{p_{dco}}\right)\left[1 + j\omega\left(\frac{W^2}{2D_p}\right)\right] \exp(j\omega t) \quad (6.14\text{-}16)$$

where eqns (6.14-5) and (9) for J_{dc} and θ respectively, have been used. The current density $J_{ac}(0)$ is seen to have in-phase and quadrature components, which can be represented respectively by the current flow in a constant conductance and a constant capacitance, the two elements being in parallel. The ratio of the capacitance to the conductance is, from eqn (6.14-16), $(W^2/2D_p)F\Omega$. The absolute magnitudes of these components will be obtained in section 8.5, where this example will be considered in more detail.

The condition, eqn (6.14-15), can be shown to be equivalent to another, namely that of assuming that the frequency is low enough for the hole distribution across the base to be able to follow changes of injection density, at the emitter, without delay. For the present example, this means that the hole distribution across the base is always linear. Again, this will be treated in more detail in section 8.5.

6.15 A.C. Current Density: Semi-Infinite Bar

In section 6.11, the steady-state current density in a semi-infinite bar of n-type semiconductor, with hole injection at the free end, was considered. In the present section, the a.c. component of current density, flowing in response to an a.c. component of injected hole density, is investigated. The problem is rather similar to that of the last section, except that now bulk recombination can no longer be neglected. The situation is depicted in fig. 6.15a which should be compared with figs

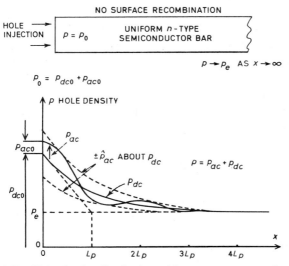

Figure 6.15a. Hole density distribution with a.c. component, along semi-infinite bar

6.11a and 6.14a. Again, as in the last section, the hole density p is written as:

$$p = p_{dc} + p_{ac} .$$ (6.15-1)

Substitution into the continuity equation, eqn (6.10-2), yields for the one-dimensional uniform bar:

$$\left\{ \left(\frac{d^2 P_{dc}}{dx^2} \right) - \left(\frac{P_{dc}}{L_p^2} \right) \right\} + \left\{ \left(\frac{\partial^2 p_{ac}}{\partial x^2} \right) - \left(\frac{p_{ac}}{L_p^2} \right) - \frac{1}{D_p} \left(\frac{\partial p_{ac}}{\partial t} \right) \right\} = 0 .$$ (6.15-2)

As in the last section, this equation reduces to two equations, namely:

$$\left(\frac{d^2 P_{dc}}{dx^2} \right) - \left(\frac{P_{dc}}{L_p^2} \right) = 0$$ (6.15-3)

and

$$\left(\frac{\partial^2 p_{ac}}{\partial x^2} \right) - \left(\frac{p_{ac}}{L_p^2} \right) - \frac{1}{D_p} \left(\frac{\partial p_{ac}}{\partial t} \right) = 0 .$$ (6.15-4)

Equation (6.15-3) has the same solution as was obtained for the steady state in section 6.11; that is an exponential decay of hole density from the injection level to the equilibrium density with a length constant L_p. This is shown in fig. 6.15a. The d.c. component of hole current density is:

$$J_{dc}(x) = \left(\frac{qD_p}{L_p} \right) P_{dc}(x) = \left(\frac{qD_p}{L_p} \right) (p_{dc}(x) - p_e)$$ (6.15-5)

and in particular, the d.c. component of current density at the free end of the bar is:

$$J_{dc}(0) = \left(\frac{qD_p}{L_p} \right) P_{dc}(0) = \left(\frac{qD_p}{L_p} \right) (p_{dco} - p_e) .$$ (6.15-6)

In order to deal with eqn (6.15-4), as in the last section, p_{ac} is written:

$$p_{ac} = \hat{p}_{ac} \exp (j\omega t)$$ (6.15-7)

and so eqn (6.15-4) becomes:

$$\left(\frac{d^2 \hat{p}_{ac}}{dx^2} \right) - \left(\frac{1}{L_p^2} \right) \left\{ 1 + j\omega \left(\frac{L_p^2}{D_p} \right) \right\} \hat{p}_{ac} = 0 .$$ (6.15-8)

The general solution of this equation may be written as:

$$\hat{p}_{ac} = A \exp(\theta x) + B \exp(-\theta x) \qquad (6.15-9)$$

where:

$$\theta = \left(\frac{1}{L_p}\right)\sqrt{\left[1 + j\omega\left(\frac{L_p^2}{D_p}\right)\right]}. \qquad (6.15-10)$$

The boundary conditions are that $\hat{p}_{ac}$ is zero for sufficiently large x, which implies that A must be zero, and that $\hat{p}_{ac}$ is $\hat{p}_{aco}$ at the free end of the bar. Thus eqn (6.15-9) becomes:

$$\hat{p}_{ac} = \hat{p}_{aco} \exp(-\theta x). \qquad (6.15-11)$$

The exact form of $\hat{p}_{ac}$ is an involved, complex, function of ω. A sketch of how it might appear at any particular instant is shown in fig. 6.15a.

The a.c. component of current density at any point is given by:

$$J_{ac}(x) = -qD_p\left(\frac{dp_{ac}}{dx}\right) = qD_p\theta\hat{p}_{aco} \exp(-\theta x) \exp(j\omega t). \quad (6.15-12)$$

In particular, at the free end of the bar, this is:

$$J_{ac}(0) = qD_p\theta\hat{p}_{aco} \exp(j\omega t). \qquad (6.15-13)$$

Again, as in the last section, the complex current density is an involved function of ω. Its real and imaginary components can be considered as flowing in a parallel combination of a conductance and a capacitance, but the values of the elements will be frequency dependent.

For frequencies such that:

$$\omega \ll \left(\frac{D_p}{L_p^2}\right) \qquad (6.15-14)$$

the expression for θ, eqn (6.15-10), reduces to:

$$\theta = \left(\frac{1}{L_p}\right)\left\{1 + j\omega\left(\frac{L_p^2}{2D_p}\right)\right\}. \qquad (6.15-15)$$

The a.c. component of current density, eqn (6.15-13), now becomes:

$$J_{ac}(0) = \left(\frac{qD_p}{L_p}\right)\hat{p}_{aco}\exp(j\omega t).\left\{1+j\omega\left(\frac{L_p^2}{2D_p}\right)\right\}$$

$$= J_{do}(0)\left(\frac{p_{aco}}{p_{dco}-p_e}\right)\left\{1+j\omega\left(\frac{L_p^2}{2D_p}\right)\right\}. \qquad (6.15\text{-}16)$$

The capacitance and conductance are now independent of frequency and the ratio of their values is seen to be $(L_p^2/2D_p)F\Omega$. It is somewhat larger than the value obtained from the base of the transistor in the last section. This is a consequence of the large charge which is stored under the exponential in the present case, compared with that under the triangle in the previous example.

The frequency limiting conditions, eqn (6.15-14), is equivalent to the statement that changes in the injection level are slow enough for the distribution along the bar to follow them without delay. The hole distribution along the bar would then always have an exponentially decaying form.

6.16 Trapping Theory of Carrier Recombination

In section 6.8, a rather restricted account of carrier recombination was presented. From this was developed a simple theory of minority carrier lifetime. In the present section, further consideration will be given to the trapping mechanism of carrier recombination. The principle work on this theory was carried out by Shockley and Read [6.2], Hall [6.3] and Rose and Sandiford [6.4]. The material of this section is largely drawn from the papers of these workers.

An important concept is that of *capture cross-section*. This cross-section is a circular area, centred on the trap, with its plane normal to the motion of the carrier whose *trapping* or *capture* is being considered. The area is chosen such that, if the carrier passes through it, it is captured. Trapping occurs, because the energy of the carrier in the trap is less than its energy as a mobile carrier. Once a carrier is captured, the cross-section of the trap becomes vanishingly small until such time as the carrier is released. This latter process will occur ultimately because of the thermal vibration of the lattice.

The cross-section is a function of the energy of the carrier being captured, being smaller the more energetic the carrier. There is an analogy here, with the too energetically *putted* golf ball which passes directly over the top of the hole. The thermal velocities of the carriers are randomly orientated in direction; it is therefore necessary to consider the cross-section of the trap in different directions. The capture cross-section is not necessarily the same in every direction. Assume, for the present, that all the carriers have the same magnitude and direction of thermal velocity **v**. The number of carriers passing through the cross-section per second would then be nvA, where A is the cross-section,

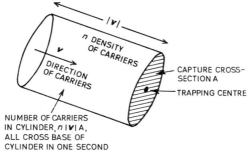

Figure 6.16a. Rate of carrier trapping by a cross-section A

v is the velocity magnitude of the carriers and n is the carrier density; see fig. 6.16a. Allowing now, random orientation in space of the carrier velocities, consider a cone of small solid angle $d\omega$, at any point and about any direction. A fraction $(d\omega/4\pi)$ of the density n of carriers, may be said to move wholly within the chosen cone. The number of carriers per second passing through the capture cross-section normal to the axis of the cone is, therefore, $nvA(dw/4\pi)$. If the cross-section is independent of orientation, integration of this last expression, over all orientations, again yields nvA as the rate of trapping of the carriers. Even when the cross-section is dependent on orientation, it is possible to introduce a mean cross-section as follows:

$$A = \left(\frac{1}{4\pi}\right) \int_{\text{all orientations}} A\binom{\text{Function of}}{\text{orientation}} d\omega . \qquad (6.16\text{-}1)$$

The rate of trapping of carriers can thus still be expressed as:

$$R = nvA . \tag{6.16-2}$$

Let now N_t be the density of traps, and n_t be the occupation density, and p_t be the density of those traps which are empty, that is occupied by holes. The rate at which the electron density decreases, as a result of trapping, is therefore:

$$-\left(\frac{dn}{dt}\right) = nvAp_t . \tag{6.16-3}$$

The restriction to the same magnitude of thermal velocity for all carriers must now be removed. Equation (6.16-3), can be applied to carriers whose energies lie in the narrow range E to $(E + dE)$. The density of carriers whose energies, lie in the range E to $(E + dE)$, is $n(E)dE$, where $n(E)$ is $F(E)N(E)$; see notation of section 4.1. Thus:

$$\left(\frac{dn(E)}{dt}\right) dE = -n(E)dE . v . A(E)p_t \tag{6.16-4}$$

or

$$\left(\frac{dn(E)}{dt}\right) = -c_n(E) . n(E) p_t \tag{6.16-5}$$

where:

$$c_n(E) = v . A(E) = \sqrt{\left[\frac{2(E - E_c)}{m}\right]} . A(E) . \tag{6.16-6}$$

The quantity $c_n(E)$ is the probability that an empty trap will capture an electron of energy E in unit time. It is called, the *capture probability per unit time*.

A special case occurs, when the density p_t of unoccupied traps is equal to the total trap density; for example, when N_t greatly exceeds the total density of electrons, or alternatively, when some, unspecified, mechanism empties the traps immediately after they become occupied. The probability $c_n(E)$ is then related to the mean lifetime $\tau_{n0}(E)$ of electrons in the energy level at E. This is seen by integration of eqn (6.16-5):

$$n(E) = n_0(E) . \exp\left(-\frac{t}{\tau_{n0}(E)}\right) \tag{6.16-7}$$

where $n_0(E)$ is the value of $n(E)$ at zero time, and where the mean lifetime is:

$$\tau_{n0}(E) = \{c_n(E)N_t\}^{-1} . \qquad (6.16\text{-}8)$$

In an exactly similar way, a probability per unit time $c_p(E)$, for the capture of holes from the valence band, can be defined.

By analogy with $c_n(E)$, it is also possible to define an emission probability, per unit time, $e_n(E)$, for the emission of an electron from the trap to a higher energy level E. Lattice vibration phonons provide the energy for such transitions. The rate of increase of $n(E)$, due to emissions from the trapping levels, is, by comparison with eqn (6.16-5):

$$\left(\frac{dn(E)}{dt}\right) = e_n(E)[N(E) - n(E)]n_t . \qquad (6.16\text{-}9)$$

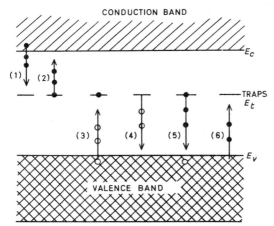

Figure 6.16b. Trapping processes:
(1) Electron from conduction band captured by empty trap
(2) Electron emitted by filled trap to conduction band
(3) Hole from valence band captured by filled trap
(4) Hole emitted by empty trap to valence band
(5) Electron emitted by filled trap to neutralize hole in valence band; equivalent to (3)
(6) Electron from valence band captured by empty trap; equivalent to (4)

Here, $[N(E) - n(E)]$ is the *hole* density in the conduction band, per unit energy range, and n_t is the density of occupied traps. Note that the total trap density N_t is such that:

$$N_t = p_t + n_t . \qquad (6.16\text{-}10)$$

An occupied trap level can loose an electron in one of two ways; firstly, by emitting it to the conduction band, or secondly, by losing it to neutralize a hole in the valence band. This latter process is, however, equivalent to the electron occupied trap *capturing* a hole from the valence band. The corresponding emission process is described by the probability, per unit time, $e_p(E)$, of hole emission from the trap level to the valence band. This process is equivalent to the capture, by a trap, of an electron from the valence band.

For the sake of uniformity, it will always be assumed that traps capture and emit electrons from the conduction band and holes from the valence band. All equivalent processes will be described as one of these four processes; which are shown schematically in fig. 6.16b as (1), (2), (3) and (4). In this scheme, recombination and generation are thought of as occurring at the trap level; recombination being the result of processes (1) and (3), in either order, and generation, the result of processes (2) and (4). Direct transitions between the conduction and valence bands are considered to be so unlikely, compared with the processes (1) to (4), as to be negligible in number.

An important relation exists between the probabilities $c_n(E)$ and $e_n(E)$. Consider a semiconductor in equilibrium, and assume that it has a density N_t of traps at an energy level E_t. The electron and hole densities, in the conduction and valence bands, respectively, are constant in time. In particular, the distributions of these densities with energy are constant, that is, $n(E)$ and $p(E)$ are constants in time. It follows that the rate of trapping, of electrons from the conduction band, must equal their rate of emission from the traps back to the conduction band. Thus by eqns (6.16-5) and (9):

$$c_n(E) . n(E) . p_t = e_n(E) [N(E) - n(E)] n_t \qquad (6.16\text{-}11)$$

or:
$$e_n(E) = c_n(E) \left(\frac{n(E)}{N(E) - n(E)} \right) \left(\frac{p_t}{n_t} \right) . \qquad (6.16\text{-}12)$$

In equilibrium, using eqns (4.1-1) and (4.2-8):

$$n(E) = N(E)F(E) \tag{6.16-13}$$

$$n_t = N_t F(E_t) \tag{6.16-14}$$

$$N(E) - n(E) = N(E) . \tilde{F}(E) \tag{6.16-15}$$

$$p_t = N_t \tilde{F}(E_t) . \tag{6.16-16}$$

Substitution into eqn (6.16-12) yields, with eqns (3.11-7) and (9) for $F(E)$ and $\tilde{F}(E)$:

$$e_n(E) = c_n(E) \exp\left[- \left(\frac{E - E_t}{kT} \right) \right]. \tag{6.16-17}$$

A similar result may be devised for the hole capture and emission probabilities per unit time, namely:

$$e_p(E) = c_p(E) \exp\left[- \left(\frac{E_t - E}{kT} \right) \right]. \tag{6.16-18}$$

Although equilibrium conditions were used for the derivation of these last two equations, it should be appreciated that the use of these equations is not restricted to such conditions. This is because the equations relate capture and emission probabilities of the traps, quantities which are not influenced by the thermodynamic state of the material.

The capture and emission probabilities discussed so far, have referred to the transit of electrons, or holes, between the trapping level and some other particular energy level. Of more significance, are the capture and emission probabilities between the trapping level and the whole of the conduction or valence band. Integrating eqn (6.16-5) over the whole of the conduction band, the total rate of capture, per unit volume, of electrons from the conduction band is:

$$U_{nc} = p_t \int_{E_c}^{\infty} c_n(E) n(E) dE = p_t n c_n \tag{6.16-19}$$

where:

$$c_n = \left(\frac{1}{n}\right) \int_{E_c}^{\infty} c_n(E) n(E) dE . \tag{6.16-20}$$

Similarly, the rate of emission of electrons, from the traps to the conduction band is:

$$U_{ne} = n_t \int_{E_c}^{\infty} e_n(E)[N(E) - n(E)]\,dE = n_t N_c e_n \qquad (6.16\text{-}21)$$

where:

$$e_n = \left(\frac{1}{N_c}\right) \int_{E_c}^{\infty} e_n(E)[N(E) - n(E)]\,dE . \qquad (6.16\text{-}22)$$

The quantities c_n and e_n are, respectively, the capture and emission probabilities, per unit time, between the trap levels and the whole of the conduction band.

It is worth noting, that in defining e_n, it is assumed that the conduction band is empty, and therefore, the density of states to which transitions can take place is N_c, the effective density of states in the conduction band. These states are imagined to be at energy E_c, that is, at the bottom of the band. It would have been more rational, to have used $(N_c - n)$ as the density of available states in the conduction band, but this leads to more involved analysis subsequently.

Provided the electron density in the conduction band is non-degenerate:

$$n(E) = N(E) \exp\left\{-\left(\frac{E - E_{Fn}}{kT}\right)\right\} \qquad (6.16\text{-}23)$$

and:

$$n = N_c \exp\left\{-\left(\frac{E_c - E_{Fn}}{kT}\right)\right\}. \qquad (6.16\text{-}24)$$

Substitution into eqn (6.16-20) gives:

$$c_n = \left(\frac{1}{N_c}\right) \int_{E_c}^{\infty} c_n(E) N(E) \exp\left\{-\left(\frac{E - E_c}{kT}\right)\right\} dE . \qquad (6.16\text{-}25)$$

This shows that c_n is independent of the electron density in the conduction band and, in particular, it shows that c_n is independent of whether, or not, the semiconductor is in equilibrium.

By analogy with eqn (6.16-8), the probability c_n can be related to the lifetime of an electron in the conduction band, thus:

$$\tau_{n0} = \{c_n N_t\}^{-1} . \tag{6.16-26}$$

It should be remembered, however, that this is the mean lifetime, on the assumption that the effective trap density p_t remains equal to the actual trap density N_t; that is, all the traps remain in the *ready to trap* state.

Consider now the integrand $e_n(E)[N(E)-n(E)]$ in the expression for e_n. It may be written as $e_n(E)N(E)[1-F_n(E)]$, where $F_n(E)$ is the Fermi function with reference energy E_{Fn}. With the aid of this expression and eqn (6.16-17), relating $e_n(E)$ and $c_n(E)$, eqn (6.16-22) for e_n may be written:

$$
\begin{aligned}
e_n &= \left(\frac{1}{N_c}\right) \int_{E_c}^{\infty} c_n(E)N(E).F_n(E) \exp\left[-\frac{E_{Fn}-E_t}{kT}\right) dE\Big] \\
&= \left(\frac{1}{N_c}\right) \exp\left[-\left(\frac{E_c-E_t}{kT}\right)\right] \int_{E_c}^{\infty} c_n(E)N(E) \exp\left[-\left(\frac{E-E_c}{kT}\right)\right] dE \\
&= c_n \exp\left[-\left(\frac{E_c-E_t}{kT}\right)\right] \tag{6.16-27}
\end{aligned}
$$

where the classical approximation to the Fermi function and eqn (6.16-25) have been used. This last equation is analogous to eqn (6.16-17) and can be regarded as an integrated form of the latter. In a similar way, transition probabilities c_p and e_p, between the trap levels and the valence band can be defined, and an equation like eqn (6.16-27) obtained:

$$e_p = c_p \exp\left[-\left(\frac{E_t-E_v}{kT}\right)\right]. \tag{6.16-28}$$

Again, the probability c_p can be related to a lifetime:

$$\tau_{p0} = \{c_p N_t\}^{-1} . \tag{6.16-29}$$

The net capture rate, per unit volume, of electrons from the conduction band, is, from eqns (6.16-19), (21) and (27):

$$U_n = U_{nc} - U_{ne} = p_t n c_n - n_t N_c e_n$$
$$= (p_t n - n_t' n_1) c_n \qquad (6.16\text{-}30)$$

where:
$$n_1 = N_c \exp\left[-\left(\frac{E_c - E_t}{kT} \right) \right] \qquad (6.16\text{-}31)$$

is a constant quantity, with the dimensions of a density, at constant temperature. Similarly, the net capture rate, per unit volume, of holes from the valence band is:

$$U_p = U_{pc} - U_{pe} = (n_t p - p_t p_1) c_p \qquad (6.16\text{-}32)$$

where:
$$p_1 = N_v \exp\left[-\left(\frac{E_t - E_v}{kT} \right) \right]. \qquad (6.16\text{-}33)$$

Note, also:
$$n_1 p_1 = N_c N_v \exp\left(\frac{E_v - E_c}{kT} \right) = n_i^2 . \qquad (6.16\text{-}34)$$

In equilibrium, the net recombination rate of electrons and holes is zero. Because recombination is assumed to occur in the trapping levels, this means that the net capture rates U_n and U_p must both be zero, as is readily verified directly from the equations concerned. Under non-equilibrium conditions, there will be a net recombination of electrons and holes at the trap levels. However, for given carrier densities in the conduction and valence bands, it will be assumed that the electron and hole capture rates at the traps are equal; that is, there is no build up of carriers, of either type, in the trap levels. This is described as the *steady-state* condition, and lifetimes associated with it, are described as *steady-state* lifetimes. This condition is described by using eqns (6.16-30) and (32):

$$U = (p_t n - n_t n_1) c_n = (n_t p - p_t p_1) c_p . \qquad (6.16\text{-}35)$$

Writing p_t as $(N_t - n_t)$, n_t may be eliminated, giving:

$$U = \frac{(np - n_1 p_1) N_t}{(n + n_1)\left(\dfrac{1}{c_p} \right) + (p + p_1)\left(\dfrac{1}{c_n} \right)} \qquad (6.16\text{-}36)$$

Using eqns (6.16-26), (29) and (34), this is:

$$U = \frac{(np - n_i^2)}{(n + n_1)\tau_{p0} + (p + p_1)\tau_{n0}}.$$ (6.16-37)

This last equation should be used as the recombination term in *steady-state* versions of the charge conservation, that is continuity, equations of section 6.9. It gives the net rate at which both excess electrons and excess holes are removed, from their respective bands, by recombination. Further, eqn (6.16-37), shows to what extent the assumptions of the simple recombination theory, presented in section 6.8, are valid. The constant C, of eqns (6.8-2) through (5), is to be identified with the denominator $\{(n + n_1)\tau_{p0} + (p + p_1)\tau_{n0}\}^{-1}$ of eqn (6.16-37), and so the earlier theory is valid, to the extent that this quantity is a constant.

As in section 6.8, it is more convenient to deal with a carrier lifetime than a recombination rate, especially if the former is a constant. However, some difficulty arises in the definition of *excess carrier lifetime* in this trapping model. Let thermal equilibrium be disturbed by, say, injecting a *steady-state* excess density P, of holes, into an n-type semiconductor. Charge equilibrium may be maintained by drawing in an excess density P of electrons, from the other contact. Not all these electrons necessarily remain in the conduction band; some may enter unoccupied traps, thereby changing the occupation density of the traps. The conversation condition is then expressed as:

$$P = N + \Delta n_t$$ (6.16-38)

where N is the excess density in the conduction band and Δn_t is the change in the density of occupied traps. It is important to realize, that this is a steady-state phenomenon. Both in equilibrium and *steady-state* non-equilibrium, there is no build up, in time, of carriers at the trap level. It is simply that a different density of traps is occupied in the non-equilibrium condition compared with that in the equilibrium condition.

When the total trap density N_t is small, compared with p_e, or n_e, Δn_t will be small compared with P, or N. Then the simple P and N equality condition is retained, as in section 6.8. In this circumstance, the *steady-*

state excess carrier lifetimes, are equal and readily defined by reference to eqn (6.8-8).

Thus, from eqn (6.16-37):

$$\tau = \left(\frac{P}{U}\right) = \left[\frac{(P+n_e+n_1)\tau_{p0}+(P+p_e+p_1)\tau_{n0}}{(n_e+P)(p_e+P)-n_i^2}\right] P$$

$$= \frac{(P+n_e+n_1)\tau_{p0}+(P+p_e+p_1)\tau_{n0}}{P+p_e+n_e}. \qquad (6.16\text{-}39)$$

One conclusion which can be drawn from this result, is the inverse proportionality of the *lifetime* τ on the trap density N_t. This is a consequence of the same dependence on N_t of τ_{p0} and τ_{n0}, as shown by eqns (6.16-26) and (29).

For low injection levels, the excess density P, in eqn (6.16-39), may be neglected compared with the other densities. Then, τ is a constant and the validity of the result of section 6.8, for this condition, is established. For a heavily doped, *n*-type, semiconductor, the equilibrium density n_e will greatly exceed all other densities, including n_1 and p_1*.

In this case eqn (6.16-39) becomes:

$$\tau \simeq \tau_{p0} \qquad (6.16\text{-}40)$$

a result expected intuitively, for when the electron density is high, almost all the trap will be occupied by electrons and hence be in the *ready to capture a hole* condition. Similarly, in the case of a heavily doped, *p*-type semiconductor:

$$\tau \simeq \tau_{n0}. \qquad (6.16\text{-}41)$$

A somewhat better approximation, for an *n*-type semiconductor at low injection levels, is obtained when either n_1 or p_1 is retained, according to which is the larger. When p_1 is neglected, eqns (6.16-39) and (31) yield:

* All the effective recombination traps are in the middle region of the forbidden gap, otherwise lifetimes of the same order as, or larger than, those of the direct-photon radiative process would result. Hence eqns (6.16-31) and (33), predict lower values for n_1 and p_1 than the equivalent equation for n_e.

$$\tau \simeq \left(\frac{n_e + n_1}{n_e}\right) \cdot \tau_{p0} = \left\{1 + \left(\frac{N_c}{n_e}\right) \exp\left[-\left(\frac{E_c - E_t}{kT}\right)\right]\right\} \tau_{p0}. \quad (6.16\text{-}42)$$

On the other hand, when n_1 is neglected:

$$\tau \simeq \tau_{p0} + \left(\frac{p_1}{n_e}\right) \tau_{n0} = \left\{\tau_{p0} + \left(\frac{N_v}{n_e}\right) \exp\left[-\left(\frac{E_t - E_v}{kT}\right)\right] \tau_{n0}\right\}. \quad (6.16\text{-}43)$$

Experimentally [6.3], [6.5], by investigating the temperature dependence of lifetime, these relations have been used to locate the recombination trap energy levels. This is possible since τ_{n0} and τ_{p0} have, at most, power dependence on temperature. Thus for temperatures for which the exponential term predominates, a logarithmic plot of lifetime against reciprocal temperature yields a straight line from which $(E_c - E_t)$ or $(E_t - E_v)$ can be deduced. Because there are two equations, ambiguity remains as to which of these quantities has been obtained.

When the trap density N_t is not small, compared with the carrier densities, Δn_t, in eqn (6.16-38), is not negligible compared with P and N. In this case, there is a distinction between the electron and hole lifetimes, which are defined by:

$$\tau_n = (N/U) \qquad\qquad (6.16\text{-}44)$$

$$\tau_p = (P/U). \qquad\qquad (6.16\text{-}45)$$

The analysis in this case, is somewhat involved algebraically, although no more difficult in concept, and will not be presented here. The ambiguity, mentioned above, can be resolved if the difference in the carrier lifetimes is known; for details of this and a detailed account of eqns (6.16-44) or (45), see reference [6.6].

Under large signal conditions, the carrier densities become large, compared with the trap density N_t, and so the excess densities P and N again become equal. Further, at sufficiently high-injection-levels, eqn (6.16-39), is:

$$\tau \simeq \tau_{p0} + \tau_{n0}. \qquad\qquad (6.16\text{-}46)$$

Denoting by τ_0, the carrier lifetime of eqn (6.16-39), for very low-injection-levels, it is readily shown that τ increases monotonically from τ_0 to $\tau_{p0} + \tau_{n0}$, as the injection level is raised from zero to large values.

If the injection level, or the carrier generation rate, is suddenly increased, the carrier densities are subsequently controlled by the *transient lifetimes*. These differ from the *steady-state lifetimes* because the occupation density of the traps, following the sudden change, is altering with time. In this circumstance, the rates U_n and U_p cannot be equated, and a pair of simultaneous differential equations must be solved for the carriers densities. The analysis of *transient lifetimes*, is beyond the scope of this book and the reader should consult ref [6.7] for an account of this topic.

Carrier lifetimes, in both germanium and silicon, range from less than one microsecond to about one millisecond. Impurity atoms, usually from group II or VI of the Periodic Table, often act as recombination centres, but lattice defect sites may also play this role.

6.17 Non-Recombination Traps

When one or other of the probabilities c_n or c_p is negligible, the traps are said to be *non-recombination* traps. Thus, when c_p is effectively zero, electrons from the conduction band can be trapped, but not holes from the valence band. Ultimately a trapped electron will be emitted back into the conduction band. Such traps obviously have no effect on *steady-state* recombination rates. Under transient conditions, however, they appear to act as recombination traps, for, with minority carrier injection, their density of occupation changes. They thus absorb a net number of carriers from one of the bands, just as if recombination were occurring. Having adjusted to the new injection level, they have no further effect on the carrier lifetimes. Transient lifetimes can be assigned to such traps in a similar manner as for recombination traps.

References

[6.1] VAN ROOSBROECK (1953), 'The transport of added current carriers in a homogeneous semiconductor', *Phys. Rev.*, **91**, 282–289.

[6.2] SHOCKLEY, W. and READ, W. T. (1952), 'Statistics of the recombination of holes and electrons', *Phys. Rev.*, **87**, 835–842.

[6.3] HALL, R. N. (1952), 'Electron-hole recombination in germanium', *Phys. Rev.*, **87**, 387.

[6.4] ROSE, F. W. G. and SANDIFORD, D. J. (1955), 'An easy derivation of the hole life-time in an n-type semiconductor with acceptor traps', *Proc. Phys. Soc.*, **69B,** 894—897.

[6.5] PELL, E. M., and ROE, G. M. (1956), 'Reverse current and carrier lifetime as a function of temperature in silicon junction diodes,' *Journ. Appl. Phys.*, **27,** 768–772.

[6.6] TILLMAN, J. R., and ROBERTS, F. F. (1961), *The theory and practice of transistors*, p. 56, Pitman.

[6.7] SANDIFORD, D. J. (1957), 'Carrier lifetime in semiconductors for transient conditions', *Phys. Rev.*, **105,** 524.

CHAPTER 7

Current Flow across Semiconductor Junctions

7.1 Introduction

Junctions between two types of semiconductor, or between semiconductor and metal contacts, will be considered in this chapter. Such junctions may exhibit non-ohmic, that is rectifying, properties. The rectifying action of a junction depends of the presence of a *depletion layer* across the junction. Depletion layers arise when high electric intensities usually caused by internal electric fields, remove carriers from a region faster than they can be replenished. The layer is said to be *depleted* of mobile carriers and a net space charge exists because of the presence of the unneutralized charges of the donor and acceptor centres. Why such a layer gives rise to rectifying properties will be discussed in later sections of the chapter. Outside a depletion layer, the principle of charge neutrality is valid. This principle has been used extensively in previous chapters. The present chapter commences with a study of the conditions necessary to maintain charge neutrality. Subsequently, conditions under which the principle is violated, and the mechanism for the formation of a depletion layer will be considered.

7.2 The Principle of Charge Neutrality

Experimental verification of the principle of charge neutrality is an indirect consequence of the drift mobility determinations of Shockley, Pearson and Haynes [7.1], and of Prince [7.2]. For interpretation of these experiments, the reader is referred to the paper by Shockley, Pearson and Haynes [7.1].

The principle of charge neutrality for a uniform semiconductor in equilibrium is readily established. Each atom in the crystal lattice, including donor and acceptor impurity atoms, is electrically neutral and so the lattice as a whole is electrically neutral. Because the semiconductor is uniform, the net space-charge density is everywhere zero on a macroscopic scale, that is when averaged over any region containing a hundred or so donor or acceptor centres. The validity of the condition was implied in chapter 4 where charge conservation was used to determine the position of the Fermi level.

If a semiconductor is not uniform, the same conclusion is not immediately obvious. Although the semiconductor as a whole is electrically neutral, it is possible that the net density may be positive in some regions and negative in others. This is precisely what occurs in a depletion layer. To investigate the case of a non-uniform semiconductor, Poisson's equation of electrostatics can be used. This differential equation, which relates the charge density and the electric intensity, is considered in all books on electrostatics and electromagnetics, and in one form [7.3] may be expressed as:

$$\nabla \cdot \mathbf{E} = \frac{\rho(\mathbf{r})}{\varepsilon}. \qquad (7.2\text{-}1)$$

Here, $\mathbf{E}$ is the electric intensity, $\rho(\mathbf{r})$ is the charge density as a function of a position, and ε is the permittivity of the medium. The permittivity may be written as $\varepsilon_0 \varepsilon_r$ where ε_0 is the permittivity of free space and ε_r is the relative permittivity of the medium.

A crude justification for charge neutrality in a non-uniform semiconductor can be obtained in the following way. Let a transition from uniform p-type to uniform n-type material take place in a distance L and let the total electrostatic potential drop across the transition be V: see fig. 7.2a. A very rough approximation to $\nabla \cdot \mathbf{E}$ is then (V/L^2). Now ε is of the order of $10^{-10} \mathrm{Fm}^{-1}$ for both germanium and silicon and so eqn (7.2-1) indicates a space charge density of the order of $(V/L^2)10^{-10}$ C m^{-3}. If the semiconductor is equilibrium, the Fermi level E_F is constant across the junction and because for semiconductors it always lies within the forbidden gap, the potential drop across the transition intrinsic carrier density n_i is qn_i which is approximately 1 C cm^{-3} for

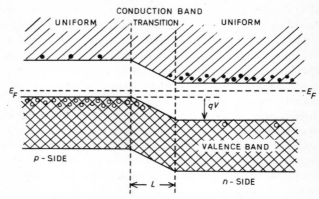

Figure 7.2a. Transition from uniform *p*-type to uniform *n*-type semiconductor

germanium at room temperatures. Thus, provided L is greater than 10^{-5} m, the space charge density in the transition region is less than that due to the intrinsic carrier density, and hence the region may be considered electrically neutral. However, if L is appreciably smaller than 10^{-5} m, a space-charge density must exist in the transition region and depletion of mobile carriers must occur.

The solution of Poisson's equation, eqn (7.2-1), will now be considered in a little more detail. The intensity **E** may be replaced by $(1/q)\nabla E_{Fi}$, eqns (5.8-3) and (4). Also, the charge density is given by:

$$\rho(\mathbf{r}) = q(p - n + N_d^+ - N_a^-) \qquad (7.2-2)$$

where N_d^+ and N_a^- are the densities of ionized donors and acceptors respectively*. All the quantities p, n, N_d^+ and N_a^- are in general functions of position. At room temperatures, N_d^+ and N_a^- may be replaced by N_d and N_a respectively, for virtually all the impurity centres are ionized: see section 4.8. This last statement needs some qualification: for example, in a net *n*-type material, acceptor centres may be compensated by donors; that is the electrons from the donors drop into the acceptor

---

* Note that by ionization of acceptors is meant removal of their holes. That is the centre is occupied by the electron.

levels which are therefore ionized, thus justigying the statement. With these substitutions, eqn (7.2-1) is:

$$\nabla^2 E_{\text{Fi}} = \left(\frac{q^2}{\varepsilon}\right)(p - n + N_{\text{d}} - N_{\text{a}}) . \tag{7.2-3}$$

In equilibrium, p and n are given by eqns (6.2-1) and (2) respectively. Substitution into eqn (7.2-3) then yields:

$$\nabla^2 E_{\text{Fi}} = \left(\frac{q^2}{\varepsilon}\right)\left[2n_{\text{i}} \sinh\left(\frac{E_{\text{Fi}} - E_{\text{F}}}{kT}\right) - (N_{\text{a}} - N_{\text{d}})\right]. \tag{7.2-4}$$

The intrinsic density n_{i} is a function only of the semiconductor material and temperature; it is independent of position. The argument of the hyperbolic function of eqn (7.2-4) is a normalized, dimensionless, potential which will be denoted by the symbol u. Because in equilibrium E_{F} is independent of position, the equation can be expressed in terms of u:

$$\nabla^2 u = \left(\frac{1}{L_{\text{D}}^2}\right)[\sinh u - F(\mathbf{r})] \tag{7.2-5}$$

where

$$L_{\text{D}} = \sqrt{\left(\frac{\varepsilon kT}{2q^2 n_{\text{i}}}\right)} \tag{7.2-6}$$

and:

$$F(\mathbf{r}) = \left(\frac{N_{\text{a}} - N_{\text{d}}}{2n_{\text{i}}}\right) . \tag{7.2-7}$$

The quantity L_{D} is known as the *Debye* length. At room temperatures its magnitude is about 10^{-4} cm for germanium and 10^{-3} cm for silicon. The function $F(\mathbf{r})$ is a dimensionless expression for the net acceptor density at any point.

If N_{a} and N_{d} are known functions of position, in theory eqn (7.2-5) can be solved for the potential u. It would then be possible to say to what extent charge neutrality is valid, that is, how closely the right-hand side of eqn (7.2-5), and hence that of eqn (7.2-1), approaches zero. However, eqn (7.2-5) cannot be solved in terms of known functions and approximate or numerical methods of solution must be used. For most cases of interest, the net density $(N_{\text{a}} - N_{\text{d}})$ of acceptors varies in one direction only and then Shockley [7.4] has shown that, subject to the correct physical boundary conditions, the equation always has a solution. In addition, he considers the case where the net density $(N_a - N_d)$ of acceptors is a linear function of distance, and writes:

$$F(\mathbf{r}) = F(x) = \left(\frac{x}{L_a}\right) \tag{7.2-8}$$

where L_a is a characteristic length of the impurity gradient at a given temperature; see eqn (7.2-7). It is the distance over which the net acceptor density changes by twice the intrinsic carrier density. The analysis presented by Shockley is beyond the scope of the present book but the main conclusions of his work will be listed here. First, in regions of the semiconductor where $(N_a - N_d)$ is appreciably larger than n_i, charge neutrality is assured if L_a is of the same order as, or larger than, the Debye length L_D. Secondly, in the near intrinsic regions of the semiconductor, where $(N_a - N_d)$ is of the order of n_i or less, charge neutrality is only assured when L_a is an order or so larger than L_D. If L_a is of the same order as, or less than, L_D, the near intrinsic region is depleted of mobile carriers to some extent. It should be noted however, that the *intrinsic* point itself, that is where x is zero and hence N_a equal to N_d, is electrically neutral. This follows because $F(x)$ is an odd function of x, from which it can be deduced* that $u(x)$ is an odd function also. Thus both the net densities of acceptors and mobile carriers vanish at the *intrinsic* point. It follows also that E_F and E_{Fi} coincide at this point, as might be expected. It is also obvious intuitively that charge neutrality must hold at the intrinsic point, for the sign of the net charge must change at this point.

It is concluded, therefore, that charge neutrality is maintained for gradual spatial variations of the donor and acceptor densities. Abrupt, or rapid variation with distance, produces a depletion layer. The approximate integration of Poisson's equation carried out at the beginning of the section is seen not to contradict these conclusions.

* Let $T: x \rightarrow -x$, then $T: F(x) \rightarrow -F(-x)$ by hypothesis. Also $T: (d/dx) \rightarrow -[d/d(-x)]$ and $T: (d^2/dx^2) \rightarrow [d^2/d(-x)^2]$. Then $T:$ eqn $(7.2\text{-}5) \rightarrow d^2 u(-x)/d(x)^2 = (1/L_D^2)[\sinh u(-x) + F(-x)]$; but the differential equation should be invariant under change of x-axis direction. Hence $u(-x)$ must equal $-u(x)$.

Before leaving the topic of charge neutrality under equilibrium conditions, one particular solution of eqn (7.2-5) will be considered. For a uniform semiconductor $F(x)$ is a constant for all x, and in equilibrium it is electrically neutral everywhere. Consider now a semiconductor that is uniform throughout a substantial, continuous, part of its volume, but which is not uniform everywhere. For example, a semiconductor which is uniform except for a rectifying p–n junction, or a metal contact at one end, might be considered. The depletion layer associated with the junction or contact will disturb the equilibrium density of mobile carriers, and hence the charge neutrality, in the bordering uniform region. Let the constant value of $F(x)$ in the uniform region be denoted by F_0 and the value of u in the regions where charge neutrality holds be u_0. Then from eqn (7.2-5):

$$\sinh u_0 = F_0 . \tag{7.2-9}$$

For small disturbances $(u - u_0)$ from neutrality in the uniform regions, eqns (7.2-5) and (9) give:

$$\left(\frac{d^2(u - u_0)}{dx^2} \right) = \left(\frac{\cosh u_0}{L_D^2} \right)(u - u_0) . \tag{7.2-10}$$

This equation has solutions of the form:

$$(u - u_0) = A \exp\left\{ \frac{\sqrt{(\cosh u_0)}}{L_D} . x \right\} + B \exp\left\{ -\frac{\sqrt{(\cosh u_0)}}{L_D} . x \right\} \tag{7.2-11}$$

where A and B are constants. Only the solution giving an exponential decay of $(u - u_0)$ deeper into the uniform region is appropriate. The *decay length*, that is the distance in which the disturbance decays by a factor $(1/e)$, is $L_D(\cosh u_0)^{-\frac{1}{2}}$. For an extrinsic semiconductor at room temperatures, the separation of E_F and E_{Fi} will be an order or so greater than kT. It follows that the magnitude of u_0 will exceed ten and hence the decay length is less than a tenth of the Debye Length L_D. Charge neutrality is thus established at a very small distance into the uniform region. When the uniform region of the semiconductor is near intrinsic, the magnitude of u_0 will be close to, or even less than, unity. The decay length will then be approximate to L_D. These results are in general agreement with the stated conclusions of Shockley's work.

Materials with large forbidden gaps are classed as insulators and have intrinsic densities which are very small. The Debye length, eqn (7.2-6), then becomes very large. It follows that if charge neutrality is violated in some region of an insulator, say by injection of carriers into the conduction band, it is violated everywhere. This topic is considered further in chapter 9.

7.3 Non-Equilibrium Conditions and Charge Neutrality

The principle of charge neutrality is still largely valid for semiconductors under non-equilibrium conditions. The principle is of course violated in depletion regions which are present even under equilibrium conditions.

The principle is clearly valid for a uniform semiconductor in which only drift current flows, that is when no excess carriers are present. If a formal proof of this is required, it can be established as follows. The drift current density is given by:

$$\mathbf{J} = q(\mu n_e + \mu_p p_e)\mathbf{E} = \sigma_e \mathbf{E} \qquad (7.3\text{-}1)$$

where the conductivity σ_e is a constant of the material but is dependant on temperature. Taking the divergence of this equation, $\nabla . \mathbf{J}$ will be zero, for the divergence of both the hole and electron components of current density will be zero, by eqns (6.9-7) and (8), when no excess carriers are present. It follows that $\nabla . \mathbf{E}$ is also zero and hence the net space-charge density is zero by Poisson's equation.

Next, the case of a semiconductor with excess carriers present will be considered. In order to obtain some conception of the magnitudes involved, let it be supposed that charge neutrality is violated to the extent of a space-charge density equivalent to the intrinsic carrier density n_i over a short distance L. Integration of Poisson's equation, eqn (7.2-1), over this distance gives (see fig. 7.3a), a change of electric intensity equal to $[(q n_i L)/\varepsilon]$ over the distance L. This represents the net intensity tending to remove charge from the space-charge region, that is tending to re-establish neutrality. Alternatively, this result follows directly from the Gauss theorem of electrostatics [7.3] which is the integrated form

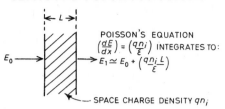

Figure 7.3a. Estimation of intensity tending to neutralize space charge

of Poisson's equation. As before, taking qn_i as approximately 1 C m^{-3} and ε as 10^{-10} Fm^{-1}, this change of intensity is $10^{10} L$ Vm^{-1}. Thus even if neutrality is only violated to this small extent over a distance as small as 1 μ, the intensity tending to restore neutrality is as high as 10^4 Vm^{-1}. Such an intensity will normally cause a drift current much in excess of any diffusion current and the latter may be neglected in the present context.

In order to consider this neutralization process in more detail, let a uniform piece of *n*-type semiconductor be in equilibrium, and let the density of electrons be suddenly increased in one part of it by some injection process. The extra electrons set up a space-charge and an electric intensity related by Poisson's equation, eqn (7.2-1). The electric field causes a drift current which is predominantly due to electrons:

$$\mathbf{J} = \sigma \mathbf{E} \tag{7.3-2}$$

whence:

$$\nabla . \mathbf{J} = \nabla \sigma . \mathbf{E} + \sigma \nabla . \mathbf{E} . \tag{7.3-3}$$

By eqn (6.9-10), $\nabla . \mathbf{J}$ is also equal to $-(\partial \rho / \partial t)$, and $\nabla . \mathbf{E}$ is (ρ/ε) by Poisson's equation, hence eqn (7.3-3) is:

$$\left(\frac{\partial \rho}{\partial t} \right) + \left(\frac{\sigma}{\varepsilon} \right) \rho = -\nabla \sigma . \mathbf{E} . \tag{7.3-4}$$

For low-level-injection, the term in $\nabla \sigma$ can be ignored, thus:

$$\left(\frac{\partial \rho}{\partial t} \right) + \left(\frac{\sigma_e}{\varepsilon} \right) \rho = 0 \tag{7.3-5}$$

whence:

$$\rho = \rho_0 \exp\left(-\frac{t}{\tau_R}\right) \tag{7.3-6}$$

where:

$$\tau_R = \left(\frac{\varepsilon}{\sigma_e}\right). \tag{7.3-7}$$

The constant τ_R is called the *dielectric relaxation time*. Equation (7.3-6) shows that the space-charge decays from its initial value ρ_0 towards zero with the time constant τ_R. For an ε of $10^{-10}\,\mathrm{Fm}^{-1}$ and σ_e values $1\,\mho\mathrm{m}^{-1}$ to $10^5\,\mho\mathrm{m}^{-1}$, τ_R is of the order of $10^{-10}\,\mathrm{s}$ to $10^{-15}\,\mathrm{s}$ respectively, for near intrinsic and heavily doped semiconductor. Thus any space-charge created by the injection of electrons is eliminated in less than $10^{-10}\,\mathrm{s}$. The excess electrons are rapidly dispersed by drift, and equilibrium is restored.

A similar situation occurs if holes, minority carriers, are injected into the uniform *n*-type semiconductor. Once more, a local space-charge and an electric field are set up. Again a predominantly electron drift current flows to neutralize the local space-charge. The same theory as previously applies and eqn (7.3-6) gives the decay of the space-charge. In this case, the electron density is increased above the equilibrium density. This occurs in such a way as everywhere to neutralize the charge of the injected holes. As the holes diffuse into the semiconductor, so the electron density is modified to maintain charge neutrality. Similarly, if holes are withdrawn from a region of a semiconductor, the electron density drops exponentially with time, time constant τ_R, until neutrality is achieved.

In discussing the phenomenon of space-charge relaxation, the contribution of the current density resulting from diffusion of carriers has been neglected. This is permissable since diffusion effects are on a longer time scale, as was mentioned previously in this section. The two processes can be considered as sequential. Firstly, the space-charge of the injected minority carriers is neutralized by a rapid majority carrier flow. Secondly, the minority carriers diffuse under their concentration gradient, neutralization always being maintained by movement of the majority carriers.

In the foregoing account of charge neutrality, low-level-injection was assumed, see section 6.2, thus allowing the term in $\nabla\sigma$, eqn (7.3-4), to be dropped. Often this assumption is not justified and there is then a slight departure from charge neutrality. An example of this effect has already been noted in section 6.11. In general, the treatment of such cases is rather involved and will not be pursued here.

For a non-uniform semiconductor, some slight modifications to the foregoing theory are necessary. In equilibrium appreciable diffusion current may flow, but the net current is zero:

$$\sigma_e \mathbf{E} + \mathbf{J}(\text{diff}) = 0 \tag{7.3-8}$$

whence:

$$\nabla\sigma_e \cdot \mathbf{E} + \nabla \cdot \mathbf{J}(\text{diff}) = 0 \tag{7.3-9}$$

since $\nabla \cdot \mathbf{E}$ is zero for equilibrium conditions by Poisson's equation. If now equilibrium is disturbed by majority or minority carrier injection, eqn (7.3-2) must be replaced by:

$$\mathbf{J} = \sigma\mathbf{E} + \mathbf{J}(\text{diff}) \tag{7.3-10}$$

whence:

$$\nabla \cdot \mathbf{J} = \sigma\nabla \cdot \mathbf{E} + \nabla\sigma \cdot \mathbf{E} + \nabla \cdot \mathbf{J}(\text{diff}) . \tag{7.3-11}$$

For low-level-injection, the last two terms of this equation are zero by eqn (7.3-9). Equations (7.3-5), (6) and (7) then follow as previously, and hence the charge neutrality principle is established for this case.

7.4 The Abrupt p–n Junction in Equilibrium

In this and the next section, the depletion layer existing at the junction between p-type and n-type material, in a single crystal, will be considered. Junctions can be constructed by a variety of processes of which alloying, diffusion and epitaxial growth techniques are currently the most important. The technology allows the net impurity profile across the junction to be controlled and a wide range of transition rates can be produced. The technology of semiconductors, and of transistor manufacture, is not considered in this book; the reader is referred elsewhere [7.5],

[7.6], [7.7] for an account of this topic. In what follows all the junctions will be assumed planar and perpendicular to the direction of x.

As was explained in section 7.2, no depletion layer exists for a sufficiently gradual transition across the junction. For less gradual transitions depletion layers may exist.

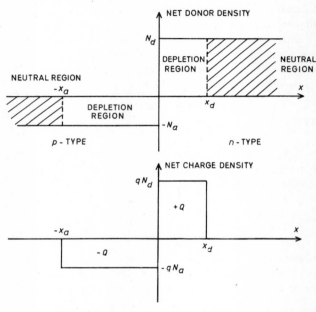

Figure 7.4a. Impurity and charge densities of the abrupt *p–n* junction

An abrupt *p–n* junction is one in which the transition from a uniform *p*-type region to a uniform *n*-type region is a step function. This is of course an idealization but some junctions, particularly alloyed junctions, approximate to this case. The situation is depicted in fig. 7.4a where the origin of the *x*-co-ordinate is taken at the junction. For negative x, the semiconductor is *p*-type and the charge density of the acceptor type impurities is $-qN_a$. For positive x, the material is *n*-type and the impurity charge density is qN_d. The characteristic length of such a junction can be interpreted as zero and consequently is less than the Debye length L_D. It follows that a depletion region is formed. The edges of the depletion layer are assumed to be sharp, that is the transition between the completely depleted and completely neutral regions occurs abruptly. The extent to which this is valid will be investigated later in the section. One further point concerning fig. 7.4a is the equality of the areas of the depleted regions, or total charges, on either side of the junction. This follows because the semiconductor as a whole is electrically neutral, and so:

$$Q = qx_d N_d = qx_a N_a \tag{7.4-1}$$

where Q is the total un-neutralised charge per unit junction area on either side of the junction. This result will also arise out of the solution of Poisson's equation which now follows.

It is possible to work either with the dimensionless form of Poisson's equation, eqn (7.2-5), or with the usual form eqn (7.2-1); the solutions will differ only by normalizing constants. Because one of the results required of the present analysis is a junction capacitance, it is more convenient to work with the latter equation. For one-dimension, this is:

$$\left(\frac{d^2 V}{dx^2}\right) = -\left(\frac{\rho}{\varepsilon}\right) \tag{7.4-2}$$

where V is the potential in volts. This equation is to be applied in two regions:

(I) $\qquad\qquad -x_a \leqslant x \leqslant 0, \quad \text{where} \quad \rho = -qN_a \qquad\qquad$ (7.4-3)

(II) $\qquad\qquad 0 \leqslant x \leqslant x_d, \quad \text{where} \quad \rho = qN_d. \qquad\qquad$ (7.4-4)

Outside these regions, the semiconductor is neutral and V is taken equal to constants V_a and V_d in the p and n regions respectively. If appreciable current is flowing these constant values are not justified, but this will be considered later. Integration of eqn (7.4-2) in region (I) yields:

$$\left(\frac{dV}{dx}\right) = \left(\frac{qN_a}{\varepsilon}\right)(x + x_a) \tag{7.4-5}$$

since (dV/dx) is zero at $-x_a$. A second integration gives:

$$V = \left(\frac{qN_a}{\varepsilon}\right)\left(\frac{x^2}{2} + xx_a\right) \tag{7.4-6}$$

where V has been set to zero at the origin of x. In particular the constant potential V_a at $-x_a$ is:

$$V_a = -\left(\frac{qN_a}{2\varepsilon}\right) x_a^2. \tag{7.4-7}$$

Similarly, integration of eqn (7.4-2) for the region II yields:

$$\left(\frac{dV}{dx}\right) = \left(\frac{qN_d}{\varepsilon}\right)(x_d - x) \tag{7.4-8}$$

$$V = \left(\frac{qN_d}{\varepsilon}\right)\left(xx_d - \frac{x^2}{2}\right) \tag{7.4-9}$$

$$V_d = \left(\frac{qN_a}{2\varepsilon}\right)x_d^2. \tag{7.4-10}$$

A vanishingly thin layer about the origin of x contains no charge, hence eqn (7.4-2) or its equivalent the Gauss electrostatic theorem, indicates continuity of (dV/dx) at the origin. Equations (7.4-5) and (8) thus verify the condition of eqn (7.4-1).

The total voltage across the junction can be obtained in terms of x_a and x_d, the depletion layer widths, from eqns (7.4-7) and (10):

$$V_J = V_d - V_a = \left(\frac{q}{2\varepsilon}\right)(N_a x_a^2 + N_d x_d^2). \tag{7.4-11}$$

The polarity of this voltage is such as to oppose the flow of majority carriers across the junction. The distances x_a and x_d are simply related, by eqn (7.4-1); consequently eqn (7.4-11) implies that if the voltage across the junction is known, then so is also the width of the depletion layer, and conversely. In equilibrium, the voltage across the junction can be obtained from a knowledge of the position of the Fermi level E_F relative to the band edges, on each side of the junction. The equations of chapter 4 give this information. The voltage across the junction can then be deduced because E_F is constant, across the junction. This is indicated in fig. 7.4b. This equilibrium potential is often referred to as the *internal* or *inherent* potential barrier at the junction and will be

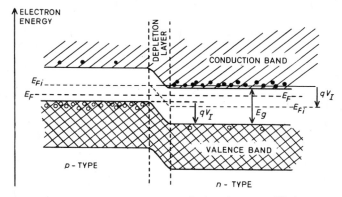

Figure 7.4b. Energy level diagram of a junction at equilibrium

denoted by V_I. Equation (4.8-5) gives the position of E_F for an n-type semiconductor. Using this and a similar equation for a p-type semiconductor, and referring to fig. 7.4b, the internal barrier is found as:

$$V_I = \left(\frac{E_g}{q}\right) - \left(\frac{kT}{q}\right) \ln \left(\frac{N_c N_v}{N_a N_d}\right). \qquad (7.4\text{-}12)$$

If desired, E_g and the product $N_c N_v$ can be eliminated with the aid of eqn (4.3-4) giving:

$$V_I = \left(\frac{kT}{q}\right) \ln \left(\frac{N_a N_d}{n_i^2}\right). \qquad (7.4\text{-}13)$$

By way of example, let N_a be $10^3 n_i$ on the p-side of the junction and let N_d be $10^4 n_i$ on the n-side. At room temperatures (kT/q) is about 0.026 volt. This last equation then gives the value of the junction potential V_I as about 0.43 volt. Increasing N_d, say by a factor ten, increases this V_I to 0.5 volt. Further increase in N_d would make the electron density degenerate, see section 4.1, and the equations would no longer be valid.

The elimination of x_a and x_d from eqn (7.4-11) in terms of Q, eqn (7.4-1), gives with rearrangement:

$$Q = \left\{ 2\varepsilon q \left(\frac{N_a N_d}{N_a + N_d} \right) V_J \right\}^{\frac{1}{2}}. \tag{7.4-14}$$

Alternatively, the depletion layer thicknesses may be expressed in terms of V_J:

$$x_a = \left(\frac{Q}{qN_a} \right) = \left\{ \left(\frac{2\varepsilon}{q} \right) \left(\frac{N_d}{N_a(N_a + N_d)} \right) V_J \right\}^{\frac{1}{2}} \tag{7.4-15}$$

$$x_d = \left(\frac{Q}{qN_d} \right) = \left\{ \left(\frac{2\varepsilon}{q} \right) \left(\frac{N_a}{N_d(N_a + N_d)} \right) V_J \right\}^{\frac{1}{2}}. \tag{7.4-16}$$

Very often one impurity density is much higher than the other. Suppose, for example, that N_d is much larger than N_a; the last three equations then approximate to:

$$Q \simeq \{2\varepsilon q N_a V_J\}^{\frac{1}{2}} \tag{7.4-17}$$

$$x_1 \simeq \left\{ \frac{2\varepsilon V_J}{qN_a} \right\}^{\frac{1}{2}} \tag{7.4-18}$$

and

$$x_d \simeq 0. \tag{7.4-19}$$

In this case the depletion layer extends almost entirely into the material of higher resistivity.

The validity of the assumption concerning the sharp transition between the depletion and neutral regions will now be examined. For simplicity, a symmetrical junction will be assumed, that is one with equal densities of impurities on either side of the junction. As a first approximation, the potential distribution throughout the depletion layer, obtained with the assumption of total depletion, will be used to compute the density of mobile carriers in the depletion region. This potential is given by eqns (7.4-6) and (9) and is shown plotted, in dimensionless form, in fig. 7.4c. The dimensionless potential u in this figure is the same as that of eqn (7.2-5). When the semiconductor is in equilibrium, the net density of mobile carriers in the depletion region is $(2n_i \sinh u)$ and this may be compared with N_d, or N_a, to determine the extent to which the

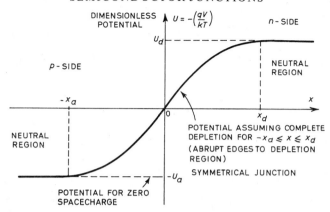

Figure 7.4c. Potential distribution across an abrupt *p–n* junction

region is depleted. Note that at the edges of the depletion layer, where neutrality is assumed, eqn (7.2-5) gives:

$$\sinh u_a = \left(\frac{N_a}{2n_i}\right) \tag{7.4-20}$$

$$\sinh u_d = \left(\frac{N_d}{2n_i}\right). \tag{7.4-21}$$

For the symmetrical junction under consideration, N_a and N_d are equal and hence are also u_a and u_d. Two cases will be investigated; for the first, N_d will be taken as $10^3 n_i$, and for the second, as $10^4 n_i$. Equation (7.4-21) then gives u_d as 6.9 and 9.2 for the two cases respectively. The value of u at $0.5x_d$ is given by eqn (7.4-6) as $0.75u_d$ and $\sinh u$ takes the values $\sinh 5.2$, that is approximately 80, and $\sinh 6.8$, that is approximately 500, respectively. These values are to be compared with the appropriate value of $(N_d/2n_i)$, that is with 500, and 5000 respectively. Thus at the point $0.5x_d$ the net densities of mobile carriers are about 16% and 10% respectively, of the appropriate impurity density. Nearer the edges of the depletion layer, these densities will be higher and will modify the potential distribution through Poisson's equation.

At best, the theory presented is very approximate, although the approximation improves as the rate of impurity to intrinsic density increases. The assumption of a sharp transition to neutrality at the edge of the depletion layer is hardly justified for the impurity densities here used, but is the best that can be achieved without recourse to more elaborate theory, or numerical integration of Poisson's equation. The validity of the assumption improves, however, when the junction is reverse biased. This latter case will be mentioned again in section 7.6. To seek a more exact theory is unnecessary. This is because the impurities are distributed in the lattice in a random fashion, and so the assumption of uniform densities N_a and N_d within a small volume of the depletion regions is subject to doubt. It is likely that random variations of these densities will cause errors of similar magnitude to those of the inexact theory here presented.

7.5 The Linearly-Graded p–n Junction in Equilibrium

In this section the potential distribution across a linearly-graded junction will be considered. As in section 7.2, the net impurity density across the *intrinsic* point of such a junction can be described in terms of n_i and a characteristic length L_a:

$$N_a - N_d = 2n_i \left(\frac{x}{L_a} \right). \tag{7.5-1}$$

Note that 'x greater than zero' is the p-region in contrast to the last section: this arrangement has been adopted to avoid confusion of signs with section 7.2. Equation (7.5-1) is often an adequate approximation even for non-linearly-graded junctions, for the depletion layer is restricted to the neighbourhood of the *intrinsic* point, over which the gradient of the net impurity density may be considered constant. Most diffused junctions, and some alloy and epitaxially grown junctions, may be considered as linearly-graded junctions. Figure 7.5a(i) shows a typical impurity profile for a diffused junction.

A depletion layer is formed about the intrinsic point provided the characteristic length L_a is of the order of, or less than, the Debye length L_D: see section 7.2. Assuming this is so, the net impurity density and

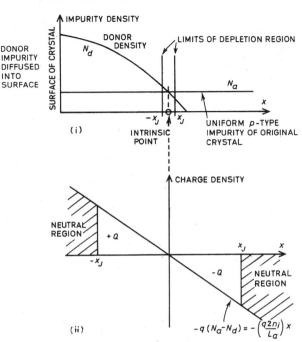

Figure 7.5a. The linearly graded junction
(i) Diffused junction impurity profile
(ii) Space charge density across the junction

net space-charge density are shown in fig. 7.5a(ii). The symmetry through the origin implies that the depletion layer extends to equal distances on either side of the intrinsic point. The un-neutralized charge per unit area on either side of the junction is:

$$Q = \left(\frac{qn_{i}}{L_{a}}\right) x_{J}^{2} . \qquad (7.5\text{-}2)$$

Poisson's equation for the range $-x_{J}$ to x_{J} is:

$$\left(\frac{d^2 V}{dx^2}\right) = \left(\frac{q}{\varepsilon}\right)\left(\frac{2n_{i}}{L_{a}}\right) x \qquad (7.5\text{-}3)$$

on the assumption that the region is completely depleted of mobile carriers. This implies an abrupt transition from the depletion region to neutral regions at $-x_J$ and x_J. The extent to which this is justified will be examined later in this section. The boundary conditions are (dV/dx) equal to zero at x_J and V equal to zero at the origin. Integration of eqn (7.5-3) then yields:

$$V = \left(\frac{qn_i}{\varepsilon L_a}\right)\left(\frac{x^3}{3} - xx_J^2\right). \tag{7.5-4}$$

This gives the total voltage drop across the depletion layer as:

$$V_J = 2\left(\frac{2qn_i}{3\varepsilon L_a}\right)x_J^3. \tag{7.5-5}$$

Eliminating x_J in terms of Q, eqn (7.5-2), and rearranging:

$$Q = \left\{\frac{9\varepsilon^2 qn_i}{16L_a}\right\}^{\frac{1}{3}} V_J^{\frac{2}{3}}. \tag{7.5-6}$$

Alternatively, x_J may be expressed in terms of V_J:

$$x_J = \left\{\frac{3\varepsilon L_a}{8qn_i}\right\}^{\frac{1}{3}} V_J^{\frac{1}{3}}. \tag{7.5-7}$$

The determination of the junction voltage V_b, for the junction in equilibrium, is much more involved for the present case than for the abrupt junction with uniform semiconductor on either side. The difficulty arises because the impurity gradient causes a variation in electrostatic potential even in the neutral regions outside the depletion layer. Reference to Poisson's equation, eqn (7.2-5), shows that for a junction in equilibrium the dimensionless potential in the electrically neutral regions is given by:

$$u = \sinh^{-1} F(x) = \sinh^{-1}\left(\frac{x}{L_a}\right). \tag{7.5-8}$$

This is plotted as the solid line in fig. 7.5b. It is only necessary to plot points for positive x and u, for u is an antisymmetric function of x and so points for negative x can be obtained by reflection in the origin of the figure. The potential distribution in the depletion region is given by

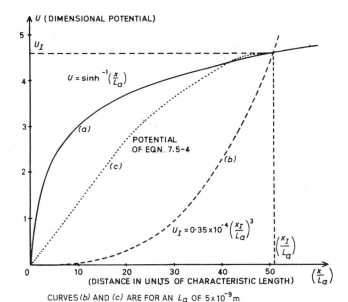

CURVES (b) AND (c) ARE FOR AN L_a OF 5×10^{-9} m

Figure 7.5b. Potential distribution across the linearly graded junction

eqn (7.5-4) and, according to the assumption under which it was deduced, this potential coincides with the potential of the neutral region when x is equal to x_I. This neutral region potential is given by eqn (7.5-5), without the factor 2 because half of V_I appears on either side of the origin. In dimensionless form, the neutral region potential is:

$$u_I = \left(\frac{2}{3}\right)\left(\frac{q}{kT}\right)\left(\frac{q}{\varepsilon}\right) n_i L_a^2 \left(\frac{x_I}{L_a}\right)^3. \qquad (7.5-9)$$

For germanium at room temperatures, n_i is about 5×10^{19} m^{-3}, (kT/q) is 0·26 volt, and ε is $16 \times 8·85 \times 10^{-12}$ Fm^{-1}. The last equation is then:

$$u_I = 1·4 \times 10^{12} L_a^2 \left(\frac{x_I}{L_a}\right)^3. \qquad (7.5-10)$$

The depletion layer width x_I for a semiconductor in equilibrium may be determined from the intersection of eqns (7.5-8) and (10) plotted as functions of (x/L_a). The curve of eqn (7.5-8) will be independent of L_a but that of eqn (7.5-10) depends on L_a. The latter equation is plotted in fig. 7.5b, broken curve, for a value of L_a of 5×10^{-9} m. This is approximately one hundredth of the Debye length L_D for germanium. The intersection of the two curves gives x_I as approximately $50L_a$ or $2 \cdot 5 \times 10^{-7}$ m, while the corresponding value of u_I is about $4 \cdot 6$. The symbols x_I and u_I are used for x_J and u_J when the junction is in equilibrium. It is now possible, using this value of u_I, to plot the potential distribution across the layer as given by eqn (7.5-4). This distribution is shown as the dotted curve of fig. 7.5b.

Examination of the figure shows a discrepancy in the boundary conditions at x_I. At this point (dV/dx) was taken as zero, whereas it is clear from the neutrality potential curve, solid line, that (dV/dx) is not zero at any point in the neutral region, although it tends to small values at great distances from the junction. It would have been more appropriate, to have matched the slopes of the neutrality curve and the depletion region solution at the point x_I. From the figure, it can be seen that the slopes are equal at a point very close to x_I. However, the potentials differ slightly at this point of equal slopes. It is not difficult to visualize the form of dotted curve, which would give a better match of potential, and its derivative, at the point x_I. Such a curve would not depart appreciably from the dotted curve of the figure over the larger part of the depletion region.

Finally, the density of mobile carriers at the point $0 \cdot 5 x_I$ will be estimated in a similar way to that used for the abrupt junction. At x_I, u_I was found to be $4 \cdot 6$ for the example considered. Now sinh $(4 \cdot 6)$ is about 50, and hence the corresponding figure for the space-charge density of the impurities at $0 \cdot 5 x_I$ is 25. This follows because the gradient of the net impurity density is constant. The potential distribution of eqn (7.5-4) shows that u is $0 \cdot 69$ of u_I, that is $3 \cdot 15$, at $0 \cdot 5 x_I$. Thus, sinh $(3 \cdot 15)$, that is $11 \cdot 3$, is the figure which represents the density of mobile carriers at $0 \cdot 5 x_I$. This figure of $11 \cdot 3$ is to be compared with 25, and so the density of mobile carriers is just less than 50% of the net impurity density at $0 \cdot 5 x_I$. This hardly justifies the assumption of a sharp transition, and hence once more, the theory must be considered very approximate. The situation improves somewhat with decreasing L_a. The L_a of the above example was only one hundredth of the Debye length and it is known that some sort of depletion layer exists even when L_a approaches L_D. However, it is not worth pursuing a more exact theory for the same reason as was given for the abrupt junction.

With an external reverse bias across the junction, the depletion layer widens and the approximation should be more reliable. The biasing of a junction will be considered in the next section.

7.6 The Reverse Biased p–n Junction

If an external voltage is applied across a p–n junction in such a way as to enhance the internal potential barrier, the junction is said to be reverse biased. In equilibrium the net current flow across the junction is zero; the flow of majority carriers across the junction being just balanced by the flow of minority carriers in the opposite sense. With reference to fig. 7.4b, this dynamic balance can be explained in the following way. Most of the holes on the p-side, and electrons on the n-side, are not sufficiently energetic* to surmount the internal barrier. Some minority carriers, electrons on the p-side and holes on the n-side, may diffuse to the junction provided they are generated within approximately one diffusion length from the junction. Such carriers are then swept across the depletion layer by the favourable electric field there. This flow of minority carriers is just balanced by the more energetic majority carriers overcoming the barrier, the net current being zero. The height V_I of the internal potential barrier is automatically adjusted such that the majority and minority carrier flows just annul each other. If, for example, the majority carrier flow were to predominate, the n-side would acquire positive charge from the excess of holes and the p-side, negative charge from the excess of electrons. Thus the n-side would be made more positive relative to the p-side and so V_I would increase. The majority carrier flow would then be reduced until zero net current is re-established. Theoretically, this dynamic balancing process is expressed in the equality of the Fermi level E_F on either side of the junction, as was shown in

* Note that a hole is more energetic the lower it is in the valence band.

section 4.10. It was just this latter fact which was used to determine the internal barrier voltage V_I in the numerical example of section 7.4.

When the junction is reverse biased, the enhanced potential barrier reduces the majority carrier flow and then the minority carrier flow predominates. It will be shown in the next section, that at room temperatures, an enhancement of the junction voltage by as little as 0·2 volt is sufficient virtually to eliminate majority carrier flow across the junction.

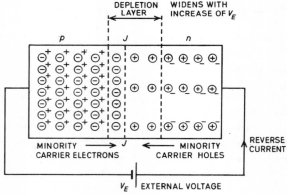

⊖ ACCEPTOR CENTRE, CHARGE −q

⊕ DONOR CENTRE, CHARGE +q

+ MOBILE HOLE, CHARGE + q

− MOBILE ELECTRON, CHARGE -q

Figure 7.6a. Schematic model of a reverse biased *p–n* junction

The reverse biased junction is shown in highly schematic form in fig. 7.6a. Both the minority carrier flow of holes from *n*-side to *p*-side, and the minority carrier flow of electrons from *p*-side to *n*-side, are in the correct sense of current flow with regard to the bias V_E. When a *p–n* junction is reverse biased, positive charge is removed from the *p*-side and placed on the *n*-side. This is manifested as a withdrawal of electrons from the *n*-side and an equal number of holes from the *p*-side. The field existing across the depletion layer repels majority carriers and thus the electrons on the n-side, and holes on the p-side, are effectively withdrawn from the edges of the depletion region. The depletion layer thus widens with reverse bias. Similarly, with forward bias the layer will narrow. This is also apparent from eqns (7.4-15) and (16), which show that the depletion layer width is proportional to the square root of the total voltage across the junction, for the abrupt junction, or from eqn (7.5-7) which shows it is proportional to the cube root of the voltage, for the linearly-graded junction. In addition the junction has capacitance, called the depletion or transition capacitance, for a change of voltage across the junction causes charge to be transferred from one side of the junction to the other.

The magnitude of the reverse current across the junction is generally small. This is because it arises out of the diffusion of minority carriers with small density gradient. Consequently, very little of the applied voltage V_E appears across the neutral regions of the semiconductor as ohmic potential drops. Almost all of V_E enhances the internal barrier V_I, and so the total voltage V_J across the junction is approximately $(V_E + V_I)$. The integrations of Poisson's equation in the last two sections were not restricted to equilibrium conditions. This restriction was used only to evaluate the internal voltage V_I. The main assumption of the integrations was the absence of mobile carriers in the depletion regions, and this becomes more nearly true with increasing reverse bias and widening layers. To justify this theoretically is difficult and beyond the scope of this book. That the statement is qualitatively correct can, however, be established. The height of the potential barrier at the junction is approximately proportional to the reverse bias, while the width of the depletion layer is approximately proportional to the square root, or cube root for linearly-graded junction, of the reverse bias. The electric intensity in the depletion region thus increases approximately as the square root, or to the power two-thirds for the linearly-graded junction, of the reverse bias. The greater the electric intensity in the depletion region, the greater the extent to which it will be depleted and so the approximation can be expected to improve with increasing reverse bias.

The results of the last two sections may therefore be used for the reversed biased junction, provided that V_J is interpreted as $(V_I + V_E)$. For the abrupt junction eqns (7.4-14) through (19) are thus valid for the present case. Similarly, eqns (7.5-6) and (7) for the linearly-graded junction are valid when the junction is reverse biased.

The capacity associated with the depletion layer can be obtained by finding the change in charge ΔQ on either side of the layer, corresponding to a change in applied voltage ΔV_E. The quotient of these quantities gives the depletion layer incremental capacitance. Thus from eqn (7.4-14), for the abrupt junction

$$C = \left(\frac{dQ}{dV_E}\right) = \left\{\left(\frac{\varepsilon q}{2}\right)\left(\frac{N_a N_d}{N_a + N_d}\right)\right\}^{\frac{1}{2}} (V_E + V_I)^{-\frac{1}{2}} \qquad (7.6-1)$$

and from eqn (7.5-6), for the linearly-graded junction:

$$C = \left(\frac{dQ}{dV_E}\right) = \left\{\frac{\varepsilon^2 q n_i}{6 L_a}\right\}^{\frac{1}{3}} (V_E + V_I)^{-\frac{1}{3}} . \qquad (7.6-2)$$

These depletion capacitances vary as the inverse square root, and inverse cube root, of the total junction voltage respectively. These results appear to be true for most junctions in practice, despite the shortcoming of the theory used to predict them.

In transistors, depletion capacitances are considered to be parasitic elements which may limit the maximum frequency of operation of the device and which, in certain instances, introduce unwanted feedback between output and input. However, the voltage dependent depletion capacitance can be used to advantage for *parametric* amplification [7.8] and junctions designed specifically for this purpose are termed *varactor diodes* [7.9].

It is interesting to note that these results for the depletion capacitances, can be obtained without integrating Poisson's equation, but by using instead the formula for the capacitance of a parallel plate capacitor. Of course, this last formula is really the result of an integration of Poisson's equation for the special case of constant electric intensity. The parallel plate capacity formula is usually derived from the Gauss electrostatic theorem, which is a once integrated form of Poisson's equation. The derivation of the depletion capacitance by this method for the abrupt junction is as follows.

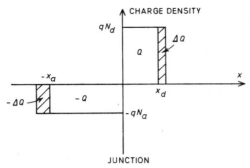

Figure 7.6b. Widening of the depletion layer with reverse biasing of the junction

With reference to fig. 7.6b, which is similar to fig. 7.4a, let ΔQ be the charge added to one side, and subtracted from the other side, of the junction when the voltage across it is increased by ΔV. When ΔQ is small it can be thought of as the charge added to a parallel plate capacitor, of plate separation $(x_a + x_d)$ and dielectric permittivity ε, when the voltage across it is increased by ΔV. Now the capacitance per unit area is:

$$\left(\frac{dQ}{dV}\right) = C = \frac{\varepsilon}{x_a + x_d}. \tag{7.6-3}$$

Also, from fig. 7.6b, or eqn (7.4-1):

$$Q = qx_a N_a = qx_d N_d. \tag{7.6-4}$$

Eliminating x_a and x_d from the expression for C yields:

$$\left(\frac{dQ}{dV}\right) = \left(\frac{\varepsilon q}{Q}\right)\left(\frac{N_a N_d}{N_a + N_d}\right). \tag{7.6-5}$$

Integration of this equation, with Q taken as zero when the total junction voltage V is zero, gives:

$$\tfrac{1}{2}Q^2 = \varepsilon q\left(\frac{N_a N_d}{N_a + N_d}\right)V \tag{7.6-6}$$

which is the same eqn (7.4-14). The depletion capacitance then follows as previously, as do also expressions for x_a and x_d in terms of V.

An almost identical approach can be followed to obtain the formulae for the linearly-graded junction.

7.7 Current Flow Across the Reverse Biased p–n Junction

Let it be supposed that a p–n junction is reverse biased by an external voltage source in excess of 0·2 volt. At room temperatures, the majority carrier flow across the junction is then virtually eliminated: see section 7.8. The reverse current across the junction is then due exclusively to diffusion of minority carriers to the junction. The edges of the depletion layer act as a *sink* for minority carriers, holding their densities zero at these points. The energy level diagram appropriate to this case is shown in fig. 7.7a. Donor and acceptor centres are omitted from this figure for

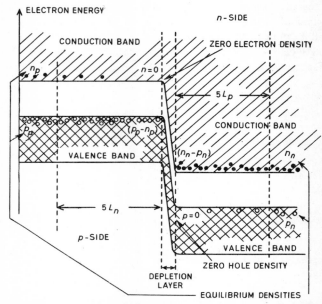

Figure 7.7a. Energy level diagram for a reverse biased p–n junction

the sake of clarity. At sufficiently large distances on either side of the depletion layer, say greater than five diffusion lengths* from the junction, all the carrier densities will take their equilibrium values, p_p and n_p on the p-side and n_n and p_n on the n-side: see the notation of section 6.3.

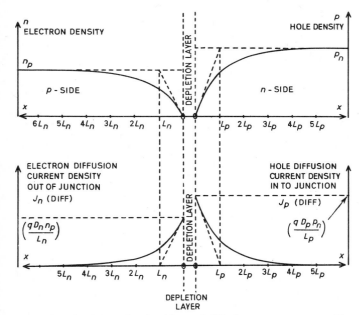

Figure 7.7b. Minority carrier densities and diffusion currents, reverse biased junction

The minority carrier densities decay exponentially from their equilibrium values to zero at the edge of the depletion layer. This follows from the solution of the continuity equation, section 6.10, for the diffusion of minority carriers in the steady state. The present case is that of section 6.11, except that the injected excess density is negative and equal to

* Note: This strictly only applies to uniform semiconductor on either side of the junction, for simplicity it will be assumed valid even for the linearly-graded junction.

$-p_n$. Figure 7.7b shows the densities of the minority carriers and the diffusion current densities on either side of the junction. The hole current, for example, comes about in the following way: the hole distribution on the n-side is:

$$p(x) = p_n \left[1 - \exp \left(-\frac{x}{L_p} \right) \right]. \tag{7.7-1}$$

The hole diffusion current is therefore:

$$J_{p(\text{diff})} = -qD_p \left(\frac{dp}{dx} \right) = \left(\frac{qD_p}{L_p} \right) [p_n - p(x)]. \tag{7.7-2}$$

This becomes zero when $p(x)$ is equal to p_n. The total current density across the junction flows from n to p-side. It is

$$J_{\text{sat}} = \left(\frac{qD_p}{L_p} \right) p_n + \left(\frac{qD_n}{L_n} \right) n_p \tag{7.7-3}$$

and is known as the reverse saturation current density. Very often one or other of the two terms of this last equation predominates. If, for example, the p-side is of much lower resistivity material than that of the n-side, p_n will be much smaller than n_p, and then:

$$J_{\text{sat}} \simeq \left(\frac{qD_n}{L_n} \right) n_p \tag{7.7-4}$$

that is, J_{sat} depends on the resistivity of the lightly doped side.

In any event, J_{sat} is small compared with any ohmic current density that would be produced in the semiconductor by the same applied voltage. This is because the densities of the minority carriers in eqn (7.7-3) are small compared with majority carrier densities. The decay of the diffusion currents away from the junction, implies that an increasing fraction of the total current must be carried by a drift component in these regions; as was the case in section 6.11. However, the magnitude of the electric intensity required to support the drift component is very small. Consequently almost all the external voltage appears across the junction, as previously stated.

The densities of the majority carriers at the edges of the depletion layer, as shown in fig. 7.7a, should be noted. These are below their equilibrium values by amounts equal to the densities of the minority carriers at equilibrium. This is brought about by the maintenance of charge neutrality, the densities of the minority carriers being zero at these edges. Zero net majority carrier flow occurs at the junction, because drift and diffusion components of current density cancel. Therefore a small electric field near the depletion region exists, but this field has a negligible effect on the minority carrier current for the low-level-injection condition.

The reverse saturation current is strongly temperature dependent. Apart from any dependence of the diffusion constant on the mobility, through the Einstein relation, and hence on some small power of the temperature, section 5.3, the densities of the minority carriers are exponentially dependent on the temperature. This dependence is shown in the equations of chapter 4. It follows that J_{sat} will also be exponentially dependent on the temperature.

According to the theory presented here, the reverse saturation current is independent of the applied voltage. This is not quite the case. In the first place, with increasing junction voltage, the depletion layer widens and minority carriers are collected from a larger volume. Note, no allowance was made in eqn (7.7-3) for carriers generated in the depletion layer. The reverse saturation current will thus increase slightly with increasing reverse bias. A second effect, which has so far been omitted, is *avalanching* of minority carriers in the depletion layer. With increasing reverse bias the electric intensity in the depletion layer increases. Minority carriers crossing the depletion layer are accelerated to comparatively large energies per free path, and in subsequent collision, may break covalent bonds thereby forming electron-hole pairs. The number of minority carriers in the depletion layer increases with consequent increase in the reverse current. The multiplication of the number of minority carriers by this process can be described by a factor [7.10], [7.11]:

$$M = \frac{1}{\left\{ 1 - \left(\dfrac{V}{V_B} \right)^m \right\}} \tag{7.7-5}$$

where V is the voltage across the junction, and V_B and m are constants for the particular junction. According to the type of junction, m is between about 1·5 and 6, while V_B varies from a few volts to about a hundred volts. This latter quantity is the breakdown voltage of the junction, for when V is equal to V_B the factor becomes infinite and the reverse current is limited only by external circuit conditions. At values of V appreciably less than V_B, the factor M is approximately unity and only increases slightly with increasing V. Figure 7.7c shows the factor M plotted for an index m of 3, a typical value for a germanium junction. In practice, for a suitable choice of the index m, the factor M seems to represent the observed increase of J_{sat} with bias satisfactorily. The reader is referred to the references [7.11] and [7.12] for more details of this topic.

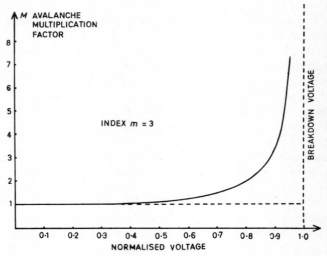

Figure 7.7c. Plot of the Miller function for m equal to 3

Finally, another mode of breakdown of a reverse biased p–n junction will be briefly mentioned. Referring to fig. 7.7a, which shows the energy levels of a reverse biased junction, it will be seen that in the depletion layer, the very high density of electrons in the valence band is separated from a high density of vacant energy levels in the conduction band by a very small horizontal distance. This distance decreases with increasing reverse bias for, as explained earlier, the barrier height increases more rapidly with reverse bias than the depletion layer widens. Quantum Mechanics shows [7.12] that there is a finite probability of electrons from the valence band *tunnelling* their way into the vacant conduction band levels, provided the forbidden gap, measured horizontally, is sufficiently narrow. At high reverse biases, appreciable *tunnel* currents may flow in spite of a low tunnelling probability, primarily because of the very high density of electrons in the valence band. This latter density is of the order of $10^{29} \, \text{m}^{-3}$.

Physically, this mechanism, which is known as the Zener [7.13] effect, can be thought of as occurring when the electric intensity in the depletion layer becomes large enough to cause the direct rupture of covalent bonds by electrostatic force.

In practice, as the reverse bias is increased, most junctions attain the avalanche breakdown voltage before that for Zener breakdown. Only very abrupt junctions with a very high density of impurities on one or both sides of the junction normally break down by the Zener mechanism.

Beyond breakdown resulting from either mechanism, the voltage across the junction is substantially constant for a wide range of reverse currents. For this reason, p–n junction diodes, operated in breakdown mode, are often used as voltage reference sources.

In conclusion, it might just be mentioned that the tunnel effect of the Zener breakdown mechanism is deliberately employed in the tunnel diode [7.14]. This device, which exhibits a negative incremental resistance over a range of its characteristic, has high speed switching and microwave applications.

7.8 Current Flow Across a Forward Biased p–n Junction

When the external voltage is opposite in polarity to the internal potential barrier, the junction is said to be forward biased. Part of the external voltage annuls part of the internal barrier and the rest of the external voltage appears as ohmic potential difference across the neutral regions of the semiconductor. The net junction voltage is $(V_{\mathrm{I}} - V_{\mathrm{E}}')$ where V_{E}' is that part of the external voltage which appears across the junction. In practice, $(V_{\mathrm{I}} - V_{\mathrm{E}}')$ is always greater than, or at the best equal to, zero. It is the voltage which must be used in the expressions for depletion layer thicknesses and capacitances of the last three sections. It should, however, be remembered that these expressions will not be so reliable for the forward biased junction, for the assumption of complete depletion of the layer is hardly justified in this case.

The reduction of the net junction voltage lowers the barrier to majority carriers and allows a greater number of these to cross the depletion layer. The balance between the flows of majority and minority carriers is thus upset and the former predominates. Majority carriers, which have crossed the junction, become minority carriers on the other side. Thus the densities of minority carriers on both sides of the junction are increased above their equilibrium values and the carriers diffuse away from the junction.

The hole, or electron, current across the depletion layer has both drift and diffusion components, neither component necessarily being small compared with the other. An expression for the hole current density, which includes both components, is that of eqn (6.4-5); in one-dimension:

$$J_p = p\mu_p \left(\frac{dE_{\mathrm{F}p}}{dx} \right) \tag{7.8-1}$$

where $E_{\mathrm{F}p}$ is the hole Imref. It will now be shown that $E_{\mathrm{F}p}$ remains practically constant across the depletion layer. It is noted first, that there will be negligible recombination in the depletion layer because its width is small compared with a diffusion length. This means that the hole current is practically constant throughout the depletion layer. It is therefore possible to integrate eqn (7.8-1), treating J_p as a constant, to give the change in Imref across the layer:

$$\Delta E_{\mathrm{F}p} = \left(\frac{J_p}{\mu_p} \right) \int_0^{\Delta x} \frac{dx}{p} \tag{7.8-2}$$

where Δx is the width of the depletion layer. This last equation may be made into an inequality:

$$|\Delta E_{\mathrm{F}p}| \leqslant \left(\frac{J_p}{\mu_p}\right)\left(\frac{\Delta x}{p_0}\right) \qquad (7.8\text{-}3)$$

where p_0 is the hole density on the n-side of the layer, and also the minimum value of p across the layer. Now p_0 is the injection density of minority carriers on the n-side of the junction. In the example of section 6.11, which is identical with the present case, the hole current density injected into the n-type material is given by eqn (6.11-8), namely:

$$J_p = \left(\frac{qD_p}{L_p}\right)(p_0 - p_n). \qquad (7.8\text{-}4)$$

The inequality (7.8-3) thus becomes:

$$|\Delta E_{\mathrm{F}p}| \leqslant \left(\frac{qD_p}{\mu_p}\right)\left(\frac{p_0 - p_n}{p_0}\right)\left(\frac{\Delta x}{L_p}\right) < kT\left(\frac{\Delta x}{L_p}\right) \qquad (7.8\text{-}5)$$

where the Einstein relation has been used. Because Δx is a small fraction of L_p, it follows that the change of Imref across the depletion layer is small fraction of kT; the latter quantity being 0·026 electron volt at room temperatures. The hole Imref is thus practically constant across the layer. A similar result can be deduced for the electron Imref.

It was explained in section 6.2, that for low-level-injection in an extrinsic semiconductor, the majority carrier Imref is approximately coincident with the Fermi level of equilibrium conditions. Hence $E_{\mathrm{F}p}$ may be assumed to coincide with E_{F} on the p-side of the junction, and $E_{\mathrm{F}n}$ with E_{F} on the n-side. At distances of the order of five diffusion lengths from the junction, both majority and minority carrier Imrefs will coincide with the Fermi level, for the densities at such points have their equilibrium values. Neglecting for the present the ohmic resistance of the neutral regions of the semiconductor, the Fermi levels some five diffusion lengths from the junction and on either side of it, will differ in energy by the external voltage V'_{E}. This is shown, together with the Imrefs, in the energy level diagram of fig. 7.8a. The Imref $E_{\mathrm{F}p}$ is constant on the p-side and remains so through the depletion layer, and then

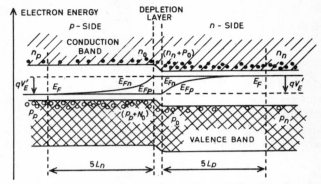

Figure 7.8a. Energy level diagram for the forward biased *p–n* junction

rises exponentially to E_F on the *n*-side in a distance of approximately $5L_p$. Similarly, E_{Fn} is constant on the *n*-side, and in the depletion layer, and then falls exponentially to E_F on the *p*-side in a distance $5L_n$. Continuity of an Imref through the system has been assumed for this figure. This follows because a step discontinuity of an Imref would imply a step discontinuity of a carrier density, which is physically impossible. The minority carrier Imrefs, on either side of the junction, give the minority carrier densities. Thus from eqn (6.3-4), on the *p*-side:

$$n = n_p \exp\left(\frac{E_{Fn} - E_{Fp}}{kT}\right) \tag{7.8-6}$$

and from eqn (6.3-5), on the *n*-side:

$$p = p_n \exp\left(\frac{E_{Fn} - E_{Fp}}{kT}\right). \tag{7.8-7}$$

For both equations the majority carrier Imref has been used for the equilibrium Fermi level. In particular, at the edges of the depletion layer these last equations give the minority carrier injection densities as:

$$n_0 = n_p \exp\left(\frac{qV_E'}{kT}\right) \tag{7.8-8}$$

$$p_0 = p_n \exp\left(\frac{qV_E'}{lT}\right) \tag{7.8-9}$$

on the p-side and n-side respectively, because $(E_{Fn} - E_{Fp})$ is qV_E' at the depletion layer. These equations show by how much the minority carrier densities are lifted above their equilibrium values by the injection voltage; that is the forward external bias. The problem of finding the injected diffusion currents, in terms of the injected densities, was carried out in section 6.11. Equation (7.8-4) was deduced from the results of this section; substitution of eqn (7.8-9) into eqn (7.8-4) gives the hole current density which is injected into the n-side:

$$J_p(0) = \left(\frac{qD_p p_n}{L_p}\right)\left[\exp\left(\frac{qV_E'}{kT}\right) - 1\right]. \tag{7.8-10}$$

Similarly, the electron current density injected into the p-side is:

$$-J_n(0) = -\left(\frac{qD_n n_p}{L_n}\right)\left[\exp\left(\frac{qV_E'}{kT}\right) - 1\right]. \tag{7.8-11}$$

The total current density which flows from p-side to n-side is therefore:

$$J = J_s\left[\exp\left(\frac{qV_E'}{kT}\right) - 1\right] \tag{7.8-12}$$

where J_s, the reverse saturation current density is given by eqn (7.7-3) or (4), as appropriate.

If V_E' is negative and of magnitude greater than $5(kT/q)$, that is about 0·12 volt at room temperatures, the exponential term in this last equation is less than 0·01 and may be neglected compared with unity. The current J is then $-J_s$, in agreement with the results of section 7.7 for the reverse biased junction. On the other hand, if V_E' is positive and greater than $5(kT/q)$, the exponential term exceeds 100 and -1 can be neglected in comparison. Equation (7.8-12), the characteristic of the junction, is sketched as the broken curve in fig. 7.8b.

Although minority carriers account for the current flow across the junction, at distances in excess of about five diffusion lengths from the junction, all the current is carried by the drift of majority carriers. In this distance of five diffusion lengths, the diffusion current falls exponen-

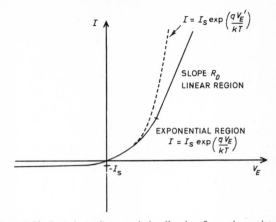

Figure 7.8b. Junction characteristic allowing for series resistance

tially, and the drift current rises such that the total current is constant: this was explained in section 6.11. Beyond these five diffusion lengths, the voltage drop across the semiconductor, can be expressed in terms of its ohmic resistance. This is readily calculated from its conductivity and dimensions. The voltage drop across the semiconductor within the five diffusion lengths from the junction must, however, be examined in more detail.

Let the electron current on the *n*-side of the junction be considered. It may be expressed in terms of the electron Imref, by analogy with eqn (7.8-1), or from eqn (6.4-6):

$$J_n(x) = n\mu_n \left(\frac{dE_{Fn}}{dx}\right) \tag{7.8-13}$$

and also as:

$$J_n(x) = J - J_p(x) \tag{7.8-14}$$

where J is the total current density and $J_p(x)$ the hole current density. At a given V_E', the former is a constant and the latter is:

$$J_p(x) = J_p(0) \exp\left(-\frac{x}{L_p}\right). \tag{7.8-15}$$

These three equations give:

$$\left(\frac{dE_{\mathrm{F}n}}{dx}\right) = \left(\frac{1}{n_n \mu_n}\right)\left[J - J_p(0)\exp\left(-\frac{x}{L_p}\right)\right] \qquad (7.8\text{-}16)$$

where n has been replaced by n_n, an approximation which is valid for low-level-injection. Integration of this last equation yields:

$$E_{\mathrm{F}n}(x) - E_{\mathrm{F}n}(0) = \left(\frac{1}{\mu_n n_n}\right)\left\{Jx - J_p(0)L_p\left[1 - \exp\left(-\frac{x}{L_p}\right)\right]\right\}. \qquad (7.8\text{-}17)$$

As already assumed, for low-level-injection $E_{\mathrm{F}n}$ does not depart significantly from the E_{F} of equilibrium conditions. In turn, for a uniform semiconductor, E_{F} has a constant separation from $E_{\mathrm{F}i}$ and hence $E_{\mathrm{F}n}$ may be used as a measure of electrostatic potential in the electrically neutral n-type region. Thus taking x equal to $5L_p$, eqn (7.8-17) gives:

$$V(0) - V(5L_p) = \left(\frac{1}{q\mu_n n_n}\right)\left[J \cdot 5L_p - J_p(0)L_p\right]. \qquad (7.8\text{-}18)$$

Now, at the junction:

$$J = J_p(0) + J_n(0) \qquad (7.8\text{-}19)$$

while from eqns (7.8-10) and (11):

$$\left(\frac{L_p}{p_n D_p}\right)J_p(0) = \left(\frac{L_n}{n_p D_n}\right)J_n(0). \qquad (7.8\text{-}20)$$

Eliminating $J_n(0)$ between these last two equations:

$$J_p(0) = \frac{J}{\left[1 + \left(\dfrac{D_n}{D_p}\right)\left(\dfrac{L_p}{L_n}\right)\left(\dfrac{n_p}{p_n}\right)\right]}. \qquad (7.8\text{-}21)$$

Substitution into eqn (7.8-18) then yields:

$$V(0) - V(5L_p) \simeq \left(\frac{J\,5L_p}{\sigma_n}\right)\left\{1 - \frac{1}{5\left[1 + \left(\dfrac{D_n}{D_p}\right)\left(\dfrac{L_p}{L_n}\right)\left(\dfrac{n_p}{p_n}\right)\right]}\right\} \qquad (7.8\text{-}22)$$

where σ_n is the ohmic conductivity of the n-side.

This last equation shows that the voltage across the region of n-type semiconductor from the junction to a distance $5L_p$ from the junction, can be represented by an ohmic potential drop across a material of conductivity σ_{eff} given by:

$$\sigma_{\text{eff}} = \sigma_n \Bigg/ \left\{ 1 - \frac{1}{5\left[1 + \left(\dfrac{D_n}{D_p}\right)\left(\dfrac{L_p}{L_n}\right)\left(\dfrac{n_p}{p_n}\right)\right]} \right\}. \qquad (7.8\text{-}23)$$

A similar expression can be obtained for the p-side of the junction. For most practical diodes one or other of n_p or p_n predominates, then σ_{eff} approximates to the normal conductivity on one side of the junction and to 1·25 times the normal conductivity on the other side. For low-level-injection, it is therefore possible to represent the total external voltage by:

$$V_E = V_E' + R_D I \qquad (7.8\text{-}24)$$

where V_E' is the voltage applied to the junction itself, I is the forward current and R_D is an ohmic resistance. This resistance R_D is calculated as four resistances in series, corresponding to the four parts into which the neutral regions of the semiconductor were split for the foregoing analysis. The junction may thus be represented by a characteristic of the form shown in fig. 7.8b.

The treatment of the more difficult case of high-level-injection is beyond the scope of the present book. For an account of this topic the reader is referred elsewhere [7.15]. Very often, the high resistivity side of practical p–n junction diodes is terminated by an ohmic metal contact at a distance of the order of one diffusion length from the junction. This is done to obtain a low forward resistance for the diode in spite of the high resistivity of the material. It is desirable to have a high resistivity material on one side of the junction in order that the reverse breakdown voltage shall not be too low. The derivation of the diode characteristic for this case is left as an exercise for the reader.

7.9 Small Signal A.C. Characteristic of a p–n Junction

A reverse biased p–n junction has a small signal equivalent circuit of the form shown in fig. 7.9a(i). The capacitance C_{Tr} is the depletion capacitance at the mean operating voltage of the junction, and r_s is the total series resistance of the semiconductor on both side of the junction. The conductance g_p is the ohmic conductance arising from the flow of reverse current across the junction. The resistance r_s is usually small compared with the reactance of C_{Tr}, except at the highest frequencies, and hence r_s can usually be omitted from the circuit. At all but the lowest frequencies, the conductance g_p will be negligible compared with the susceptance of C_{Tr}. Thus for most purposes, the junction can be represented simply by C_{Tr} as far as its small signal a.c. behaviour is concerned.

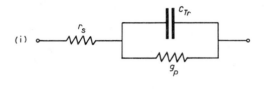

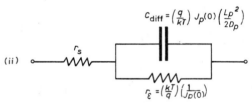

Figure 7.9a. Equivalent circuit of a *p–n* junction
(i) Reverse biased
(ii) Forward biased at lower frequencies

The equivalent circuit of the forward biased junction is more complicated. For simplicity, discussion will be restricted to the case where the *p*-side of the junction is of much lower resistivity than the *n*-side. Then, virtually all the forward current across the junction arises from the injection of holes into the *n*-material. The frequency dependent behaviour of the junction then follows that of the example of section 6.15. From the work of that section, it is apparent that no simple, lumped parameter, equivalent circuit for the junction exists at high frequencies. Equations

(6.15-10) and (13) give the small signal, a.c., current density crossing the forward biased junctions in terms of the small signal density $\hat{p}_{aco}$ of injected holes. This latter quantity, may be related to the small signal voltage across the junction by differentiation of eqn (7.8-9):

$$\hat{p}_{aco} = \left(\frac{q}{kT}\right) p_0 \, \hat{v}_{ac} \tag{7.9-1}$$

where:

$$v_{ac} = \hat{v}_{ac} \exp(j\omega t) \tag{7.9-2}$$

is the small signal voltage. Thus, when the series ohmic resistance is neglected, the small signal, a.c., admittance of the junction is

$$y = \left(\frac{q}{kT}\right) q D_p p_0 \theta \, . \tag{7.9-3}$$

Eliminating p_0 with the aid of eqns (7.8-9) and (10):

$$y = \left(\frac{q}{kT}\right) J_p(0) \left\{ \frac{\exp\left(\dfrac{qV'_E}{kT}\right)}{\exp\left(\dfrac{qV'_E}{kT}\right) - 1} \right\} L_p \theta \tag{7.9-4}$$

where $J_p(0)$ is the d.c. component of current density. Provided V'_E exceeds approximately $5(kT/q)$, that is about 0·12 volt at room temperatures, the admittance may be written as:

$$y = \left(\frac{q}{kT}\right) J_p(0) L_p \theta \, . \tag{7.9-5}$$

The form of θ, eqn (6.15-10), shows that no lumped parameter circuit, frequency independent passive components, can be used to represent the admittance y. At any frequency, it is possible to represent y by a parallel combination of a conductance and a susceptance, capacitive or inductive. However, the values of the conductance and the capacitance, or inductance, will be different at other frequencies.

As in section 6.15, eqn (6.15-14), at frequencies such that:

$$\omega \ll \left(\frac{D_p}{L_p^2}\right) \tag{7.9-6}$$

θ approximates to, eqn (6.15-15):

$$\theta \simeq \left(\frac{1}{L_p}\right)\left[1 + j\omega\left(\frac{L_p^2}{2D_p}\right)\right]. \tag{7.9-7}$$

The admittance is then:

$$y \simeq \left(\frac{q}{kT}\right) J_p(0)\left[1 + j\omega\left(\frac{L_p^2}{2D_p}\right)\right]. \tag{7.9-8}$$

This may be represented by a conductance of $(q/kT)J_p(0)$ in parallel with a capacitance of $(q/kT)J_p(0)(L_p^2/2D_p)$, called the diffusion capacitance, giving a break angular frequency of $(2D_p/L_p^2)$ which is independent of the mean operating current. This approximate, lower frequency equivalent circuit is shown in fig. 7.9a(ii). Again r_s represents the series resistance of the semiconductor and may be considered negligible for many purposes.

7.10 Metal-Semiconductor Junctions

In this section, metal-semiconductor junctions will be briefly discussed. In order to be specific, the junction between a metal and an n-type semiconductor will be considered: the case of a metal to p-type semiconductor is similar and will be left for the reader to investigate. In fig. 7.10a, the energy level diagrams corresponding to the surface of a metal and the surface of an n-type semiconductor are shown. In the upper part of the figure, the metal and semiconductor are isolated, and have work functions, see section 1.1, of ϕ_m and ϕ_s respectively. The two surfaces have been brought together in intimate contact in the lower part of the figure. In equilibrium, the equality of the Fermi level on either side of the junction, demands the formation of the depletion layer indicated in the figure. This arises because, when the junction is first made, electrons from the semiconductor flow into the metal. The metal thus becomes negatively charged and semiconductor positively charged. A potential barrier is set up at the junction which opposes the further flow of electrons, and the junction comes to equilibrium with the Fermi level constant throughout. The barrier potential, equal to the difference in the work functions, repels the electrons in the semiconductor, thus producing the depletion region. It has been assumed that ϕ_m is greater than ϕ_s, which is usually the case of interest for a rectifying junction. When ϕ_s is greater than ϕ_m, there will be an excess of electrons in surface layers of the semiconductor, and the junction will not exhibit rectifying properties.

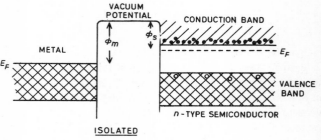

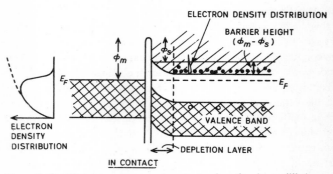

Figure 7.10a. Metal to *n*-type semiconductor junction in equilibrium

When the semiconductor, of fig. 7.10a, is made positive relative to the metal with the aid of an external bias, the barrier potential is enhanced. Electron flow from the semiconductor to the metal is completely cut off, but a limited flow of electrons from the metal to the semiconductor still occurs. Holes, in the semiconductor, diffuse to the edge of the depletion layer under their concentration gradient and

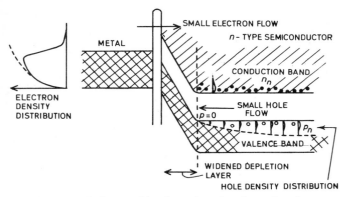

Figure 7.10b. Reverse biased metal-semiconductor junction

enhance the reverse current across the junction. The situation is depicted in fig. 7.10b.

Making the semiconductor negative relative to the metal, biases the junction in the forward sense. The junction barrier is partially annulled and the depletion layer is narrowed. Figure 7.10c shows the energy level diagram for this case. The reduction in the barrier height allows appreciable electron flow from the semiconductor to the metal. In addition, some hole injection from the metal to semiconductor occurs. This has the effect of increasing the forward current, across the junction, in two ways. Firstly, there is the direct contribution resulting from the hole diffusion current in the semiconductor. Secondly, the electron density in the semiconductor increases with hole injection in order to maintain charge neutrality. This increases the electron injection across the barrier, into the metal, and also reduces the ohmic resistance of the semiconductor. The latter effect is very marked for point contact rectifiers, and has the effect of greatly reducing the *spreading* resistance of the semiconductor about the point contact.

It is apparent from fig. 7.10c, that the electrons crossing the potential barrier to enter the metal have energies appreciably greater than the Fermi energy of the metal. This excess of energy may amount to an electron-volt or so, and hence the electrons are termed *hot electrons**. Subsequently electron-phonon interaction, that is collisions with the lattice, average out the excess energy and the injected electrons become indistinguishable from others in the metal.

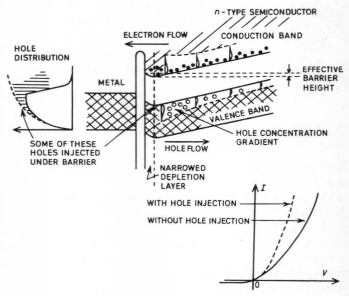

Figure 7.10c. Forward biased metal-semiconductor junction

A semiconductor-metal junction which behaves in the manner described above is called a Schottky junction [7.16], after the person who first presented an account of its rectifying action, or *hot electron* emitter. In section 8.11, a device which is dependent on *hot electron* emission is briefly discussed.

According to the foregoing account of the metal-semiconductor junction, a rectifying characteristic should be a function of $(\phi_m - \phi_s)$,

* Note: 1 electron volt of energy, the equivalent to (kT/q), corresponds to a temperature of about 10^4 °K.

that is the difference of the work functions of the metal and semiconductor. This is not borne out by experiment. Point contacts, using different metals but the same semiconductor surface, often produce substantially similar rectifying characteristics. This suggests that the rectifying characteristic is a function of the semiconductor and its surface and is largely independent of the work function of the metal. An explanation of this can be found in the theory of surface states [7.17], [7.18].

In this theory, it is supposed that the surface of the semiconductor has energy levels which may act as traps for electrons or holes. These traps may possibly arise as a result of unsatisfied atomic bonds at the surface of an otherwise regular array of atoms, or as a result of lattice imperfections at the surface, or, more likely, as the result of surface contamination. The surface traps *capture* mobile carriers which then

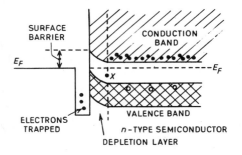

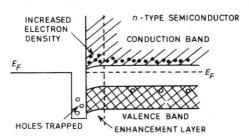

Figure 7.10d. Surface states, depletion and enhancement layers

repel, or attract, other carriers and hence cause depletion, or enhancement, layers to be formed at the surface. Two possible situations are shown in fig. 7.10d, both for an n-type semiconductor. In the upper part of the figure, surface electron traps cause the depletion of electrons from the surface layer, and the production of a surface barrier even in the absence of a metal contact. In the lower part of the figure, hole traps attract electrons to the surface producing an enhancement layer. The hole traps, may be energy levels, which are normally occupied by electrons, but which have given up their electrons to the conduction band. Two similar diagrams can be drawn for a p-type semiconductor.

When, as in the upper part of fig. 7.10d, the density of surface traps is such that the surface layer of the semiconductor is changed in type, compared with the bulk, the layer is called an *inversion* layer. The criterion for inversion, in this way, is that the Fermi level in the layer should move to the other half of the forbidden gap. Inversion layers of this kind are important in connection with insulated-gate transistors, as will be discussed in section 9.7.

When a metal contact is made to a semiconductor surface, it is usually assumed that the Fermi levels on either side of the junction are equated, by adjustment of the carriers in the surface states. Electrons are drawn from, or given to, the metal to effect the balance. Thus differences in the work function, from one metal to another, might be expected to have only second order effects on the rectifying characteristics. It must be admitted, however, that surface effects in semiconductors are the least fully understood part of the subject. There are many effects which have yet to be explained satisfactorily.

This section will be concluded with a brief mention of non-rectifying semiconductor contacts. When the surface layer of the semiconductor is of the enhancement type, it will not exhibit rectifying properties. Only junctions with strong inversion layers have rectifying properties. Again, if the transition from the metal to the semiconductor is gradual, the junction will not rectify; this is analogous to the gradual p–n junction, with a characteristic length L_a larger than the Debye length L_D; see section 7.2. Gradual metal to semiconductor junctions are usually formed by soldering, particularly when the solder is doped with appropriate n

or p-type impurity. The heat causes a large number of dislocations in the surface layers of the semiconductor, and also causes impurities to diffuse into these layers, thus giving rise to a gradual transition from metal to semiconductor.

7.11 Surface Recombination

The topic of carrier recombination in the bulk of a semiconductor was considered in section 6.16. The present section is concerned with recombination at the surface of a semiconductor. As was explained in the last section, there is usually a high area density of carrier traps at the surface of a semiconductor. Many of these traps act as recombination centres, and excess carriers which reach the free surface usually recombine there very rapidly.

The discussion of surface recombination is simplified with the aid of the concept of *surface recombination velocity*; this is defined in the following way. Consider, for example, holes. Let P be the excess hole density in the bulk material just beyond the surface layer, that is, at a point such as X in fig. 7.10d. Also, let U_{cps} be the flux of holes crossing from the bulk material into the surface layer. Then, the surface recombination velocity S_p of the holes is defined by:

$$S_p = \left(\frac{U_{cps}}{P} \right). \tag{7.11-1}$$

A similar definition exists for the surface recombination velocity S_n of the electrons.

$$S_n = \left(\frac{U_{cns}}{N} \right). \tag{7.11-2}$$

Because the bulk semiconductor is electrically neutral, in the steady state, S_p and S_n will be equal for there can be no build up in time of either type of carrier in the surface states. The recombination velocity is then denoted by S without a suffix. A strong analogy exists between S and $(1/\tau)$, where τ is the *bulk* lifetime. Thus, by analogy with eqn (6.16-39) the recombination velocity S may be expressed as:

$$S = \frac{P + p_e + n_e}{(P + n_e + n_1)\tau_{pos} + (P + p_e + p_1)\tau_{nos}} \tag{7.11-3}$$

where:

$$\tau_{nos} = \{c_{ns}N_{ts}\}^{-1} \tag{7.11-4}$$

and:

$$\tau_{pos} = \{c_{ps}N_{ts}\}^{-1}. \tag{7.11-5}$$

Here, N_{ts} is the area density of surface recombination traps and c_{ns} and c_{ps} are the total capture probabilities, per unit time, of the traps for electrons from the conduction band and for holes from the valence band respectively: see eqns (6.16-6), (20) and (26).

For the low-level-injection condition, eqn (7.11-3) approximates to:

$$S = \frac{p_e + n_e}{(n_e + n_1)\tau_{pos} + (p_e + p_1)\tau_{nos}} \tag{7.11-6}$$

which is a constant. Thus, subject to this condition, the surface recombination velocity can be assumed to be constant.

The magnitude of S for mechanically worked, semiconductor surfaces, for example, sandblasted or lapped, is in excess of 10^2 m/sec. Chemical etch treatments can reduce this velocity to below 1 m/sec. Silicon surfaces, passivated by a silicon oxide layer as in planar technology, usually have recombination velocities below 10 m/sec. Equation (7.11-1), or (2), is used as a boundary condition for solutions of the continuity equation, section 6.9, when some boundaries of the semiconductor are free surfaces. The form used is:

$$U_{cs} = PS . \tag{7.11-7}$$

When S is a constant, as discussed above, the solutions of the continuity equation remain linear and, in principle, are readily obtained. When S is not constant, similar difficulties arise to those which occur when τ is not constant. Equation (7.11-7) may also be used as a boundary condition at non-rectifying metal to semiconductor contacts. In such cases, an equivalent surface recombination velocity is defined. It will not, however, be necessary to solve the continuity equation subject to such boundary conditions for any purpose in this book.

References

[7.1] SHOCKLEY, W., PEARSON, G. L. and HAYNES, J. R. (1949), 'Hole injection in germanium – Quantitative studies and filamentary transistors', *Bell Syst. Tech. Journ.*, **28**, 344–366.

[7.2] PRINCE, M. B. (1953), 'Drift mobilities in semiconductors: I, Germanium.' *Phys. Rev.*, **92**, 681–687.

[7.3] HEADING, J. (1964), *Electromagnetic theory and special relatively*, p. 13, Univ. Tutorial Press.

[7.4] SHOCKLEY, W. (1949), 'The theory of p–n junctions in semiconductors and p–n junction transistors', *Bell Syst. Tech. Journ.*, **28**, 435–489, app. VII.

[7.5] BIONDI, F. J. (1958), *Transistor technology*, Vol. III, Chaps 1–9, Van Nostrand.

[7.6] ROTH, E. A., GOSSENBERGER, H. and AMICK, J. A. (1963), 'The Growth of germanium epitaxial layers by pyrolysis of germane', *R.C.A. Rev.*, **24**, 499–510.

[7.7] BHOLA, S. R. and MAYER, A. (1963), 'Epitaxial deposition of silicon by thermal deposition of silane', *R.C.A. Rev.*, **24**, 511–522.

[7.8] NERGAARD, L. S. and GLICKSMAN, M. (1964), *Microwave solid state engineering*, pp. 78–85, Van Nostrand.

[7.9] do. pp. 45–48.

[7.10] MILLER, S. L. (1955), 'Avalanche breakdown in germanium', *Phys. Rev.*, **99**, 1234–1241.

[7.11] MILLER, S. L. (1957), 'Ionisation rates for holes and electrons in silicon', *Phys. Rev.*, **105**, 1246–1249.

[7.12] See for example: ROJANSKI, V. (1939), *Introductory quantum mechanics*, pp. 211–221, Blackie.

[7.13] ZENER, C. (1934), 'A theory of the electrical breakdown in solid dielectrics,' *Proc. Roy. Soc.*, (London), **145A**, 523–529.

[7.14] See for example: NERGAARD, L. S. and GLICKSMAN, M. (1964), *Microwave solid state engineering*, pp. 54–60, Van Nostrand.

[7.15] FLETCHER, N. H. (1957), 'The high-current limit for semiconductor junction devices', *Proc. I.R.E.*, **45**, 862–872.

[7.16] SCHOTTKY, N. and SPENKE, E. (1939), 'Quantitative treatment of space-charge and boundary-layer theory of the crystal rectifier', *Wiss. Veröff. Siemens Werke*, **18**, 1–67.

[7.17] BARDEEN, J. (1947), 'Surface states and rectification at a metal semiconductor contact', *Phys. Rev.*, **71**, 717–727.

[7.18] BRATTAIN, W. H. and BARDEEN, J. (1953), 'Surface properties of germanium', *Bell Syst. Tech. Journ.*, **32**, 1–41.

CHAPTER 8

Minority Carrier Transistors

8.1 Introduction

The minority carrier transistor has already been introduced in earlier chapters. Both the *diffusion, uniform-base*, transistor, and the somewhat more complex *drift, graded-base*, transistor, have been briefly considered. In the present chapter, these devices will be considered in more detail, both with regard to their d.c. characteristics and their small signal a.c. equivalent circuits. The one-dimensional planar flow model, used in earlier chapters, will be retained for the present chapter, but the effects of departures from one-dimensional flow will also be noted. The behaviour of the diffusion transistor will be the main theme of the chapter, but where appropriate and not too difficult, the drift transistor will also be discussed. Throughout, consideration will be restricted to low-level-injection conditions. The detailed behaviour of transistors, particularly the drift variety, under high-level-injection conditions is rather involved and is beyond the scope of the present volume.

8.2 D.C. Characteristics of the Uniform-Base Transistor

In section 6.13, the one-dimensional diffusion, uniform-base, transistor, with allowance for base recombination, was considered. In this example, the emitter junction was forward biased and the collector junction was reverse biased. The work of the section culminated in eqns (6.13-11), (12) and (13), which related the emitter and collector currents, and which introduced the current gain α and the collector leakage current I_{CBO}. The connection between the emitter bias and the emitter current was not investigated. The developments of chapter 7 now enable this latter relation to be obtained, as will be shown below. In addition, the restriction to a reverse biased collector junction will be removed.

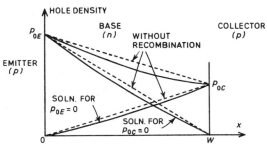

Figure 8.2a. Hole density distribution across the base of a diffusion transistor, both junctions forward biased.

Referring to fig. 8.2a, let p_{0E} and p_{0C} be the hole densities injected into the base by the forward biases across the emitter and collector junctions respectively. It is assumed, that the whole of the base from x equal to zero to x equal to W is electrically neutral. That is, the widths of the depletion layers are to be neglected for the present: the effect of these layers will be discussed later. At this stage, the ohmic resistances will also be neglected; the externally applied voltages thus appear entirely across the junctions. This is usually a satisfactory assumption as far as the emitter and collector regions are concerned, since these regions usually have low resistivity, but it is not so satisfactory for the high resistivity base region. However, the base current is usually small, being the difference between the emitter and collector currents, and so the ohmic voltage drop in the base region, between the junctions and the base metallic contact, will not be large. An ohmic resistance, called the *base spreading resistance*, can be used to represent the voltage drop between the active base region and the base metallic contact.

Equation (7.8-9) relates the injected densities, p_{0E} and p_{0C}, to the voltages, V_{EB} and V_{CB} across the emitter-base and collector-base junctions, respectively:

$$p_{0E} = p_n \exp\left(\frac{qV_{EB}}{kT}\right) \tag{8.2-1}$$

$$p_{0C} = p_n \exp\left(\frac{qV_{CB}}{kT}\right) \tag{8.2-2}$$

or, in terms of the excess densities:

$$P_{0E} = p_n \left[\exp\left(\frac{qV_{EB}}{kT}\right) - 1 \right] \tag{8.2-3}$$

$$P_{0C} = p_n \left[\exp\left(\frac{qV_{CB}}{kT}\right) - 1 \right] . \tag{8.2-4}$$

The one-dimensional, steady-state, continuity equation is now to be solved subject to these boundary conditions. Referring to section 6.10, eqn (6.10-2), the continuity equation for the present case is:

$$\left(\frac{d^2 P}{dx^2}\right) - \left(\frac{P}{L_p^2}\right) = 0 . \tag{8.2-5}$$

The general solution of this last equation is:

$$P = A \exp\left(-\frac{x}{L_p}\right) + B \exp\left(\frac{x}{L_p}\right). \tag{8.2-6}$$

Substitution of the boundary conditions:

$$\begin{aligned} P &= P_{0E} \; ; \; \text{at} \; x = 0 \\ P &= P_{0C} \; ; \; \text{at} \; x = W \end{aligned} \tag{8.2-7}$$

yields:

$$\left. \begin{aligned} A &= \tfrac{1}{2} \operatorname{csch}\left(\frac{W}{L_p}\right)\left[P_{0E} \exp\left(\frac{W}{L_p}\right) - P_{0C}\right] \\ B &= -\tfrac{1}{2} \operatorname{csch}\left(\frac{W}{L_p}\right)\left[P_{0E} \exp\left(-\frac{W}{L_p}\right) - P_{0C}\right] \end{aligned} \right\} \tag{8.2-8}$$

Assuming unity injection efficiency γ for both junctions, the emitter and collector current densities are respectively:

$$J_E = -qD_p \left(\frac{dP}{dx}\right)_0 = \left(\frac{qD_p}{L_p}\right)(B - A) =$$

$$= \left(\frac{qD_p}{L_p}\right)\left[P_{0E} \coth\left(\frac{W}{L_p}\right) - P_{0C} \operatorname{csch}\left(\frac{W}{L_p}\right)\right] \tag{8.2-9}$$

$$J_C = qD_p \left(\frac{dP}{dx}\right)_W = \left(\frac{qD_p}{L_p}\right)\left[B \exp\left(\frac{W}{L_p}\right) - A \exp\left(-\frac{W}{L_p}\right)\right]$$

$$= \left(\frac{qD_p}{L_p}\right)\left[-P_{0E} \operatorname{csch}\left(\frac{W}{L_p}\right) + P_{0C} \coth\left(\frac{W}{L_p}\right)\right] \quad (8.2\text{-}10)$$

where eqn (8.2-8) has been used, and where the convention that currents flowing into the base are positive has been adopted. The symmetry of these last two equations results from the symmetry between the emitter and collector inherent in a one-dimensional model of a *uniform-base* transistor.

The linearity of the last two equations in the excess densities of injected carriers at the emitter and collector junctions, shows that the problem could have been solved by superimposing two solutions, one for p_{0C} zero and the other for p_{0E} zero. Either one of these solutions would have been identical, in principle, to the problem of section 6.13. That is, for the first, the collector junction would have been assumed reverse biased, and for the second, the emitter junction would have been reverse biased. These two solutions are indicated in fig. 8.2a. The superposition of the two special solutions, to give the general solution, when base recombination is negligible, is immediately obvious from the figure.

Eliminating P_{0E} and P_{0C} from eqns (8.2-9) and (10), with the aid of eqns (8.2-3) and (4), gives:

$$J_E = \left(\frac{qD_p p_n}{L_p}\right)\left\{\left[\exp\left(\frac{qV_{EB}}{kT}\right) - 1\right] \coth\left(\frac{W}{L_p}\right)\right.$$
$$\left. - \left[\exp\left(\frac{qV_{CB}}{kT}\right) - 1\right] \operatorname{csch}\left(\frac{W}{L_p}\right)\right\} \quad (8.2\text{-}11)$$

$$J_C = \left(\frac{qD_p p_n}{L_p}\right)\left\{-\left[\exp\left(\frac{qV_{EB}}{kT}\right) - 1\right] \operatorname{csch}\left(\frac{W}{L_p}\right)\right.$$
$$\left. + \left[\exp\left(\frac{qV_{CB}}{kT}\right) - 1\right] \coth\left(\frac{W}{L_p}\right)\right\}. \quad (8.2\text{-}12)$$

When, as in normal operation, the collector junction is reverse biased by several times (kT/q), $\exp(qV_{CB}/kT)$ becomes negligible compared with unity and can be neglected. Then, eliminating $[\exp(qV_{EB}/kT)-1]$ between the last two equations:

$$\operatorname{csch}\left(\frac{W}{L_p}\right) J_E + \coth\left(\frac{W}{L_p}\right) J_C$$

$$= \left(\frac{qD_p p_n}{L_p}\right)\left[\operatorname{csch}^2\left(\frac{W}{L_p}\right) - \coth^2\left(\frac{W}{L_p}\right)\right] = -\left(\frac{qD_p p_n}{L_p}\right) \quad (8.2\text{-}13)$$

or: $$-J_C = \alpha J_E + J_{CB0} . \quad (8.2\text{-}14)$$

This is eqn (6.13-11) again, where:

$$J_{CB0} = \left(\frac{qD_p p_n}{L_p}\right) \tanh\left(\frac{W}{L_p}\right) \quad (8.2\text{-}15)$$

and:

$$\alpha = \operatorname{sech}\left(\frac{W}{L_p}\right) \quad (8.2\text{-}16)$$

as in section 6.13.

If W is small compared with L_p:

$$J_{CB0} \simeq \left(\frac{qD_p p_n}{L_p}\right)\left(\frac{W}{L_p}\right) \quad (8.2\text{-}17)$$

and:

$$\alpha \simeq 1 - \tfrac{1}{2}\left(\frac{W}{L_p}\right)^2 . \quad (8.2\text{-}18)$$

Using eqns (8.2-15) and (16), it is readily shown that:

$$\left(\frac{qD_p p_n}{L_p}\right)\coth\left(\frac{W}{L_p}\right) = J_{CB0}\coth^2\left(\frac{W}{L_p}\right) = \frac{J_{CB0}}{(1-\alpha^2)} \quad (8.2\text{-}19)$$

and:

$$\left(\frac{qD_p p_n}{L_p}\right)\operatorname{csch}\left(\frac{W}{L_p}\right) = J_{CB0}\coth^2\left(\frac{W}{L_p}\right)\operatorname{sech}\left(\frac{W}{L_p}\right) = \frac{\alpha J_{CB0}}{(1-\alpha^2)} . \quad (8.2\text{-}20)$$

It is thus possible to eliminate the quantities on the left-hand side of the last two equations, in favour of the electrically measurable parameters α and J_{CB0}, from eqns (8.2-11) and (12) for the emitter and collector currents.

$$J_E = \frac{J_{CB0}}{(1-\alpha^2)} \left\{ \left[\exp\left(\frac{qV_{EB}}{kT}\right) - 1 \right] - \alpha \left[\exp\left(\frac{qV_{CB}}{kT}\right) - 1 \right] \right\} \quad (8.2\text{-}21)$$

$$J_C = \frac{J_{CB0}}{(1-\alpha^2)} \left\{ -\alpha \left[\exp\left(\frac{qV_{EB}}{kT}\right) - 1 \right] + \left[\exp\left(\frac{qV_{CB}}{kT}\right) - 1 \right] \right\}. \quad (8.2\text{-}22)$$

These equations are known as the Ebers-Moll [8.1] equations, in this case restricted to a symmetrical transistor. The main features of the d.c. characteristics can be deduced from these equations. As has already been shown, eqn (8.2-14) results when the collector junction is reverse biased and the terms in V_{EB} are eliminated. More generally, if these terms are eliminated, without necessarily requiring the collector to be reverse biased, the following equation is obtained:

$$-J_C = \alpha J_E - J_{CB0} \left[\exp\left(\frac{qV_{CB}}{kT}\right) - 1 \right]. \quad (8.2\text{-}23)$$

This, of course, includes eqn (8.2-14) as a special case. The characteristics of J_C as a function of V_{CB}, for a given J_E, can be drawn from eqn (8.2-23). A set of such characteristics is shown in fig. 8.2b for values of J_E of J,

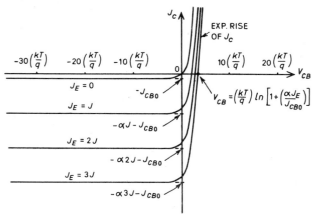

Figure 8.2b. Collector characteristic of a *pnp* transistor

$2J$ and $3J$, where J is some unit of current density. The characteristics of this figure, are based on an equivalent p–n junction characteristic:

$$J_C = J_{CB0} \left[\exp \left(\frac{qV_{CB}}{kT} \right) - 1 \right] . \tag{8.2-24}$$

This is the transistor characteristic for J_E equal to zero, that is, no injection at the emitter. The characteristics for the other values of J_E, can be obtained from this p–n junction characteristic by simply displacing it down, relative to the J_C axis, by a current αJ_E.

Care should be taken, however, not to identify J_{CB0} with any physically measurable reverse saturation current density. Although J_{CB0} is the collector-base leakage current density, it is not the reverse saturation current of the collector-base junction. This latter quantity cannot ever be measured owing to the close proximity of the emitter junction. It is also possible to define J_{CBS}, which is the collector-base leakage current when the collector is reverse biased but the emitter is short circuited to the base, that is V_{EB} is zero. Equations (8.2-12) and (19) show that J_{CBS} is equal to $J_{CB0}/(1 - \alpha^2)$.

In the third quadrant of fig. 8.2b, the characteristics are horizontal and equally spaced for equal increments of J_E; for this quadrant, eqn (8.2-14) is adequate because the collector-base junction is reverse biased. Transistors are normally operated in this quadrant. In the first and fourth quadrants, the transistor is said to be *saturated* or *bottomed*, and the collector-base junction is forward biased. The circuit configuration, however, seldom allows the collector current to become positive*. The supply voltage polarity is such that current is always withdrawn from the collector. This means that operation in the first quadrant does not occur and so a saturated transistor operates in the fourth quadrant.

The characteristics of fig. 8.2b are called the *common-base* characteristics and are used when the base terminal of the transistor is *common* to both input and output circuits. In most amplifiers, transistors are operated in *common-emitter* configuration, that is the emitter terminal is *common* to both input and output circuits. The circuit engineer then

---

* For an n–p–n transistor, this would be negative.

uses the *common-emitter* characteristics; these can be derived from the *common-base* characteristics which are being considered here. It is not within the scope of this book to consider why the *common-emitter* configuration is to be preferred for certain applications. Such considerations will be found in books on transistor circuit engineering [8.2]. The derivation of the *common-emitter* characteristics from those for *common-base* is considered in Appendix II.

Referring once more to fig. 8.2b, the value of V_{CB} for which J_C is zero is, from eqn (8.2-23):

$$V_{CB} = \left(\frac{kT}{q}\right) \ln \left[1 + \left(\frac{\alpha J_E}{J_{CB0}}\right)\right]. \qquad (8.2\text{-}25)$$

This value is only an order greater than (kT/q), equal to 0·026 volt at room temperatures, even when J_E is as much as four or five orders greater than J_{CB0}. Thus comparatively small voltages are all that is required to reduce J_C to zero, and then all the emitter current must flow out of the base terminal.

The emitter input characteristic will next be considered. Referring to eqns (8.2-21) and (22), it is seen that J_E is a function of both V_{EB} and V_{CB} or, if the terms in V_{CB} are eliminated, of both V_{EB} and J_C. That is, the emitter input conditions are a function of the collector output conditions. The device is said to be *bilateral*, in that changes at either emitter or

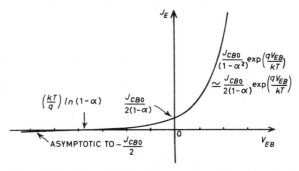

Figure 8.2c. Emitter characteristics of a *pnp* transistor, collector junction reverse biased

collector region affects the behaviour of the other region. When, however, the collector junction is reverse biased, the collector-base voltage does not affect the emitter input conditions, at least, in the model as developed so far. To show this, when $\exp(qV_{CB}/kT)$ is negligible compared with unity; eqn (8.2-21) becomes:

$$J_E = \frac{J_{CB0}}{(1-\alpha^2)} \left[\exp\left(\frac{qV_{EB}}{kT}\right) - (1-\alpha) \right]. \qquad (8.2\text{-}26)$$

Now, α is only slightly less than unity, and hence the term $(1-\alpha)$ can nearly always be neglected compared with the exponential term for positive values of V_{EB}. The characteristic corresponding to eqn (8.2-26) is shown in fig. 8.2c.

8.3 Base Width Modulation

In the previous section, the base width W was assumed to be the fixed separation of the two junctions. More exactly, it should be defined as the distance between the edges of the depletion layers in the base. This is indicated in fig. 8.3a. Two points should be noted; firstly, because the base region is of higher resistivity than either that of the emitter or collector regions, both depletion layers extend mainly into the base, as was shown in section 7.4. Secondly, with normal operation, the emitter junction is forward biased, while the collector junction is reverse biased, and hence the depletion layer at the emitter is usually much narrower

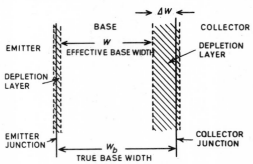

Figure 8.3a. Effective base width

than that at the collector junction. This follows from section 7.6, where it was shown that the width of the depletion layer increases with reverse bias, and tends to zero with forward bias. As a first approximation, to what will be shown ultimately as a second order effect, the collector depletion layer width will be taken into account, but that of the emitter will be neglected. The effective base width is therefore assumed to be:

$$W = W_b - \Delta W \qquad (8.3\text{-}1)$$

where ΔW is proportional either to $(V_I + |V_{CB}|)^{\frac{1}{2}}$, or to $(V_I + |V_{CB}|)^{\frac{1}{3}}$, section 7.6, as appropriate.

The quantities, in the analysis of the previous section, which were dependent on W, and hence on V_{CB}, are J_{CB0} and α. For the present purpose, these may be assumed to have their approximate values as given by eqns (8.2-17) and (18). According to these equations and eqn (8.3-1), J_{CB0} should decrease slightly, and α should increase slightly, with increasing reverse bias of the collector junction. In practice, J_{CB0} increases with increasing reverse bias. This occurs because the decrease associated with decreasing W, is swamped by other effects tending to increase J_{CB0}. These latter effects are the same as those discussed in the last chapter, section 7.7, in connection with the reverse biased p–n junction. They are, increasing volume from which minority carriers, forming the reverse saturation current, can be collected, and avalanching effects of the minority carriers in the depletion layer. In addition, in certain types of transistor, leakage current across the free surface of the base contributes to both J_{CB0} and its increase with reverse bias. The net effect is to cause a slight increase of J_{CB0} with increasing reverse bias, until voltages are approached at which one of the three breakdown mechanisms occurs. These are: avalanche breakdown, Zener breakdown and *punch through*. The first two of these have been discussed in the last chapter, section 7.7, and the third occurs [8.3] when W becomes zero owing to the extension of the depletion layers throughout the whole basewidth W_b. At the onset of breakdown, by any mechanism, J_{CB0} increases sharply with small increases in reverse bias of the collector junction. No further account of breakdown in transistors will be given here.

Excepting breakdown, as described above, the increase in α with the increase of reverse bias, has a more marked effect on the transistor characteristics than that caused by the slight increase in J_{CB0}. When the collector junction is reverse biased by several times (kT/q), eqn (8.2-23) gives:

$$-J_C = \alpha J_E + J_{CB0} . \qquad (8.3\text{-}2)$$

The magnitude of J_C, at constant J_E, increases with increasing reverse bias of the collector junction, through both terms on the right-hand side of the equation. The J_{CB0} contribution is slight, as is also that of αJ_E when J_E is small. At larger J_E, and hence larger magnitude of J_C, the increase in the latter with reverse bias is predominantly due to the αJ_E term. For a given change in α, the change in the magnitude of J_C is proportional to J_E. The $J_C - V_{CB}$ characteristics of fig. 8.2b are replotted

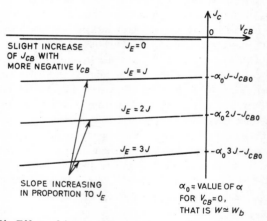

Figure 8.3b. Effect of base width variation on the collector characteristics

in fig. 8.3b, with allowance for this effect. The slope of the characteristics will depend on the base width, the type of collector junction, the value of V_{CB}, and other factors in the equation for the depletion layer thickness. Typically, for a low frequency transistor operating with an emitter current of 1 mA, the slope will be about 1 $\mu\mho$.

The variation of the effective base width with collector junction bias also influences the emitter characteristics of the transistor. Equation (8.2-26) approximates to:

$$J_E = \frac{J_{CB0}}{(1-\alpha^2)} \exp\left(\frac{qV_{EB}}{kT}\right) \qquad (8.3\text{-}3)$$

when the emitter junction is forward biased. The leakage current density J_{CB0} increases slightly with increase of the collector junction reverse bias, but this effect is largely masked by the increase in J_E caused by the denominator factor $(1-\alpha^2)$. The current density J_E, for a given V_{EB}, thus increases with reverse bias of the collector junction. The forward biased part of the characteristic of fig. 8.2c is redrawn in fig. 8.3c

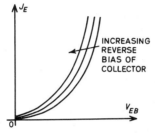

Figure 8.3c. Effect of base width variation on the emitter characteristics

to show this effect. The variation of the input characteristics in this way is often termed the *internal feedback* of the transistor; all the manifestations of base width variation with collector bias are usually referred to as the *Early* [8.4] effect.

8.4 Emitter Injection Efficiency

Up to the present, when considering the emitter junction of a transistor, the current across the junction has been assumed to be exclusively due to holes, injected from the emitter into the base. The validity of this assumption will now be investigated. For the purpose of this discussion, it will be assumed that the collector junction is reverse biased, the normal operating condition; other cases are readily investigated in a manner similar to that to be presented. Base width variation effects will also be neglected.

The forward biasing of the emitter junction, gives rise to an injected hole density p_{0E} in the base, as described in section 8.2. The bias will also cause electrons from the base to be injected into the emitter. Let the electron density on the emitter side of the junction be n_{0E}. The hole density across the base, will drop from p_{0E} to zero at the collector, in an approximately linear fashion. The electron density in the emitter will decay exponentially from n_{0E} to n_p in a distance of approximately

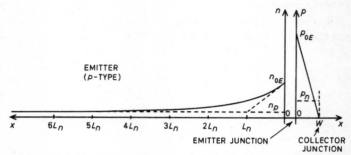

Figure 8.4a. Minority carrier injection across the emitter junction

$5L_n$. The situation is shown in fig. 8.4a. The hole current density across the junction is, when base recombination is neglected:

$$J_p = \left(\frac{qD_p}{W}\right) p_{0E} \qquad (8.4\text{-}1)$$

while the electron current density across the emitter junction is:

$$J_n = \left(\frac{qD_n}{L_n}\right)(n_{0E} - n_p). \qquad (8.4\text{-}2)$$

The injection densities p_{0E} and n_{0E} are given in terms of the equilibrium densities, and the forward bias, by eqns (7.8-8) and (9):

$$n_{0E} = n_p \exp\left(\frac{qV_{EB}}{kT}\right) \qquad (8.4\text{-}3)$$

and:
$$p_{OE} = p_n \exp\left(\frac{qV_{EB}}{kT}\right). \qquad (8.4\text{-}4)$$

From these four equations, and neglecting unity compared with $\exp(qV_{EB}/kT)$, the emitter injection efficiency, γ, which is defined as $J_p/(J_p+J_n)$, is

$$\gamma = \left\{ \frac{D_p\left(\dfrac{p_n}{W}\right)}{D_p\left(\dfrac{p_n}{W}\right) + D_n\left(\dfrac{n_p}{L_n}\right)} \right\}. \qquad (8.4\text{-}5)$$

Because the base resistivity is normally much higher than that of the emitter, n_p will be much less than p_n. Also, W will normally be much less than L_n. The diffusion constants D_p and D_n are of a similar order of magnitude, and so γ will be very close to unity. Values of γ closer to unity than 0·998 are not uncommon. At high-injection-levels, γ tends to decrease as a result of the increased electron density in the base. This effect is not apparent from the equations above, because they are strictly valid only at low injection levels.

The hole current density at the collector junction is $\gamma \alpha J_E$, and hence the emitter to collector current transfer ratio α should be replaced by $\gamma \alpha$. More exactly, this ratio is $\gamma \alpha M$, where M, the avalanche multiplication factor, is given by eqn (7.7-5). This follows, because the current $\alpha \gamma J_E$ is multiplied by M in crossing the collector junction. It is, of course, possible for $\alpha \gamma M$ to be unity or greater, but then operation is very close to the collector breakdown voltage.

8.5 A.C. Characteristics of the Uniform-Base Transistor

Some of the work necessary for a study of the small signal a.c. response of the transistor, at not too high frequencies, has already been carried out in section 6.14 as an example of the solution of the continuity equation. The discussion was restricted to the normal case of reverse biased collector junction. Recombination in the base was neglected, and γ was taken as unity. Equation (6.14-16), of that section, gives the the small signal current density across the emitter junction as:

$$J_{ac}(0) = J_{dc}\left(\frac{\hat{p}_{aco}}{p_{dco}}\right)\left[1 + j\omega\left(\frac{W^2}{2D_p}\right)\right]\exp(j\omega t) \qquad (8.5\text{-}1)$$

for frequencies such that:

$$\left(\sqrt{\frac{\omega}{2D_p}}\right) \cdot W \ll 1 . \qquad (8.5\text{-}2)$$

This condition is equivalent to assuming that the linear distribution of hole density across the base is always maintained in response to changes in the injection density. The injection density p_{dco} is given by eqn (8.2-1), while the total injection density is:*

$$p_0 = p_n\exp\left(\frac{qV_{eb}}{kT}\right) . \qquad (8.5\text{-}3)$$

Taking the differential of this equation, and equating Δp_0 to p_{aco} and ΔV_{eb} to V_{eb}, the small signal emitter voltage:

$$\hat{p}_{aco} = \left(\frac{q}{kT}\right)p_n\exp\left(\frac{qV_{EB}}{kT}\right) \cdot \hat{v}_{eb} = \left(\frac{q}{kT}\right)p_{dco}\hat{v}_{eb} \qquad (8.5\text{-}4)$$

where eqn (8.2-1) has been used again. The small signal a.c. input admittance of the emitter is now obtained from this last equation and eqn (8.5-1):

$$y_{in} = \left(\frac{q}{kT}\right)I_E\left[1 + j\omega\left(\frac{W^2}{2D_p}\right)\right] \qquad (8.5\text{-}5)$$

where I_E is the d.c. component of emitter current.

This admittance corresponds to a resistance:

$$r_\varepsilon = \left(\frac{kT}{q}\right)\left(\frac{1}{I_E}\right) \qquad (8.5\text{-}6)$$

---

* An attempt is being made to use B.S.I. symbols where possible. Thus this equation is similar to eqn (8.2-1), where V_{EB} is the steady or d.c. component of voltage. In the present case, V_{eb} is the total voltage, which includes both d.c. and a.c. components. Unfortunately, B.S.I. notation does not extend to all the symbols and quantities used in this book. In particular, carrier densities cannot be denoted by B.S.I. symbols because of the necessity to distinguish between the total density p and the excess density P.

shunted by a capacitance:

$$C = \left(\frac{q}{kT}\right) I_E \left(\frac{W^2}{2D_p}\right) = \left(\frac{1}{r_\varepsilon}\right)\left(\frac{W^2}{2D_p}\right). \qquad (8.5\text{-}7)$$

The capacitance C is termed the *diffusion* capacitance. In practice, except for the very highest frequency transistors with very narrow base widths, it is always much larger than the depletion capacitance of the emitter junction. This is despite the fact that the net voltage across the junction is small, and so this latter capacitance, eqn (7.6-1 or 2), is in its range of larger values. The reciprocal of the resistance r_ε, is the slope at any point of the emitter input characteristic of fig. 8.2c in the forward biased region; provided this characteristic is plotted in terms of I_E, which is $A J_E$, A being the cross-section area of the junction.

As far as the collector output admittance is concerned, in the absence of base width variation with collector bias, it has a zero conductance as indicated by the characteristics in the third quadrant of fig. 8.2b. It does, however, have a susceptive component corresponding to the depletion capacitance across the collector junction. When base width variation is considered, there is also a conductance component in the output admittance. Base width variation also affects the input impedance. Both these effects will be considered in the next section.

8.6 The Early Equivalent Circuit [8.4]

The results of the previous section, together with some from the consideration of base width variation with collector bias, can be obtained from a simple picture of the hole density distribution across the base of the transistor. Referring to fig. 8.6a(i), p_0 is given by eqn (8.5-3) as previously. Taking γ equal to unity*, and the area of the junction as A, the emitter current is given by:

$$I_e = -q D_p A \left(\frac{dp}{dx}\right) = q D_p A \left(\frac{p_0}{W}\right). \qquad (8.6\text{-}1)$$

The incremental input resistance r_ε is:

* For γ not unity, see J. M. Early [8.4].

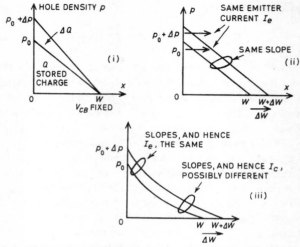

Figure 8.6a. Changes in hole density distribution across the base under small signal conditions, diffusion transistor

(i) Change in V_{eb} while V_{cb} is held constant

(ii) Feedback caused by base width variation at constant I_e

(iii) Change in collector current at constant I_e, with base recombination

$$r_\varepsilon = \left(\frac{\partial V_{eb}}{\partial I_e}\right)_{V_{cb}} = \left(\frac{dV_{eb}}{dp_0}\right)\left(\frac{\partial p_0}{\partial I_e}\right)_W \tag{8.6-2}$$

whence by eqns (8.5-3) and (8.6-1):

$$r_\varepsilon = \left(\frac{kT}{q}\right)\left(\frac{1}{p_0}\right)\left(\frac{W}{qD_p A}\right) = \left(\frac{kT}{q}\right)\left(\frac{1}{I_E}\right). \tag{8.6-3}$$

Now the holes in the base account for a charge Q, called the *stored charge*, which is related to the area of the triangle of fig. 8.6a(i). Thus:

$$Q = \tfrac{1}{2}qAp_0 W. \tag{8.6-4}$$

When V_{eb} is changed, p_0 changes to $(p_0 + \Delta p_0)$, and assuming the hole distribution across the base remains linear, that is the condition of eqn (8.5-2) is valid, Q changes to $(Q + \Delta Q)$ where ΔQ is shown in the figure. The incremental diffusion capacitance is therefore:

$$C = \left(\frac{\partial Q}{\partial V_{eb}}\right)_{V_{cb}} = \left(\frac{\partial Q}{\partial p_0}\right)_W \left(\frac{dp_0}{dV_{eb}}\right) \qquad (8.6\text{-}5)$$

whence by eqns (8.5-3), (8.6-4), (1) and (3):

$$C = \tfrac{1}{2}qAW\left(\frac{q}{kT}\right)p_0 = \left(\frac{q}{kT}\right)\left(\frac{W^2}{2D_p}\right) = \left(\frac{1}{r_\varepsilon}\right)\left(\frac{W^2}{2D_p}\right) \qquad (8.6\text{-}6)$$

which is eqn (8.5-7) again.

To account for effects associated with base width variation with collector bias, Early introduced the concept of a voltage generator, in the emitter circuit, which would be equivalent to a small signal variation of base width. When the emitter is driven from a constant current source, any voltage change at the emitter, consequent on a change of collector bias, is caused by base width variation. Thus in fig. 8.6a(ii), an increase in V_{cb}, that is a reduction of the reverse bias since voltages are measured positively relative to the base, causes an increase in W, and hence in p_0 and V_{eb}, in such a way that I_e remains constant. Now:

$$\Delta W = \left(\frac{dW}{dV_{cb}}\right)\Delta V_{cb} \qquad (8.6\text{-}7)$$

where (dW/dV_{cb}) is positive and can be estimated from eqn (8.3-1) with the aid of eqn (7.4-15) or (7.5-7) as appropriate. From fig. 8.6a(ii) and eqn (8.6-7),

$$\Delta p_0 = \left(\frac{p_0}{W}\right)\Delta W = \left(\frac{p_0}{W}\right)\left(\frac{dW}{dV_{cb}}\right)\Delta V_{cb}\,. \qquad (8.6\text{-}8)$$

But from eqn (8.5-3), and using eqn (8.6-8):

$$\Delta V_{eb} = \left(\frac{kT}{q}\right)\left(\frac{\Delta p_0}{p_0}\right) = \left(\frac{kT}{q}\right)\left(\frac{1}{W}\right)\left(\frac{dW}{dV_{cb}}\right)\Delta V_{cb} = \mu\Delta V_{cb} \qquad (8.6\text{-}9)$$

whence:

$$\mu = \left(\frac{\partial V_{eb}}{\partial V_{cb}}\right)_{I_e} = \left(\frac{kT}{q}\right)\left(\frac{1}{W}\right)\left(\frac{dW}{dV_{cb}}\right). \qquad (8.6\text{-}10)$$

The voltage μv_{cb} is known as the *Early feedback voltage*, or *voltage generator*. The magnitude of μ is generally in the range 10^{-4} to 10^{-3}. The factor μ is related to the input characteristics of fig. 8.3c in that, at any fixed emitter current, it describes the separation of the characteristics of that figure.

It is apparent from inspection of fig. 8.6a(i) and (ii), and from consideration of the foregoing equations, that only minor second order changes would have to be made in the expressions for r_ε, C and μ, if a limited amount of base recombination were allowed. It has been shown in previous parts of the book, that recombination causes only a slight *sag* in the linear distribution of hole density across the base. Such a *sag*, does not significantly effect the arguments used to obtain the expressions for r_ε, C and μ. It is therefore possible to introduce the current transfer ratio α, without altering r_ε, C and μ.

The same approximation is not valid when considering the small signal a.c. output conductance, under the condition of an a.c. open circuit in the emitter; that is constant I_e. Figure 8.6a(ii), shows that the conductance:

$$g_c = \left(\frac{\partial I_c}{\partial V_{cb}} \right)_{I_e} \tag{8.6-11}$$

vanishes to a first order. It will be necessary, therefore, to consider the second order effect of recombination in the base, if a value of g_c is to be obtained. Figure 8.6a(ii) must now be replaced by fig. 8.6a(iii), in which recombination *sag* is shown and where once again ΔI_e is made zero. Equation (8.3-2) may be written as:

$$-I_c = \alpha I_e + I_{CB0} . \tag{8.6-12}$$

Differentiating with respect to V_{cb} gives the conductance:

$$g_c = \left(\frac{\partial I_c}{\partial V_{cb}} \right)_{I_e} = -\left(\frac{d\alpha}{dV_{cb}} \right) I_E - \left(\frac{dI_{CB0}}{dV_{cb}} \right) . \tag{8.6-13}$$

The second term on the righ-hand side is negligible compared with the first, as explained in section 8.3, for all except the lowest I_e. Hence:

$$g_c = -\left(\frac{d\alpha}{dW} \right) \cdot \left(\frac{dW}{dV_{cb}} \right) I_E . \tag{8.6-14}$$

Now by eqn (8.2-18):

$$1-\alpha \simeq \tfrac{1}{2}\left(\frac{W}{L_p}\right)^2 . \tag{8.6-15}$$

It is convenient, with regard to a later section, to consider a more general case; namely:

$$1-\alpha \simeq KW^2 \tag{8.6-16}$$

where K is a constant. Differentiation with respect to W yields:

$$\left(\frac{d\alpha}{dW}\right) \simeq -2KW = -\left(\frac{2}{W}\right)(1-\alpha) . \tag{8.6-17}$$

Substituting into eqn (8.6-14):

$$g_c \simeq 2I_E(1-\alpha)\left(\frac{1}{W}\right)\left(\frac{dW}{dV_{cb}}\right) \tag{8.6-18}$$

Finally, with the aid of eqns (8.6-2) and (10):

$$g_c \simeq \frac{2\mu(1-\alpha)}{r_\varepsilon} . \tag{8.6-19}$$

This is the first, non-zero, approximation to g_c. This conductance gives the slope of the collector characteristics of fig. 8.3b.

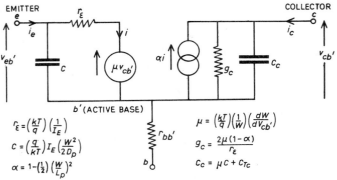

Figure 8.6b. The 'Early' equivalent circuit

The results of this section lead to the formulation of the equivalent circuit of fig. 8.6b, which is commonly known as the *Early* equivalent circuit. This circuit is the basis of a number of other equivalent circuits. The derivations of these circuits from the Early circuit will be found in books on circuit theory. For convenience, however, these circuits are considered in Appendix 1.

The resistor $r_{bb'}$, in the circuit of fig. 8.6b, represents the resistance from the base contact b to the active base region b'. In some transistors this may be quite high, 80 ohms or so. The voltage $V_{cb'}$, between the collector and active base region, is therefore to be used in place of V_{cb} in the expressions of this section. When the a.c. component $v_{cb'}$ of this voltage is zero, the effective base width is held constant and the *Early* voltage is zero. The input admittance between the emitter and the active base region, is then represented by r_ε and C in parallel. Strictly C should be augmented by C_{Te}, the emitter depletion capacitance, but this is usually so small compared with C as to be negligible, as explained previously. The output admittance, when the emitter is open circuit to a.c., that is when the emitter current I_e is held fixed, is the conductance g_c, of eqn (8.6-19) above, shunted by C_{Tc}, the depletion capacitance of the reverse biased junction, plus μC. The *Early* voltage generator is placed in series with r_ε, and not r_ε and C in parallel as might be thought at first. The justification for this, and for the addition of μC to C_{Tc}, will now be considered.

As already explained, when $v_{cb'}$ is zero, the generator $\mu v_{cb'}$ is a short circuit, and C, the input capacity, is correctly placed. On the other hand, when the emitter-active base voltage $V_{eb'}$ is held constant, equivalent to an a.c. short circuit, the influence of C is removed from the circuit of fig. 8.6b altogether. The appropriate diagram is then that of fig. 8.6c(i), the injection density p_0 being held constant despite change of $V_{cb'}$ and hence W. A capacitance, exclusive of the depletion capacitance, then appears between the collector and active base, and has the value:

$$\left(\frac{\partial Q}{\partial V_{cb'}}\right)_{V_{eb'}} = \left(\frac{\partial Q}{\partial W}\right)_{p_0}\left(\frac{dW}{dV_{cb'}}\right) = (\tfrac{1}{2})Aqp_0\left(\frac{dW}{dV_{cb'}}\right) \qquad (8.6\text{-}20)$$

where eqn (8.6-4) has been used. Using eqns (8.6-6) and (10):

$$\left(\frac{\partial Q}{\partial V_{cb'}}\right)_{V_{eb'}} = \left(\frac{kT}{q}\right)\left(\frac{1}{W}\right)\left(\frac{dW}{dV_{cb'}}\right)C = \mu C. \qquad (8.6\text{-}21)$$

This justifies the addition of the capacitance μC to the collector depletion capacitance under the present condition of an a.c. short circuit input. The two elements, C across the input and μC across the output, then represent all the diffusion capacity effects in the base, under general conditions of input and output. This can be seen by examination of fig. 8.6c(ii); the change in charge in the base can be made up of two parts, one part on C and the other part on μC; provided only small signal operation is considered.

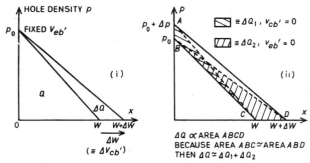

Figure 8.6c. The collector output capacitance:
(i) Effect of base width variation at constant V_{eb}
(ii) Total change of stored base charge

The presence of the current generator αi in the circuit of fig. 8.6b, is almost self explanatory; it represents the fraction of injected current which becomes collector current. It should be noted that the current i is distinguished from the small signal emitter current i_e, because some of the latter flows into the diffusion capacitance. At sufficiently low frequencies, however, i becomes equal to i_e and α is the current gain with zero $v_{cb'}$. At higher frequencies, the effective current gain, with zero $v_{cb'}$, is:

$$\alpha_{h} = \frac{\alpha\left(\dfrac{1}{j\omega C}\right)}{\left(\dfrac{1}{j\omega C} + r_{\varepsilon}\right)} = \frac{\alpha}{\left[1 + j(\omega/\omega_{\alpha})\right]} \qquad (8.6\text{-}22)$$

where:

$$\omega_{\alpha} = \left(\frac{1}{Cr_{\varepsilon}}\right) = \left(\frac{2D_{p}}{W^{2}}\right) \qquad (8.6\text{-}23)$$

is called the α cut-off angular frequency. The dependence of ω_{α} on the inverse square of W should be noted. Transistors for operation at very high frequencies require very narrow base widths W. Plotted on an Argand diagram, the locus of α_{h} is a semicircle as shown in fig. 8.6d.

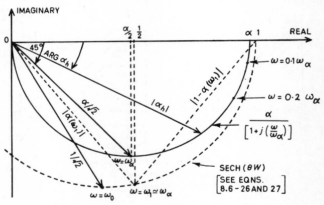

Figure 8.6d. Locus of current gain for diffusion transistor

In practice, departures from this circular locus start to occur even at frequencies appreciably below ω_{α}; for eqn (8.6-23) should be compared with the condition of eqn (8.5-2), which is violated as ω approaches ω_{α}. At such frequencies, the base of the transistor has transmission line like properties and it becomes increasingly difficult to represent the device by lumped parameter equivalent circuits [8.5], [8.6].

A better approximation can be obtained from the equations of section

6.14, prior to the introduction of the condition of eqn (8.5-2) or (6.14-15). Thus from eqn (6.14-13), the a.c. component of emitter current density is:

$$J_{ac}(0) = \left(\frac{qD_p\hat{p}_{aco}}{W}\right) (\theta W) \coth (\theta W) . \tag{8.6-24}$$

In addition, from eqns (6.14-11) and (12), the a.c. component of current density from the base to the reverse biased collector, can be obtained as:

$$J_{ac}(W) = \left(\frac{qD_p\hat{p}_{aco}}{W}\right) (\theta W) \operatorname{csch} (\theta W) . \tag{8.6-25}$$

The ratio of these last two quantities gives an expression for α_h:

$$\alpha_h = \operatorname{sech} (\theta W) \tag{8.6-26}$$

where:

$$\theta = \left(\sqrt{\frac{\omega}{2D_p}}\right) . (1+j) . \tag{8.6-27}$$

It is readily verified, that, under the condition eqn (8.5-2), this reduces to eqn (8.6-22) with α equal to unity. The latter fact is not surprising, for base recombination was neglected in section 6.14. This inaccuracy is easily corrected, the results of section 6.14 being only slightly more involved with allowance for base recombination than without it, but there is little point in doing so for the following reason. Equation (8.6-22) is an accurate description of α_h for those frequencies for which the magnitude of this quantity is not greatly different from α. Equation (8.6-26) would only be used at the higher frequencies, for which the magnitude of α_h departs appreciably from α, and then the error in putting α equal to unity is negligible. Equation (8.6-26) is also plotted on the Argand diagram of fig. 8.6d.

To a first approximation, eqn (8.6-26) once again gives the cut-off frequency as ω_α, eqn (8.6-23). A better approximation is obtained when the magnitude of α_h is written equal to $(1/\sqrt{2})$; then eqns (8.6-26) and (27) give:

$$2 \simeq |1 + \tfrac{1}{2}(\theta W)^2 + \tfrac{1}{24}(\theta W)^4|^2$$

$$= \left| 1 + \tfrac{1}{2}j\omega_0 \left(\frac{W^2}{D_p}\right) - \tfrac{1}{24}\omega_0^2 \left(\frac{W^2}{D_p}\right)^2 \right| \simeq 1 + \tfrac{1}{6}\omega_0^2 \left(\frac{W^2}{D_p}\right)^2 \tag{8.6-28}$$

or:
$$\omega_0 = (\sqrt{6}).\left(\frac{D_p}{W^2}\right) = 2\cdot45\left(\frac{D_p}{W^2}\right). \tag{8.6-29}$$

This cut-off frequency ω_0 is $22\frac{1}{2}\%$ higher than ω_α. The phase shift at ω_0 is approximately, from eqn (8.6-28):

$$\phi_0 \simeq -\tan^{-1}\left\{\frac{\omega_0\left(\dfrac{W^2}{D_p}\right)}{2\left[1 - \dfrac{\omega_0^2}{24}\left(\dfrac{W^2}{D_p}\right)^2\right]}\right\}$$

$$= -\tan^{-1}\left(\frac{2\sqrt{6}}{3}\right) = -58° \tag{8.6-30}$$

compared with $-45°$ at ω_α in eqn (8.6-22).

The simplicity of form of eqn (8.6-22) makes it very suitable for use in circuit analysis. It is unfortunate, therefore, that it is inaccurate except for frequencies which are very small compared with ω_α. One simple way of extending its usefulness, is to replace ω_α with another frequency, determined experimentally or theoretically, to give a more accurate representation of α_h. A suitable frequency for this purpose is ω_1, fig. 8.6d, at which the real part of α_h is equal to a half. This is closely equal to the frequency for which the magnitude of α is equal to the magnitude of $(1-\alpha)$. Experimentally, this latter frequency is readily measured, for it corresponds to the case when the magnitude of the common emitter current gain β, which is equal to $\alpha/(1-\alpha)$, is unity. There are, however, some difficulties with such measurements, see for example ref. [8.7].

To the order of approximation adopted in eqn (8.6-28), it is readily shown that ω_1 is equal to ω_α and so, to this order, eqn (8.6-22) is accurate for frequencies up to say one fifth of ω_α.*

Before concluding this section, the significance of eqn (8.6-24) for the determination of the input admittance at the emitter, at higher frequen-

---

* There is a possibility of confusion here; some authors and manufacturers define ω_α as the experimentally determined frequency corresponding to ω_0 of the present text. In this text ω_α is always $(2D_p/W^2)$.

cies, will be noted. Thus if $\hat{p}_{aco}$ is eliminated using eqn (8.5-4), and subsequently p_{dco} with eqn (8.4-1), the input admittance becomes:

$$y_{in} = \left(\frac{q}{kT}\right) I_E.(\theta W) \coth (\theta W) . \tag{8.6-31}$$

This equation enables the input conductance and susceptance at any frequency to be calculated.

8.7 D.C. Characteristics of the Graded-Base Transistor

Some account of the one-dimensional *drift*, i.e. *graded-base*, transistor has been given in section 6.7. The extent to which that account can be elaborated here, is limited by the complexity of the device. The principle difficulty, which arises in any attempt to analyse the behaviour of the drift transistor, is associated with the solution of the continuity equation. In the first instance, it is not possible to specialize to the diffusion continuity equation, because appreciable drift currents flow in the base of the transistor. Also, the equations to be solved no longer have constant coefficients, for the diffusion lengths and lifetimes are functions of the impurity content.

A start will be made by reiterating the results of section 6.7, wherein base recombination was neglected and low-level-injection was assumed. In that section, the hole current density across the base was shown to be, eqn (6.7-5):

$$J_p = \left(\frac{qD_p p_0}{\chi W}\right) \tag{8.7-1}$$

where, from eqn (6.7-4):

$$\chi = \left(\frac{1}{n_n(0)\,W}\right) \int_0^W n_n(x)dx \tag{8.7-2}$$

for the case when the collector junction is reverse biased. In addition, the hole density across the base was given by, eqn (6.7-6):

$$p(x) = \left(\frac{p_0}{\chi W}\right)\left(\frac{\int_x^W n_n(x')dx'}{n_n(x)}\right). \tag{8.7-3}$$

The density $n_n(x)$, of majority carriers in the base, is assumed to be equal to the net donor density at any point, and for practical transistors, it is a monotonically decreasing function of x. A close approximation to what would be obtained in a transistor manufactured by one of the impurity diffusion processes is:

$$n_n(x) = n_n(0) \exp \left(-m \frac{x}{W}\right). \tag{8.7-4}$$

For this distribution, the ratio of impurity concentration at the emitter edge of the base to that at the collector edge of the base is $\exp(m)$, where m is a positive quantity. Although in theory, the method of analysis to be presented can be used with any impurity distribution law, that of eqn (8.7-4) leads to simple analytical results. It is used therefore for this reason, in preference to a more exact law, for example, the $\mathrm{erf}c(x)$ relation [8.8]. The distribution of eqn (8.7-4) will be referred to as the *exponentially-graded-base* distribution.

Using eqns (8.7-2) and (4), calculation of χ for the *exponentially-graded-base* case yields:

$$\chi = \left(\frac{1}{W}\right) \int_0^W \exp \left(-\frac{mx}{W}\right) dx = \left(\frac{1}{m}\right)[1 - \exp(-m)]. \tag{8.7-5}$$

As m increases from zero, the *uniform-base case*, χ decreases from unity monotonically towards zero. For values of m in excess of three, χ is approximately $(1/m)$.

The hole distribution is obtained from eqns (8.7-3) and (4) and is:

$$p(x) = \left(\frac{p_0}{\chi W}\right) \left\{ \frac{\int_x^W \exp \left(-\frac{mx'}{W}\right) dx'}{\exp \left(-\frac{mx}{W}\right)} \right\}$$

$$= p_0 \left\{ \frac{\exp(m) - \exp \left(\frac{mx}{W}\right)}{\exp(m) - 1} \right\} \tag{8.7-6}$$

For m in excess of three, this approximates to:

$$p(x) = p_0 \left\{ 1 - \exp \left[-m \left(1 - \frac{x}{W} \right) \right] \right\} \qquad (8.7\text{-}7)$$

which indicates that $p(x)$, for the larger values of m, remains substantially equal to p_0 over most of the base width, and then drops fairly abruptly to zero as x closely approaches W; see fig. 8.7a. For such values of m,

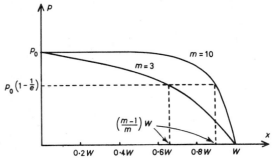

Figure 8.7a. Hole density distribution, exponentially graded base transistor

as a rough estimate, the *stored charge* of the holes in the base is twice that of the *uniform base* transistor, for the same injection level p_0, but the current flow supported is m times as large. Alternatively, the same current flow may be supported in a transistor with *exponentially-graded-base*, as in a *uniform-base* transistor, but with a stored charge which is a factor $(2/m)$ lower than that for the latter transistor. This, as will be explained subsequently, allows higher frequencies of operation.

As explained earlier in this section, estimation of recombination in the base cannot now be made from a solution of the continuity equation for the diffusion of minority carriers. The magnitude of the recombination current can, however, be estimated from the hole density distribution of eqn (8.7-3) and the more general continuity equation of section 6.9. For the one-dimensional transistor under consideration, eqn (6.9-7) becomes, in the steady state:

$$\left(\frac{dJ_p}{dx} \right) = -q \left[\frac{p(x) - p_n(x)}{\tau_p} \right]. \qquad (8.7\text{-}8)$$

Integrating this equation:

$$J_p(x) = J_p(0) - q \int_0^x \left[\frac{p(x) - p_n(x)}{\tau_p} \right] dx . \qquad (8.7\text{-}9)$$

The second term on the right-hand side of this equation, represents the loss of hole current caused by recombination in the distance 0 to x. In the present case $J_p(0)$ is the injected current density at the emitter junction, and the integration would be performed up to x equal to W, in order to give the current density across the collector junction. The hole density $p(x)$ used in this integral, is that given by eqn (8.7-3), which was derived in the absence of recombination. Thus, eqn (8.7-9) would give a first approximation to the recombination current, and strictly, the $J_p(x)$ obtained should be used to re-estimate $p(x)$, from which a better approximation to $J_p(x)$ could then be obtained. For the example under discussion, the first approximation will suffice. It has been pointed out already that τ_p depends on the impurity density, and hence on x. To perform the integration of eqn (8.7-9), the form of this dependence is needed. In what follows, however, for simplicity, it will be assumed that τ_p is a constant.

The integration will first be carried out for the *uniform-base* transistor. Here, χ is equal to unity and $p(x)$ falls linearly to zero across the base. The collector current density J_C is then:*

$$\begin{aligned}
-J_C = J_p(W) &= J_E - \left(\frac{q}{\tau_p} \right) \int_0^W \left\{ p_0 \left(1 - \frac{x}{W} \right) - p_n \right\} dx \\
&= J_E - \left(\frac{q}{\tau_p} \right) \left\{ \tfrac{1}{2} p_0 W - p_n W \right\} . \qquad (8.7\text{-}10)
\end{aligned}$$

The bracketed term on the right-hand side of this equation is small compared with J_E, because it represents the base recombination current. Hence the approximation; from (eqn 8.7-1):

$$p_0 \simeq \left(\frac{W}{q D_p} \right) J_E \qquad (8.7\text{-}11)$$

* Note: currents flowing into the base are positive by convention.

may be used in this term without causing undue error. Thus:

$$-J_C = \left[1 - \tfrac{1}{2}\left(\frac{W^2}{D_p \tau_p}\right)\right] J_E + \left(\frac{q p_n W}{\tau_p}\right). \tag{8.7-12}$$

Replacing $D_p \tau_p$ by L_p^2, this is:

$$-J_C = \left[1 - \tfrac{1}{2}\left(\frac{W}{L_p}\right)^2\right] J_E + \left(\frac{q D_p p_n}{L_p}\right)\left(\frac{W}{L_p}\right) \tag{8.7-13}$$

which has the form of eqn (8.2-14) and gives the approximations, eqns (8.2-17) and (18) respectively, for J_{CBO} and α obtained earlier. This calculation for the uniform-base transistor, was performed simply to show the order of accuracy which this approximation technique should yield.

For a transistor with *exponentially-graded-base*, χ and $p(x)$ are given by eqns (8.7-5) and (6) respectively. The density $p_n(x)$ is deduced from eqn (8.7-4); it is $p_n(0)\exp(mx/W)$ for the product pn is a constant, n_i^2, which is independent of x. The integration of eqn (8.7-9) in this case is:

$$-J_C = J_E - \left(\frac{q}{\tau_p}\right)\int_0^W \left\{ p_0 \left[\frac{\exp(m) - \exp\left(m\,\dfrac{x}{W}\right)}{\exp(m) - 1}\right] - p_n(0)\exp\left(\frac{mx}{W}\right) \right\} dx$$

$$= J_E - \left[\frac{\exp(m)}{\exp(m) - 1} - \frac{1}{m}\right]\left(\frac{qWp_0}{\tau_p}\right) + \left[\frac{p_n(W) - p_n(0)}{m}\right]\left(\frac{qW}{\tau_p}\right). \tag{8.7-14}$$

Equations (8.7-1) and (5) give the approximate relationship:

$$p_0 \simeq \left[\frac{\exp(m) - 1}{m \exp(m)}\right]\left(\frac{W}{q D_p}\right) J_E \tag{8.7-15}$$

which may be used in the small recombination term of eqn (8.7-14):

$$-J_C = \left\{1 - \left[\frac{(m-1)\exp(m) + 1}{m^2 \exp(m)}\right]\left(\frac{W}{L_p}\right)^2\right\} J_E +$$

$$+ \left[\frac{p_n(W) - p_n(0)}{m}\right]\left(\frac{q D_p}{L_p}\right)\left(\frac{W}{L_p}\right). \tag{8.7-16}$$

Thus:
$$\alpha = \left\{ 1 - \left[\frac{(m-1)\exp(m)+1}{m^2 \exp(m)} \right] \left(\frac{W}{L_p} \right)^2 \right\} \qquad (8.7\text{-}17)$$

and:
$$J_{\text{CB0}} = \left[\frac{p_n(W)-p_n(0)}{m} \right] \left(\frac{qD_p}{L_p} \right) \left(\frac{W}{L_p} \right). \qquad (8.7\text{-}18)$$

It is evident from eqn (8.7-17), that with increasing m, α should more closely approach unity. It is readily established that the factor multiplying $(W/L_p)^2$ in eqn (8.7-17) is $(1/2)$ for m equal to zero, the *uniform-base* case. For m greater than three, the factor is approximately $(m-1)/m^2$ and tends to $(1/m)$ for larger values of m.

Although space has not permitted presentation of all results, it should now be evident that all the work of section 8.2 on the d.c. characteristics of the *uniform-base* transistor can be repeated for the *graded-base* transistor, in particular, for the *exponentially-graded-base* transistor.

However, in view of the dependence of α and J_{CB0} on m, in the last two equations, it must be expected that the symmetry of the *Ebers-Moll* equations will be lost. It is then necessary to define two current gains α_N and α_I, the former being the α of this section and the latter being that for the transistor with the roles of the emitter and collector interchanged. Similarly, it is also necessary to distinguish between J_{CB0} for the collector junction and J_{EB0} for the emitter junction. The form of the *Ebers-Moll* equations, for a non-symmetrical transistor, will be briefly considered again in section 8.10.

Finally, it must be remembered that, in the work of this section, τ_p has been assumed constant. This is certainly not justified for the larger values of the index m. The expressions of this section must therefore be considered simply as an indication of what happens in a *graded-base* transistor. A knowledge of the variation of τ_p with n_n would allow, by the same method as here presented, more exact expressions to be obtained. Some indication of a relationship between τ_p and n_n can be found in section 6.16.

8.8 The Early Equivalent Circuit of the Graded-Base Transistor

In this section, attention will be confined to the lower frequencies of operation for which an equivalent circuit, similar to the Early circuit of section 8.6, is applicable.

The incremental input resistance r_ε of the emitter, when $V_{cb'}$ is held constant, has the same expression for the *graded-base* transistor as for the *uniform-base* transistor. This is readily seen by differentiating eqn (8.7-1), when:

$$\left(\frac{1}{r_\varepsilon}\right) = \left(\frac{qD_pA}{\chi W}\right)\left(\frac{dp_0}{dV_{eb'}}\right) = \left(\frac{qD_pA}{\chi W}\right)\left(\frac{q}{kT}\right)p_0 \qquad (8.8\text{-}1)$$

where (eqn 8.5-3) has been used. Using eqn (8.7-1) again:

$$r_\varepsilon = \left(\frac{kT}{q}\right)\left(\frac{1}{I_E}\right) \qquad (8.8\text{-}2)$$

which is identical with eqns (8.5-6) and (8.6-3).

The incremental diffusion capacitance C is deduced in a similar manner to that used in section 8.6. For this derivation, the equivalent expression to eqn (8.6-4) for the total charge of the stored holes, is required. It is:

$$Q = qA \int_0^W p(x)\,dx. \qquad (8.8\text{-}3)$$

A first approximation to this integral is readily available from eqn (8.7-3) for $p(x)$:

$$Q = \left(\frac{qAp_0}{\chi W}\right)\int_0^W \left\{\frac{\int_x^W n_n(x')\,dx'}{n_n(x)}\right\}dx. \qquad (8.8\text{-}4)$$

The diffusion capacitance is then, with the aid of eqns (8.5-3) and (8.8-2):

$$\begin{aligned}
C &= \left(\frac{\partial Q}{\partial V_{eb'}}\right)_{V_{cb'}} = \left(\frac{\partial Q}{\partial p_0}\right)_W\left(\frac{dp_0}{dV_{eb}}\right) \\[2mm]
&= \left(\frac{q}{kT}\right)p_0\left(\frac{qA}{\chi W}\right)\int_0^W \left\{\frac{\int_x^W n_n(x')\,dx'}{n_n(x)}\right\}dx \\[2mm]
&= \left(\frac{1}{r_\varepsilon D_p}\right)\int_0^W \left\{\frac{\int_x^W n_n(x')\,dx'}{n_n(x)}\right\}dx. \qquad (8.8\text{-}5)
\end{aligned}$$

It is readily shown that this reduces to eqn (8.6-6) for the *uniform-base* transistor, when $n_n(x)$ is taken as a constant. For the transistor with *exponentially-graded-base*, the majority carrier distribution of eqn (8.7-4) is used in the integrand of the last equation. The diffusion capacitance then becomes:

$$C = \left(\frac{1}{r_\varepsilon D_p}\right) \int_0^W \left\{ \frac{\int_x^W \exp\left(-\frac{mx'}{W}\right) dx'}{\exp\left(-\frac{mx}{W}\right)} \right\} dx$$

$$= \left(\frac{2}{m^2}\right) \left[(m-1) + \exp(-m)\right] \left(\frac{1}{r_\varepsilon}\right) \left(\frac{W^2}{2D_p}\right). \qquad (8.8\text{-}6)$$

The factor $(1/r_\varepsilon)(W^2/2D_p)$ is the diffusion capacitance of the *uniform-base* transistor. The other factor $(2/m^2)[(m-1) + \exp(-m)]$ is unity for m equal to zero, the *uniform-base* case, and tends to zero as m increases from zero. For large values of m, this latter factor is approximately $(2/m)$. The first approximation to the cut-off frequency ω_α, eqn (8.6-23) is:

$$\omega_\alpha = \left(\frac{1}{Cr_\varepsilon}\right) = \left[\frac{(\frac{1}{2})m^2}{(m-1) + \exp(-m)} \right] \left(\frac{2D_p}{W^2}\right) \qquad (8.8\text{-}7)$$

which for large values of m, is a factor $(m/2)$ greater than that for the *uniform-base* transistor.

Next, it is necessary to consider the *Early* feedback effect. From section 8.6, it will readily be seen that:

$$\mu = \left(\frac{kT}{q}\right) \left(\frac{1}{p_0}\right) \left(\frac{\partial p_0}{\partial W}\right)_{I_e} \left(\frac{dW}{dV_{cb'}}\right). \qquad (8.8\text{-}8)$$

In that section, for the *uniform-base* transistor, $(\partial p_0/\partial W)_{I_e}$ was obtained from fig. 8.6a(i) as (p_0/W), which, on substitution into eqn (8.8-8), yields the expression for μ given by eqn (8.6-10). For the *graded-base* transistor, $(\partial p_0/\partial W)$ is more complex than (p_0/W). Great care must be exercised in the choice of equation to be used for deducing the required derivative. Equation (8.7-15) must be avoided, for it involves an impurity distribution having a specified value at W, namely a factor $\exp(m)$ down on the density at x equal to zero. Any derivative with respect to W, would erroneously maintain this condition at the collector junction. It is necessary to revert to the original eqns (8.7-1) and (2), which combined give the following approximate relation:

$$p_0 \simeq \left(\frac{J_E}{qD_p n_n(0)}\right) \int_0^W n_n(x)\, dx\ . \tag{8.8-9}$$

Differentiating with respect to W;

$$\left(\frac{\partial p_0}{\partial W}\right)_{J_E} \simeq \left(\frac{J_E}{qD_p}\right)\left(\frac{n_n(W)}{n_n(0)}\right) = \left(\frac{p_0}{W}\right)\left(\frac{1}{\chi}\right)\left(\frac{n_n(W)}{n_n(0)}\right) \tag{8.8-10}$$

whence:

$$\mu \simeq \left(\frac{1}{\chi}\right)\left(\frac{n_n(W)}{n_n(0)}\right)\left(\frac{kT}{q}\right)\left(\frac{1}{W}\right)\left(\frac{dW}{dV_{cb'}}\right). \tag{8.8-11}$$

This differs by the factor $(1/\chi)(n_n(W)/n_n(0))$ from that for the *uniform-base* transistor.

This factor is $m/[\exp(m)-1]$ for the *exponentially-graded-base* transistor and decreases from unity as m increases from zero, the *uniform-base* case. When m is in excess of three, the factor is about a third, and it decreases rapidly for larger values of m.

The derivation of the collector conductance g_c, of the circuit of fig. 8.6b, for the *graded-base* transistor, is similar to that for the *uniform-base* case, as far as eqn (8.6-18). This follows because $(1-\alpha)$ for the *graded-base* transistor is proportional to W^2, see eqn (8.7-17), and so the working through eqns (8.6-15) to (18) is unchanged. The expression for g_c is best left in the form of the last of these equations, that is as:

$$g_c = 2I_E(1-\alpha)\left(\frac{1}{W}\right)\left(\frac{dW}{dV_{cb'}}\right) \tag{8.8-12}$$

or using eqn (8.8-2), as:

$$g_c = \left[\frac{2(1-\alpha)}{r_\varepsilon}\right]\left(\frac{kT}{q}\right)\left(\frac{1}{W}\right)\left(\frac{dW}{dV_{cb'}}\right) \tag{8.8-13}$$

which are both independent of the form of the impurity distribution across the base. When expressed in terms of μ, with the aid of eqn (8.8-11), g_c becomes:

$$g_c = \chi \left[\frac{n_n(0)}{n_n(W)} \right] \left[\frac{2\mu(1-\alpha)}{r_\varepsilon} \right]. \tag{8.8-14}$$

The feedback factor, μ, involves the reciprocal of $\chi[n_n(0)/n_n(W)]$ and so this last equation fails to give a direct indication of how g_c varies with impurity grading across the base.

It remains to find the fraction of the diffusion capacitance which appears between the collector and the active base, analogous to that given by eqn (8.6-21) for the *uniform-base* transistor. This capacitance is:

$$\left(\frac{\partial Q}{\partial V_{cb'}} \right)_{V_{eb'}} = \left(\frac{\partial Q}{\partial W} \right)_{p_0} \left(\frac{dW}{dV_{cb'}} \right). \tag{8.8-15}$$

The term $(\partial Q/\partial W)_{p_0}$, can be obtained from the expression for Q, eqn (8.8-4), but since χ involves W, its value, eqn (8.7-2), must be inserted into the expression for Q before differentiation with respect to W. More simply, this term may be found by differentiating eqn (8.7-3), again using the full expression for χ, to give $(\partial p(x)/\partial W)_{p_0}$, and then integrating this with respect to x over the range zero to W. Either method yields:

$$\left(\frac{dQ}{\partial V_{cb'}} \right)_{V_{eb'}} = \frac{qAp_0 n_n(0)n_n(W)}{\left[\int_0^W n_n(x).dx \right]^2} \int_0^W \left\{ \frac{\int_0^x n_n(x')dx'}{n_n(x)} \right\} dx. \tag{8.8-16}$$

With the aid of eqns (8.8-5) and (11), this may be expressed as:

$$\left(\frac{\partial Q}{\partial V_{cb'}} \right)_{V_{eb'}} = \mu C \left[\frac{\int_0^W \left\{ \frac{\int_0^x n_n(x')dx'}{n_n(x)} \right\} dx}{\int_0^W \left\{ \frac{\int_x^W n_n(x')dx'}{n_n(x)} \right\} dx} \right]. \tag{8.8-17}$$

For the *uniform-base* transistor it is readily shown that this reduces to

μC as given by eqn (8.6-21), while for the *exponentially-graded-base* it becomes, with the distribution of eqn (8.7-4):

$$\left(\frac{\partial Q}{\partial V_{cb'}}\right)_{V_{eb'}} = \mu C \left\{ \frac{\exp(m) - (m+1)}{\exp(-m) + (m-1)} \right\}. \qquad (8.8\text{-}18)$$

This increases from μC for m zero, the *uniform-base* case, to, for m large, $[\exp(m)\mu C/m]$. It must be remembered however, that μ, eqn (8.8-11), is decreased below the *uniform-base* μ by the factor $m/[\exp(m)-1]$. For large m therefore, $(\partial Q/\partial V_{cb'})_{V_{eb'}}$ is the product of C and the *uniform-base* μ, and thus it decreases with increasing m in the same way as the diffusion capacitance itself.

Before leaving the case of the *graded-base* transistor one last feature will be noted. The grading of the base resistivity results in a comparatively high resistivity adjacent to the collector junction. This reduces the collector depletion layer capacitance, that is the output capacitance. This is particularly advantageous when the transistor is used in *common-emitter* configuration, for this capacitance then acts as a feedback path between output and input circuits.

8.9 The Transistor as a Charge Controlled Device

For applications in switching circuits, it is often convenient to consider the transistor as a charge controlled device [8.9]. A brief account of this topic, applicable to a one-dimensional transistor, will be given in this section. By way of illustration, the *uniform-base* transistor will be considered. Initially it will be assumed that the collector junction is reverse biased. In the steady state, the hole density distribution across the base then falls in an approximately linear fashion from p_{0E} at the emitter junction to zero at the collector junction. The total hole charge Q_B in the base is given by, when recombination is neglected:

$$Q_B = \left(\frac{1}{2}\right) q p_{0E} A W. \qquad (8.9\text{-}1)$$

The collector current I_C is given approximately by the gradient of the hole density across the base:

$$-I_C = \left(\frac{qD_p p_{0E} A}{W}\right) = \left(\frac{Q_B}{T_C}\right) \qquad (8.9\text{-}2)$$

where:

$$T_C = \left(\frac{W^2}{2D_p}\right). \qquad (8.9\text{-}3)$$

Note that, T_C is the reciprocal of ω_α of the simple transistor model of section 8.6. The time constant T_C is also readily interpreted, from eqn (8.9-2), as the mean transit time of holes crossing the base. It can be said that the charge Q_B *controls* the collector current I_C, provided the hole density distribution across the base remains substantially linear from p_{0e} to zero. This follows because eqn (8.9-2) shows that I_C is proportional to Q_B and hence if Q_B is changed, I_C will change accordingly.

Next, the base current I_B is considered. This arises out of recombination, and so it is necessary to consider the current transfer ratio across the base. A fraction $(1-\alpha)$ of the current across the emitter junction becomes recombination current in the base. For the one-dimensional model being considered $(1-\alpha)$ is approximately $(1/2)(W/L_p)^2$, eqn (8.2-18). Thus, using eqn (8.9-2); and assuming that I_{CB0} is negligible:

$$-I_B = \left(\frac{1}{2}\right)\left(\frac{W}{L_p}\right)^2 I_C = \left(\frac{1}{2}\right)\left(\frac{W}{L_p}\right)^2 \left(\frac{Q_B}{T_C}\right) = \left(\frac{Q_B}{T_B}\right) \qquad (8.9\text{-}4)$$

where

$$T_B = \left(\frac{L_p^2}{D_p}\right). \qquad (8.9\text{-}5)$$

The time constant T_B is equal to τ_p, the excess hole lifetime in the base material. It is apparent from eqns (8.9-3) and (5) that T_B is very much greater than T_C. Again, it can be said that the base current I_B is *controlled* by the base charge Q_B. The emitter current is:*

* There is a slight inconsistency in this approach. A constant hole-density gradient across the base is assumed. The normal implication of this would be to make I_E and $|I_C|$ equal, and I_B zero. However, in this simple model, the best of both worlds is sought, namely a constant hole density gradient, but values of I_E and $|I_C|$ differing by the recombination current $|I_B|$.

$$I_E = -(I_B + I_C) = Q_B \left(\frac{1}{T_C} + \frac{1}{T_B} \right) \tag{8.9-6}$$

and so the current transfer ratio may be defined in terms of the time constants T_C and T_B:

$$\alpha \simeq \left[1 - \left(\frac{T_C}{T_B} \right) \right]. \tag{8.9-7}$$

Under transient conditions, the base charge Q_b will be a function of time. The hole current necessary, for altering the stored base charge, is drawn from the emitter, and the equal electron current, necessary to maintain charge equilibrium, from the base terminal. It is assumed, however, in common with section 8.6, that the hole distribution across the base readjusts to its approximately linear form, without delay, following changes in the injection level p_{oe}. Under transient conditions, therefore, the currents become:

$$-I_c = \left(\frac{Q_b}{T_c} \right) \tag{8.9-8}$$

$$-I_b = \left(\frac{Q_b}{T_b} \right) + \left(\frac{dQ_b}{dt} \right) \tag{8.9-9}$$

$$I_e = Q_b \left(\frac{1}{T_C} + \frac{1}{T_B} + \frac{dQ_b}{dt} \right). \tag{8.9-10}$$

When either the base current I_b, or the emitter current I_e, is a known function of time, determined by some external circuit constraint, the appropriate differential equation can be solved for the time dependent Q_b. Equation (8.9-8) then gives the time dependence of the collector current I_c. This is a very useful approach for investigating the switching times of transistors, for pulse operation, in different circuit arrangements: it is, however, left to books on circuit theory to investigate the detailed solutions of these equations [8.10]. Some simple cases are, however, considered in Appendix III.

For very low injection levels, the hole distribution across the base departs appreciably from linearity; see fig. 8.9a(i). The equations as

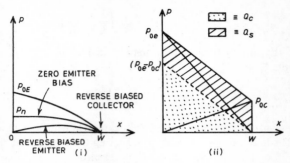

Figure 8.9a. Hole density distributions and stored charges in the base of a diffusion transistor:

(i) At very low injection levels

(ii) In the saturated condition

derived above are not then valid. The form of the equations can only be maintained with the aid of time constants T_C and T_B, which have become injection level dependent. Analytical solutions of the equations do not then in general exist. Similar remarks apply to very high levels of injection.

The same equations may be used for the *graded-base* transistor, but the values of T_C and T_B will differ from those given by eqns (8.9-3) and (5). A knowledge of the impurity distribution across the base enables the time constants to be determined. Thus, for the *exponentially-graded-base* transistor, considered in this chapter, it may be deduced from eqns (8.7-17), (8.8-7) and (8.9-4) that:

$$T_C = \left[\frac{(m-1)+\exp(-m)}{(\frac{1}{2})m^2}\right]\left(\frac{W^2}{2D_p}\right) \qquad (8.9\text{-}11)$$

$$T_B = \left[\frac{(m-1)+\exp(-m)}{(\frac{1}{2})m^2}\right]\left(\frac{L_p^2}{D_p}\right). \qquad (8.9\text{-}12)$$

For large m, the time constants are reduced by a factor $(m/2)$ compared with those for the *uniform-base* case.

Turning now to the case when both junctions are forward biased, that is the transistor is saturated, the hole distribution across the base is approximately linear, being p_{oe} at the emitter junction and p_{oc} at the collector junction. This is shown in fig. 8.2a, which also shows that the distribution can be resolved into two additive components, one corresponding to a reverse biased collector junction and the other to a reverse biased emitter junction. The total charge Q_b, can, therefore, be expressed as the sum of two charges, Q_{bf} and Q_{br}, forward and reverse injection charges, corresponding to reverse biased collector and emitter junctions respectively. The linearity of eqns (8.9-8), (9) and (10), thus allows the terminal currents for the saturated transistor to be written as:

$$I_c = Q_{br}\left(\frac{1}{T_E} + \frac{1}{T_{Br}}\right) + \left(\frac{dQ_{br}}{dt}\right) - \left(\frac{Q_{bf}}{T_C}\right) \qquad (8.9\text{-}13)$$

$$-I_b = \left(\frac{Q_{bf}}{T_{Bf}}\right) + \left(\frac{dQ_{bf}}{dt}\right) + \left(\frac{Q_{br}}{T_{Br}}\right) + \left(\frac{dQ_{br}}{dt}\right) \qquad (8.9\text{-}14)$$

$$I_e = Q_{bf}\left(\frac{1}{T_C} + \frac{1}{T_{Bf}}\right) + \left(\frac{dQ_{bf}}{dt}\right) - \left(\frac{Q_{br}}{T_E}\right). \qquad (8.9\text{-}15)$$

For the symmetrical transistor under consideration, T_{Bf} and T_{Br} will be the same, so will T_C and T_E. For asymmetric transistors, for example one-dimensional drift transistors and three-dimensional transistors, the distinction between these quantities must be maintained. Practical asymmetric transistors will have T_C less than T_E and T_{Bf} less than T_{Br}.

Specification of two of the three terminal currents, as functions of time, say by some external circuit arrangement, enables eqns (8.9-13), (14) and (15) to be solved for Q_{bf}, Q_{br} and the remaining terminal current. Again, specific solutions of these equations are not within the scope of the present book; they are considered in books on transistor circuit theory.

Sometimes, it is not possible to specify the terminal currents, from external circuit conditions, without knowledge of the terminal voltages.* These may be expressed in terms of the base charge components Q_{bf}

---

* The fact that it is ever possible to specify the currents without knowledge of the terminal voltages is due to the fact that these latter voltages are often negligible compared with externally impressed e.m.f.'s.

and Q_{br}. For example, from eqn (8.2-1):

$$V_{eb} = \left(\frac{kT}{q}\right) \ln \left(\frac{p_{oe}}{p_n}\right). \tag{8.9-16}$$

Now, $$Q_{bf} \simeq q p_{oe} W A \tag{8.9-17}$$

and so eliminating p_{oe} between these two equations:

$$V_{eb} \simeq \left(\frac{kT}{q}\right) \ln \left(\frac{Q_{bf}}{p_n q W A}\right). \tag{8.9-18}$$

Also, from eqns (8.2-17) and (8.9-5); a charge Q_{B0} equal to the product of I_{CB0} and T_B can be defined:

$$p_n q W A \simeq I_{CB0} \left(\frac{L_p^2}{D_p}\right)$$

$$= I_{CB0} T_B = Q_{B0}. \tag{8.9-19}$$

Hence, $$V_{eb} \simeq \left(\frac{kT}{q}\right) \ln \left(\frac{Q_{bf}}{Q_{B0}}\right). \tag{8.9-20}$$

The terminal voltage V_{cb} can be similarly defined. Such expressions, when used in conjunction with external circuit conditions to define the terminal currents, enable eqns (8.9-8), (9) and (10) and eqns (8.9-13), (14) and (15), to be solved for the base charge Q_{bf} and Q_{br} as functions of time.

When a transistor is in saturation, it is sometimes more convenient to express the charge control relations, eqns (8.9-13), (14) and (15), in terms of two charges Q_c and Q_s, instead of Q_{bf} and Q_{br}. The charges Q_c and Q_s are defined by, see fig. 8.9a(ii) and using simple geometry:

$$Q_s = 2Q_{br} \tag{8.9-21}$$

$$Q_c = Q_{bf} - Q_{br}. \tag{8.9-22}$$

$$I_c = \frac{1}{2}\left(\frac{1}{T_E} - \frac{1}{T_C} + \frac{1}{T_{Br}}\right)Q_s + \frac{1}{2}\left(\frac{dQ_s}{dt}\right) - \left(\frac{Q_c}{T_C}\right) \tag{8.9-23}$$

$$-I_b = \tfrac{1}{2}\left(\frac{1}{T_{Bf}} + \frac{1}{T_{Br}}\right)Q_s + \left(\frac{dQ_s}{dt}\right) + \left(\frac{Q_c}{T_{Bf}}\right) + \left(\frac{dQ_c}{dt}\right) \tag{8.9-24}$$

$$I_e = \tfrac{1}{2}\left(\frac{1}{T_C} - \frac{1}{T_E} + \frac{1}{T_{Bf}}\right)Q_s + \tfrac{1}{2}\left(\frac{dQ_s}{dt}\right) + \left(\frac{1}{T_C} + \frac{1}{T_{Bf}}\right)Q_c + \left(\frac{dQ_c}{dt}\right) \tag{8.9-25}$$

The particular advantage of this form of the equations, compared with the form of eqns (8.9-13), (14) and (15), lies in the type of solutions normally obtained. Thus, in many practical cases, the charge Q_c is found to be associated with a comparatively short time constant, while the charge Q_s is associated predominantly with a longer time constant.

For specific solutions of these sets of equations, the reader is referred to textbooks on transistor circuit theory, although some simple cases are considered in Appendix III.

8.10 Transistors with Three-Dimensional Geometry

All practical transistors have geometries which depart from one-dimensional form to a lesser or greater extent. In fig. 8.10a(i), the geometrical arrangement of a typical alloy junction transistor is shown. The base of such a transistor has uniform resistivity. Both junctions are essentially plane over their centre parts and one-dimensional, that is planar, flow occurs over this region. Towards the outer extremities of the junction areas, there is an appreciable departure from planar flow, see fig. 8.10a(ii). The area of the collector junction is made larger than that of the emitter junction, in order that as many as possible of the injected holes should reach the collector. Even so, a small fraction of the holes diffuse to the free surface of the base and there recombine with electrons. The electron current, for both bulk and surface recombination, is drawn in from the base metallic contact. It is the ohmic resistance of the material, between the base contact and the active base region, which gives rise to the component $r_{bb'}$ in the equivalent circuit of fig. 8.6b.

In practice, the surface of the transistor is etched, and the unit encapsulated, in order to reduce the recombination velocity, see section 7.11, at the free base surface. The net effect of this, is to maintain a

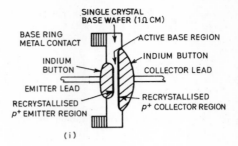

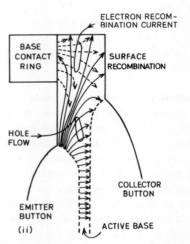

Figure 8.10a Geometrical arrangement of an alloy junction transistor:
(*i*) Construction details
(*ii*) Hole flow lines in the base of the transistor

relatively high excess density of holes at the free base surface. The hole
gradient and hence current, away from the emitter towards the free base
surface, is thereby reduced, and a closer approximation to planar flow
results over the active base region. With the reduction of the fraction
of the emitter current flowing to the free base surface the current

transfer ratio α is made closer to unity. However, the hole charge stored in the remote regions of the base may be increased.

Another type of transistor is that produced by the planar process. Figure 8.10b shows the main features of a silicon planar transistor.

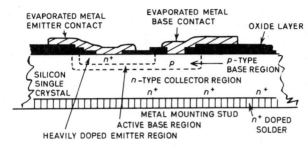

Figure 8.10b. Geometrical arrangement of a planar transistor

Photolithograpic techniques are used to define regions into which impurities are diffused to form the base and emitter. In many types of planar transistor, these diffused regions are entirely within a thin, epitaxially grown, layer of high resistivity silicon which is formed on the low resistivity base wafer. This latter construction is adopted in order to minimize the series ohmic resistance of the collector. Planar transistors, in common with all diffused base transistors, have *graded-base* resistivities and are, therefore, *drift* transistors. The planar transistor is a closer approximation to the ideal one-dimensional transistor than is the alloy junction transistor. The free base surface of a planar transistor has a low surface recombination velocity since it is passivated by an oxide layer. Almost all the minority carrier flow, from emitter to collector, occurs across the active base region which is between the plane parts of the junction. Little flow occurs elsewhere, because of the low minority carrier gradient and low drift field. The charge stored in the non-active base region, the remote charge, is much less than for the alloy junction transistor.

Other transistor geometries, for example the alloy diffused mesa construction, lie somewhere between that of the ordinary alloy junction and planar transistors.

The account of geometries of three-dimensional transistors given in the previous paragraphs, suggests that the current gain α of such transistors will be somewhat different from that predicted for the one-dimensional models. Significant errors are therefore to be expected in parameters involving $(1-\alpha)$, for example, in the common emitter current gain β, which is $\alpha/(1-\alpha)$, and in the small signal collector conductance g_c. On the other hand, the expressions for the small signal parameters r_e and μ, are expected to be substantially those given by the one-dimensional model. The stored base charge Q, and the diffusion capacitance C, will certainly be somewhat dependent on the transistor geometry because of the remote charge in the non-active region.

In conclusion, it can be said that the Ebers-Moll equations, see eqns (8.2-21) and (22), can be established for transistors of all geometries. They are:

$$I_E = -\frac{I_{EB0}}{(1-\alpha_I\alpha_N)}\left[\exp\left(\frac{qV_{EB}}{kT}\right)-1\right] + \frac{\alpha_I I_{CB0}}{(1-\alpha_I\alpha_N)}\left[\exp\left(\frac{qV_{CB}}{kT}\right)-1\right]$$

(8.10-1)

$$I_C = \frac{\alpha_N I_{EB0}}{(1-\alpha_I\alpha_N)}\left[\exp\left(\frac{qV_{EB}}{kT}\right)-1\right] - \frac{I_{CB0}}{(1-\alpha_I\alpha_N)}\left[\exp\left(\frac{qV_{CB}}{kT}\right)-1\right]$$

(8.10-2)

where a_N and α_I are the emitter to collector, and collector to emitter, current transfer ratios, and I_{EB0} and I_{CB0} are the emitter and collector leakage currents, both respectively. The same limitations apply to these equations as did to eqns (8.2-21) and (22), with the exception that they also apply to transistors with non-uniform base resistivity [8.11]. There is a third equation which is usually grouped with the Ebers-Moll equations; it is called the reciprocal relation:

$$\alpha_N I_{EB0} = \alpha_I I_{CB0}.$$

(8.10-3)

8.11 The Metal-Base Transistor

Before concluding the present chapter the *metal-base* transistor [8.12] will be briefly mentioned. This device is not strictly a minority carrier transistor but its action is sufficiently similar for it to be discussed here. The structure of the device is similar to a *npn* silicon transistor except that the *p*-type base region is replaced by a thin gold film. The *n*-type emitter injects *hot electrons*, see section 7.10, into the metallic base. Provided the base film is sufficiently thin, a few hundred A.U., the hot electrons traverse the base before their excess energy is lost by electron-phonon interaction. Most of the electrons cross the collector junction although a small fraction is reflected by the potential barrier at the junction. The device thus has a current transfer ratio α just like a conventional transistor.

At the present time, the metal-base transistor is in a very early stage of development. The device offers potentially very high frequencies of operation [8.13] in comparison with minority carrier transistors. This arises because of the extremely low transit time of carriers across the base.

References

[8.1] EBERS, J. J. and MOLL, J. L. (1954), 'Large signal behaviour of junction transistors', *Proc. I.R.E.*, **42**, 1761–72.

[8.2] See for example: ZEPLER, E. E. and PUNNETT, S. W. (1963), *Electronic devices and networks*, pp. 135–155, Blackie.

[8.3] BIONDI, F. J. (1958), *Transistor technology*, Vol. II, pp. 275–280, Van Nostrand.

[8.4] EARLY, J. M. (1952), 'Effects of space-charge layer widening in junction transistors,' *Proc. I.R.E.*, **40**, 1401–1407.

[8.5] PRITCHARD, R. L. (1954), 'Frequency variation of junction transistor parameters', *Proc. I.R.E.*, **42**, 786–789.

[8.6] OERTEL, L. (1954), 'Theory of equivalent circuits for junction transistors', *Telefunken Zeit*, **27**, 230 – 237.

[8.7] HYDE, F. J. and SMITH, R. W. (1958), 'An investigation of the current gain of transistors at frequencies up to 105 Mc/s', *Proc. I.E.E.*, **105B**, 221–228.

[8.8] WHITTAKER, E. T. and WATSON, G. N. (1927), *A Course of modern analysis*, 4th edn; p. 341, Cambridge Univ. Press.

[8.9] BEAUFOY, R. and SPARKES, J. J. (1957), 'The junction transistor as a charge controlled device', *A.T.E. Journal*, **13**, 310–327.

[8.10] See for example: CLEARY, J. F. (ed.) (1964), *Transistor manual*, pp. 158–166, G.E.C.

[8.11] BLOODWORTH, G. G. (1964), 'The significance of excess charge product in drift transistors', *Radio & Elect. Engr.*, **28,** 304–312.

[8.12] GEPPART, D. V. (1962), A metal base transistor, *Proc. I.R.E.*, **50,** 127 (1962).

[8.13] MOLL, J. L. (1963), 'Comparison of hot electron and related amplifiers', *Trans. I.E.E.*, E.D. 10, 299–303.

CHAPTER 9

Space-Charge-Limited Currents in Semiconductors and Insulators. Majority Carrier Transistors

9.1 Introduction

In this chapter, the principles governing the flow of injected carriers in high resistivity semiconductors, and insulators, will be considered. The discussion will be confined to space-charge-limited currents involving only one type of carrier. The latter part of the chapter will be concerned with majority carrier transistors; devices, which may depend on space-charge-limited currents for their operation.

The existence of a space-charge-limited current in a semiconductor, implies a violation of the principle of charge neutrality. In section 7.3, it was shown that any attempt to disturb charge neutrality in a semiconductor, was relaxed with the dielectric relaxation time, eqn (7.3-7):

$$\tau_R = \left(\frac{\varepsilon}{\sigma}\right). \tag{9.1-1}$$

Here, ε is the permittivity of the material and σ is its conductivity. According to eqn (7.3-6), when a space charge density ρ_0 is created in some region of the semiconductor, by injection or other means, the charge density decays exponentially:

$$\rho = \rho_0 \exp\left(-\frac{t}{\tau_R}\right). \tag{9.1-2}$$

In section 7.3, the value of τ_R was estimated at about 10^{-10}s for silicon of resistivity of $1\ \Omega\text{m}^{-1}$. Equation 9.1-1), shows that the relaxation time increases with increasing resistivity. For a true insulator, it becomes infinite, implying that the space-charge of injected carriers is never neutralized. This last conclusion is not surprising, for relaxation of the charge of injected carriers is normally effected by the movement of thermal carriers, and in this case, there are no thermal carriers.

9.2 Space-Charge-Limited Current in an Insulator. The Mott-Gurney Law

In this section, the law governing the flow of currents, resulting from the injection of carriers in a perfect insulator, will be considered. A uniform insulating rod, of unit area cross-section, will be supposed to have a metallic injection contact at one end, and a metallic collecting contact at the other. Both contacts may be ohmic, or the injecting contact may be a forward biased junction, and the collecting contact may be a reverse biased junction. The general principles relating to injection and collection of carriers at such contacts were considered in section 7.10. In any event, for simplicity, it will be assumed that all the voltage, V_a, applied across the contacts, appears across the insulating rod. In addition, the length L of the rod, will be assumed large compared with the widths of any depletion layers, or ohmic layers, at the metallic contacts. It is irrelevant whether electrons, injected into the conduction band, or holes, injected into the valence band, are considered, provided only one of these phenomena occurs. As an example, the injection of electrons into the conduction band will be discussed. This injection of carriers into an insulator may be likened to the injection of electrons from a cathode into a vacuum, as in thermionic valves. There will, of course, be no recombination of the injected electrons with holes, for no such holes exist in the insulator.

The potential and charge density, at any points along the rod, are related by Poisson's equation, eqn (7.4-2):

$$\left(\frac{d^2 V(x)}{dx^2}\right) = -\frac{\rho(x)}{\varepsilon}. \qquad (9.2\text{-}1)$$

The current density, at any point along the rod (eqn 5.5-1):

$$J = -\mu\rho(x)\left(\frac{dV(x)}{dx}\right) \qquad (9.2\text{-}2)$$

where μ is the carrier mobility, and J, the current density, is a constant. This follows, because there is no recombination and the rod has a uniform cross-section. Eliminating $\rho(x)$ between these equations:

$$\left(\frac{d^2 V}{dx^2}\right) = \left(\frac{1}{\varepsilon\mu}\right)\frac{J}{\left(\dfrac{dV}{dx}\right)} . \tag{9.2-3}$$

This equation integrates to:

$$\left(\frac{dV}{dx}\right)^2 = \left(\frac{2J}{\varepsilon\mu}\right)x + E_0^2 \tag{9.2-4}$$

where E_0 is the value of $+(dV/dx)$ at the origin of x. Under space-charge-limited conditions, E_0 is zero, that is, the electric intensity at the source is zero. The following argument may be used to establish this. It is first observed, from eqn (9.2-4), that if J is non-zero, (dV/dx) is a monotonic increasing function of x. Suppose, by some means it is possible to control the injection of electrons from the source into the

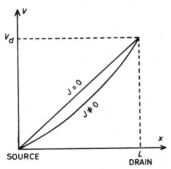

Figure 9.2a. Potential distribution along the insulating rod

insulator. When no electrons are injected, J is zero, and eqn (9.2-4) shows that (dV/dx) is equal to E_0 everywhere. The potential, V, then increases linearly from zero at the *source*, to V_d at the *drain*, as shown in fig. 9.2a. When some injection is allowed, J is non-zero, and eqn (9.2-4) indicates that (dV/dx) will be increased at the *drain*, compared with the zero current case. Because (dV/dx) is a monotonic increasing function of x, it follows that (dV/dx) at the source will be below the zero current case, as shown in the figure. Further increase in the injection will eventually cause E_0 to become zero, and, at this stage, the current becomes space-charge-limited. Any further increase in the injection tends to produce a retarding electric field at the source, thus preventing any further increase in the current. Up to the point where E_0 becomes zero, the current is said to be *injection-limited*. In the following discussion, it will be assumed that the current is not injection limited and hence E_0 will be put equal to zero. If a contact injects at all, it is not likely to cause injection-limitation of current. In practice, the electrons are injected into the conduction band with some kinetic energy. In this case, there is a small retarding field at the source, and the point of zero electric intensity occurs a little way in from the source. The effective length L is thus slightly less than the true length.

A further integration of eqn (9.2-4) then yields:

$$V(x) = \left(\frac{2}{3}\right)\left(\sqrt{\frac{2J}{\varepsilon\mu}}.x^{\frac{3}{2}}\right) \tag{9.2-5}$$

where $V(0)$ has been taken equal to zero. When x is L, $V(x)$ becomes the drain voltage V_d; this gives, with transposition:

$$J = \left(\frac{9}{8}\right)\left(\frac{\varepsilon\mu}{L^3}\right)V_d^2 . \tag{9.2-6}$$

This equation is known as the Mott-Gurney law* [9.1] and is very similar to the Child-Langmuir law of thermionics. This latter law has a $V_a^{\frac{3}{2}}$ anode voltage dependence of space-charge-limited current, which has been shown to be valid [9.2] for any two electrode geometry in vacuum. From the similarity of the two laws, and their methods of derivation, it may be concluded that the space-charge-limited current in an insulator has a V_d^2 dependance for any geometry of *source, drain* and shape of insulator.

---

* The ratio of J to V_d^2 is termed the *Perveance*.

9.3 Space-Charge-Limited Current in a Perfect Semi-Conductor

The work of this, and section 9.4, is largely based on papers by A. Rose and M. A. Lampert [9.3], [9.4], [9.5].

Let it now be supposed that the insulator of the last section has a density n_i of thermally generated carriers, but no carrier traps. No recombination can occur and such a semiconductor will be described as perfect. For simplicity, it is assumed that the thermal carriers are either electrons in the conduction band, or holes in the valence band, but not both. The results to be obtained, are readily extended to the case where carriers of both types are present.

At low *drain* voltages V_d, the ohmic conduction resulting from the thermal carriers predominates over that due to any space-charge-limiting process. This ohmic current density is given by:

$$J = \left(\frac{q\mu n_i}{L}\right)V_d \qquad (9.3\text{-}1)$$

where n_i is the density of thermal carriers, and (V_d/L) is taken as the uniform electric intensity in the rod in the absence of space-charge. At higher *drain* voltages, space-charge-limitation of current will predominate, because of its V_d^2 dependence compared with the V_d dependence of the ohmic process. The transition, from the ohmic law to the Mott-Gurney law, will occur when the current densities, given by the two laws, are approximately equal. Thus, from eqns (9.2-6) and (9.3-1), dropping the factor $(\frac{9}{8})$ in the former, the transition voltage V_T is given by:

$$\left(\frac{\varepsilon\mu}{L^3}\right)V_T^2 \simeq \left(\frac{q\mu n_i}{L}\right)V_T \qquad (9.3\text{-}2)$$

or:

$$V_T \simeq \left(\frac{qn_i L^2}{\varepsilon}\right). \qquad (9.3\text{-}3)$$

At this voltage, the transit time of a carrier along the rod is approximately:

$$t_{\text{Tr}} \simeq \frac{L}{\mu(V_T/L)} = \left(\frac{L^2}{\mu V_T}\right). \qquad (9.3\text{-}4)$$

Eliminating V_T with (eqn 9.3-3):

$$t_{Tr} \simeq \left(\frac{\varepsilon}{q\mu n_i}\right) = \left(\frac{\varepsilon}{\sigma}\right) \qquad (9.3\text{-}5)$$

that is the transit time is approximately equal to the dielectric relaxation time τ_R. Thus, the transition, from the ohmic law to the Mott-Gurney law, occurs when the transit time of the carriers is approximately equal to the dielectric relaxation time. This confirms the contention of section 9.1, namely, that a space-charge is set up once the transit time of the injected carriers is too short for them to be relaxed by thermal carriers. The transition is indicated schematically in fig. 9.3a.

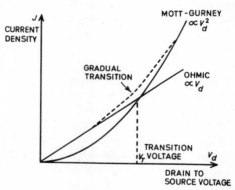

Figure 9.3a. Ohmic to Mott-Gurney law transition

One further point of interest arises: at the voltage V_T, the Mott-Gurney law, eqn (9.2-6), without the factor $(\frac{9}{8})$, gives the current density as:

$$J \simeq \left(\frac{\varepsilon\mu}{L^3}\right)V_T^2 = \left(\frac{\mu}{\varepsilon}\right)q^2 n_i^2 L. \qquad (9.3\text{-}6)$$

The charge in the rod, corresponding to this current density, can be obtained by multiplying the current density by the carrier transit time t_{Tr}, eqn (9.3-5), and so is:

$$Q \simeq (qn_i L). \qquad (9.3\text{-}7)$$

This means that the injected carrier density, required to support the space-charge-limited current at the voltage V_T, is n_i, the thermal carrier density. The transition can therefore be said to occur when the density of thermal carriers is no longer adequate to relax that of the injected carriers.

9.4 The Effect of Traps

The presence of carrier traps, in the semiconductor or insulator, has a marked effect on its current-voltage characteristic. The traps may be of either the recombination or non-recombination kind, but in effect only the latter will appear in insulators because only one type of carrier is present. Again, it will be assumed that only electrons in the conduction band are present. The density of electrons in the conduction band is then given by eqns (4.2-7) and (6.3-4):

$$n = N_c \exp \left[- \left(\frac{E_c - E_{Fn}}{kT} \right) \right] \qquad (9.4\text{-}1)$$

which is eqn (4.2-7) with E_F replaced by E_{Fn}, appropriate to non-equilibrium conditions. The occupation density of the traps is:

$$n_t = \frac{N_t}{\left[1 + \exp \left(\frac{E_t - E_{Fn}}{kT} \right) \right]} \qquad (9.4\text{-}2)$$

where N_t is the density of traps, all assumed at constant energy E_t, and where the spin degeneracy factor ($\frac{1}{2}$), eqn (3.12-17), has been set to unity for simplicity. Note that the classical approximation to the Fermi function has been used in eqn (9.4-1), but that it is necessary to use the full form of the function in eqn (9.4-2). This is because in the former case, n is expected to be much less than N_c, while in the latter case, n_t may approach N_t. An approximation, known as the *quasi-equilibrium* assumption, has been made in eqn (9.4-2). It is that the effective Fermi level for the occupation of the traps has been taken as E_{Fn}. This is valid, provided the carrier density does not change appreciably in a time which is short compared with the mean time for which a carrier is trapped.

When E_{Fn} is below E_t by more than $3kT$, the traps are said to be *shallow*. The classical approximation to the Fermi function may then be used in eqn (9.4-2):

$$n_t = N_t \exp\left[-\left(\frac{E_t - E_{Fn}}{kT}\right)\right]. \tag{9.4-3}$$

From this equation and eqn (9.4-1), a quantity θ can be defined:

$$\theta = \left(\frac{n}{n + n_t}\right) = \left[\frac{N_c}{N_c + N_t \exp\left(\dfrac{E_c - E_t}{kT}\right)}\right]. \tag{9.4-4}$$

The value of θ for *shallow* traps is thus, at any given temperature, dependant only on the density N_t and energy depth $(E_c - E_t)$ of the traps. When $N_t \exp[(E_c - E_t)/kT]$ is large compared with N_c, θ is very much less than unity. This will be the case, when N_t is large, or when E_t is well below E_c, or both. Then, most of the injected electrons go into the traps. Very few go into the conduction band and are available as charge carriers. The space-charge-limited current density, for a given voltage, will then be much less than for the trap free case. The set of traps with the smallest θ, say θ_s, is called the dominant set. This set corresponds to the maximum value of $N_t \exp[(E_c - E_t)/kT]$.

Because, for the dominant set of traps, the fraction of the injected carriers available for conduction purposes is θ_s, the space-charge-limited current will be reduced by the same fraction, thus from eqn (9.2-6):

$$J = \theta_s \left(\frac{9}{8}\right)\left(\frac{\varepsilon\mu}{L^3}\right) V_d^2. \tag{9.4-6}$$

Also, in the presence of thermal carriers (see section 9.3), the transition from ohmic conduction to space-charge-limited conduction will now occur (see eqn 9.3-3) at:

$$V_T \simeq \left(\frac{qn_i L^2}{\theta_s \varepsilon}\right). \tag{9.4-7}$$

By way of illustration, let it be supposed that N_t is 10^{20} traps per m^3, that is approximately, one trap for every 10^7 lattice ions. Thus, (N_c/N_t)

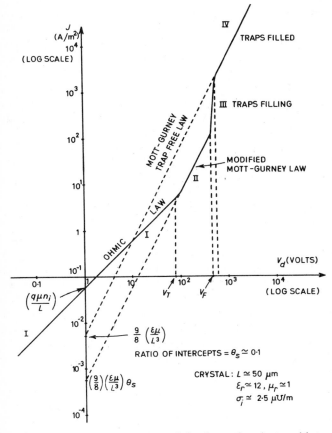

Figure 9.4a. Current-voltage characteristic of a semiconductor with traps

is of the order of 10^7. Also, let $(E_c - E_t)$ be 0·54 eV. Then at room temperatures, for which kT is about 0·03 eV, eqn (9.4-4) gives θ as approximately 0·03. Changes in N_t will change this latter figure in proportion, but doubling $(E_c - E_t)$ reduces the figure to about 10^{-10}. Thus, when the dominant shallow traps are deep lying, the space-charge-limited current, of eqn (9.4-6), will be negligible. Also, for such traps, the transition voltage V_T (eqn 9.4-7) will be very high, probably hundreds of volts for crystals 50 μ or so long, unless n_i is very small, corresponding to a very high ohmic resistivity.

On the other hand, when N_t has the same value as before, but $(E_c - E_t)$ is halved to 0·27 eV, the value of θ is unity to within one part in 10^3. In this case, therefore, the Mott-Gurney law (eqn 9.2-6) will be closely followed.

When E_{F_n} is above E_t by more than $3kT$, (eqn 9.4-2) becomes:

$$n_t \simeq N_t \qquad (9.4-8)$$

that is, almost all the traps are full. Such traps are described as *deep* traps, and it is readily shown that θ for these traps is extremely close to unity, irrespective of N_t, provided it is small compared with N_c. *Deep* traps do not influence space-charge-limited currents at all. The division of traps into *shallow* or *deep* classifications, is not absolute, but rather depends on the injection level. As the injection level rises, the electron Imref E_{F_n} rises and, as it passes through the transition regions of $3kT$ on either side of the trap energy E_t, the traps fill and their classification changes from *shallow* to *deep*.

The current-voltage characteristic for a rod with a single set of *shallow* traps, at equilibrium, will now be considered. Initially, for low voltages V_d, the characteristic will be linear, corresponding to ohmic conduction. This is shown in the log-log plot of fig. 9.4a, drawn with suitable choice of axis scale, as the straight line of unity slope of region I. With increasing V_d, eventually the *shallow* trap transition voltage V_T, eqn (9.4-7), is attained and space-charge-limitation of the current commences according to the modified Mott-Gurney law of eqn (9.4-6). This is shown as the straight line with slope of two (region II). In this region, only a fraction θ_s of the injected carriers enters the conduction band. The rest go into the traps, and the electron Imref moves up towards the trap level E_t. When sufficient charge has been injected into the rod to fill the traps, the Mott-Gurney law, eqn (9.2-6), becomes applicable. This is shown as region IV in fig. 9.4a.

An approximate value of the voltage, at which this last transition occurs, can be obtained as follows. The capacitance, per unit cross-section of the rod, is of the order of (ε/L). Also, a charge of (qN_tL), per unit cross-section of the rod, is required to fill the traps. Thus if the capacitance is charged to a voltage:

$$V_F \simeq \left(\frac{qN_tL^2}{\varepsilon}\right) \tag{9.4-9}$$

sufficient charge is available to fill the traps. Once the traps are full, a sharp rise of current with voltage occurs. This is shown as region III in fig. 9.4a, the characteristic ultimately merging with the trap-free law of region IV. This transition is abrupt, for it requires but little increase in the applied voltage to lift the electron Imref through the range of $6kT$ about the trap level E_t. Finally, if the voltage V_T tends to be larger than V_F, as is likely when θ_s is small, region II of the characteristic is absent, and a direct transition from region I to III occurs.

The magnitude of V_F itself can be very high. For a density of 10^{20} traps per m^3, a permittivity ε of 10^{-10} Fm^{-1} and a crystal length of 50 μ, V_F is about 400 volts. It follows that, in order to obtain detectable currents in insulating crystals at a few volts or so, the density of dominant traps must be less than 10^{18} per m^3, Here, dominant traps are defined as: all those with energy levels and densities giving small values of θ, at zero applied voltage. Traps with larger values of θ, particularly those with θ approaching unity, do not prevent appreciable space-charge-limited currents from flowing, as was explained previously in this section. Although V_F may be quite large for such traps, its value is of little consequence, for appreciable current flows at voltages far below it. *Deep* traps, at zero applied voltage, are also of no consequence.

The expressions obtained in this section must be regarded as very approximate. They probably indicate little more than the orders of magnitude of the quantities they are supposed to represent. To obtain more exact expressions, it would be necessary to integrate Poisson's equation, eqn (9.2-1), subject to the appropriate space-charge density. This was carried out for the perfect insulator in section 9.2. However, the problem is extremely difficult for the semiconductor, when thermal carriers and traps are present. The *trapped* carriers give rise to space-charge, which must be considered in the term $\rho(x)$ of eqn (9.2-1), but not in the term $\rho(x)$ of eqn (9.2-2). The integration of Poisson's equation is not then possible in explicit form.

The general pattern of behaviour of space-charge-limited currents in insulators, as described in this section, has been experimentally verified by a number of workers [9.6] [9.7] [9.8] [9.9]. In the first two references [9.6], [9.7], the insulator used was a cadmium sulphide single crystal. In references [9.8] and [9.9], deposited polycrystalline cadmium sulphide films were used. The semi-insulating cadmium sulphide is chosen for this work because, in the present state of technology, it is one of the very few substances into which appreciable injection of carriers can be effected and, in addition, one for which techniques for minimizing the density of traps have been developed. With advances in technology, it is likely that other suitable insulators will become available.

9.5 Majority Carrier Transistors

There are, at present, a number of different structures which may be used as majority carrier transistors. The principle of all versions of the transistor, is the use of a *gate* electrode to modulate the conductance of a *channel* along which carriers pass from *source* to *drain*. The transistors operate in one of two modes, carrier *depletion*, or carrier *enhancement*. In the first of these modes, carriers are removed from the channel, thereby reducing its conductance. In the other mode, the number of carriers in the channel is increased, with consequent increase in the channel conductance. In both modes, the modulation of the channel conductance is thought to be brought about by altering the effective cross-section of the channel at constant carrier density.

There is some doubt as to whether the mechanism described in the last paragraph is always valid. It is usually assumed that conduction in the channel is essentially ohmic. However, for high resistivity channels, and some geometries, the current in the channel may be space-charge-limited. The action of the *gate* is then to control the space-charge-density, and hence the current in the channel. This will be considered further in section 9.10.

A simplified theory for the first of these mechanisms will be presented, and then devices which operate according to this mechanism, will be described. Subsequently, section 9.9, the space-charge mechanism, will also be considered.

For the case when the conduction in the channel is considered to be ohmic, a simple theory based on that of Middlebrook [9.10] will be followed. Although this theory makes a number of simplifying assumptions, the results obtained are essentially the same as those obtained by more elaborate analyses.

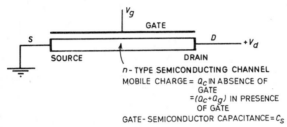

Figure 9.5a. Model of a majority carrier transistor

The method is based on a charge control principle, similar to that outlined in section 8.9. It assumes a one-dimensional flow in the source to drain channel, which is of length L; see fig. 9.5a. In addition, two major approximations are made. The first is that the electric intensity has a component along the channel, with constant value (V_d/L), where V_d is the drain to source voltage. The second is that the current flows in the channel according to the ohmic law. That is, the mobility is independant of the electric intensity and space-charge effects are neglected. With these assumptions, the channel or drain current may be written as:

$$I_d \simeq (Q/\tau) \qquad (9.5\text{-}1)$$

Here, Q is the magnitude of the charge of the mobile carriers in the channel, and τ is their mean transit time from source to drain. This equation should be compared with eqn (8.9-8).

In order to be specific, an n-type channel is considered, with electrons as the mobile majority carriers. The charge Q can be considered as the sum of two charges, Q_c and Q_g. The former is that which would be present even in the absence of the gate structure, and the latter is the additional charge, subtractive for a depletion mode, in the channel which results from the presence of the gate and its bias. Now, the carrier drift velocity, along the channel, is $(\mu V_d/L)$ and hence, the transit time is:

$$\tau = \left(\frac{L^2}{\mu V_d} \right). \tag{9.5-2}$$

From eqns (9.5-1) and (2):

$$I_d = \left(\frac{\mu Q_c}{L^2} \right) \left[1 + \left(\frac{Q_g}{Q_c} \right) \right] V_d. \tag{9.5-3}$$

The ratio of I_d to V_d, given by this equation, is the channel conductance G, and the factor $(\mu Q_c/L^2)$ is the channel conductance G_c, which would be present in the absence of the gate structure.

It is assumed that the gate is symmetrically placed with respect to the source and drain; this is usually true in practice. The mean voltage, between the gate and the channel, will then be $[V_g - (V_d/2)]$, where V_g is the gate to source voltage. Once again, this assumes a constant electric intensity component along the channel. The charge Q_g, can be expressed in terms of the mean gate to channel voltage by:

$$Q_g = C_g \left(V_g - \frac{V_d}{2} \right) \tag{9.5-4}$$

where C_g is the capacitance between the gate and the channel. Note that the induced charge in the channel is negative. Equation (9.5-3) can be written:

$$I_d = G_c \left[1 + \frac{(V_g - (V_d/2))}{(Q_c/C_g)} \right] V_d. \tag{9.5-5}$$

The incremental drain conductance is:

$$g_c = \left(\frac{\partial I_d}{\partial V_d}\right)_{V_g} = G_c \left[1 + \frac{(V_g - V_d)}{(Q_c/C_g)}\right]. \qquad (9.5\text{-}6)$$

This conductance becomes zero when:

$$V_d - V_g = \left(\frac{Q_c}{C_g}\right) \qquad (9.5\text{-}7)$$

and then the drain current, eqn (9.5-5), becomes:

$$I_{ds} = \left(\frac{G_c}{2}\right)\left(\frac{Q_c}{C_g}\right)\left[1 + \frac{V_g}{(Q_c/V_g)}\right]^2. \qquad (9.5\text{-}8)$$

For values of the drain voltage V_d greater than that given by eqn (9.5-7), the drain current saturates at the value I_{ds} given by eqn (9.5-8). To understand this saturation of the drain current, it is necessary to introduce the *pinch-off* voltage V_p. In the absence of the gate structure, the charge in the channel is Q_c. For zero drain voltage V_d, the gate voltage necessary to neutralize Q_c is:

$$V_g = -\left(\frac{Q_c}{C_g}\right) = -V_p \qquad (9.5\text{-}9)$$

where V_p is termed the *pinch-off* voltage. The minus sign arises, since it is necessary to induce a positive charge into the channel, and Q_c is the magnitude of the channel charge.

When the drain voltage is non-zero and positive, the smallest or most negative gate to channel voltage, $(V_g - V_d)$, occurs at the drain end of the channel. If the voltage $(V_d - V_g)$ is increased to the *pinch-off* voltage V_p, the mobile carriers, at the drain end of the channel, are neutralized. In practice, this means that the effective cross-section of the conducting channel is reduced to zero. It is said to be *pinched-off*, which is the origin of the terminology of V_p. With increased V_d, the *pinched-off* region, extends slightly further down the channel towards the source. The excess drain voltage, over that required to saturate the current, appears across the *depleted* drain end of the channel. The edge of this depletion region acts as a *sink* for the electrons moving towards the drain; having reached the depletion region, they are removed rapidly to the drain.

The theory which has been presented is therefore valid only for:

$$V_d \leqslant V_g + V_p \qquad (9.5\text{-}10)$$

the equality of which, is equivalent to eqn (9.5-7) giving the condition zero incremental drain conductance. Within the range of the inequality of eqn (9.5-10), substitution of V_p for (Q_c/C_g) and $(\mu Q_c/L^2)$ for G_c in eqn (9.5-5) gives:

$$I_d = \left(\frac{\mu C_g}{L^2}\right)\left[(V_g + V_p) - \left(\frac{V_d}{2}\right)\right] V_d. \qquad (9.5\text{-}11)$$

This equation has been obtained by the more exact analyses of Borkan and Weimer [9.11] and Hofstein and Heiman [9.12]. These workers however, define V_p with opposite sign to that used here.

Equations (9.5-5) and (8) may also be written respectively in the normalized forms:

$$\left(\frac{I_d}{I_{do}}\right) = 2\left\{1 + \left(\frac{V_g}{V_p}\right) - \left(\frac{1}{2}\right)\left(\frac{V_d}{V_p}\right)\right\}\left(\frac{V_d}{V_p}\right) \qquad (9.5\text{-}12)$$

$$\left(\frac{I_{ds}}{I_{do}}\right) = \left\{1 + \left(\frac{V_g}{V_p}\right)\right\}^2 \qquad (9.5\text{-}13)$$

where:

$$I_{do} = \left(\frac{1}{2}\right) G_c V_p \qquad (9.5\text{-}14)$$

is the saturated drain current for zero V_g. Equation (9.5-12) is valid below *pinch-off* and eqn (9.5-13) gives the saturation current beyond *pinch-off*. It is interesting to note that I_{do} is less than the current that would be obtained, in the absence of the gate structure, for all V_d greater than $(\frac{1}{2}) V_p$.

The characteristics given by eqns (9.5-12) and (13) are plotted in fig. 9.5b.

The incremental mutual conductance g_{mp}, beyond *pinch-off*, may be obtained from eqn (9.5-13):

$$g_{mp} = \left(\frac{dI_{ds}}{dV_g}\right) = \left(\frac{2I_{do}}{V_p}\right)\left[1 + \left(\frac{V_g}{V_p}\right)\right] = G_c\left[1 + \left(\frac{V_g}{V_p}\right)\right] \qquad (9.5\text{-}15)$$

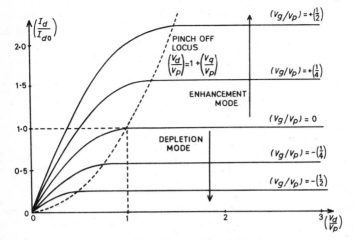

Figure 9.5b. Characteristics of the model majority carrier transistor

where eqn (9.5-14) has been used. This last result shows that the incremental mutual conductance at *pinch-off* is equal to the channel conductance G_c, both at zero gate voltage. It also shows that larger values of g_{mp} can be expected for positive values of V_g, the *enhancement* mode, than for negative V_g, the *depletion* mode.

Below pinch-off, the incremental mutual conductance g_m is obtained from eqn (9.5-12):

$$g_m = \left(\frac{\partial I_d}{\partial V_g}\right)_{V_d} = \left(\frac{2I_{d0}}{V_p}\right)\left(\frac{V_d}{V_p}\right) = G_c\left(\frac{V_d}{V_p}\right) \qquad (9.5\text{-}16)$$

where eqn (9.5-14) has been used. This shows that g_m increases linearly with V_d up to *pinch-off*, where (V_d/V_p) can be replaced by $[1+(V_g/V_p)]$ thus giving eqn (9.5-15).

In the subsequent sections, the application of this idealized theory to specific types of transistor will be considered.

9.6 The Junction Type Field-Effect Transistor

This device was first proposed by Shockley [9.13]. The first experimental versions of the device were reported by Dacey and Ross [9.14].

Epitaxial crystal growth and impurity diffusion techniques, possibly coupled with the planar technology, now make possible the construction of field-effect transistors, with accurately controlled parameters. One such structure is shown in fig. 9.6a, the upper part of which, shows a

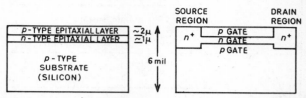

Figure 9.6a. Field-effect transistor; epitaxial-diffusion construction

p-type crystal on which has been grown a 1 micron n-type layer, and subsequently, a 2 micron p-type layer. Both layers are produced by the epitaxial process and, as such, their resistivities and thicknesses can be accurately controlled. Over the gate and channel region, an oxide mask is formed by the standard photolithographic and photo-resist techniques. The source and drain regions are then formed by diffusion of phosphorus through the mask and through the two epitaxial layers. The photo-lithographic technique ensures that the dimensions of the n-type channel are accurately controlled. The structure may be formed with the junctions passivated as for ordinary planar transistors, see section 8.10, or may be raised as a *mesa* [9.15]. Evaporated metal connections are made to the source, drain and gate regions.

A wide range of device characteristics can be achieved by control of dimensions and sheet resistivity of the channel. Typically, the sheet resistivity of the channel is about 4,000 Ω per square, and its length is about 50 micron. An extremely ingenious alternative structure, using planar technology, has been described by Roosild, Dolan and O'Neil [9.16].

In operation, the gate to channel junction of the transistor in fig. 9.6a, is reverse biased. With increasing negative bias on the gate, the space-charge depletion layer moves across the channel reducing its width and hence, its conductance. The main body of the crystal is also biased negative, relative to the channel, so as to constrain the electrons to the channel. It may also be connected to the gate, or used as a second gate [9.17].

The drain is held positive, relative to the source, usually through a load resistor. This creates the necessary drift field along the channel.

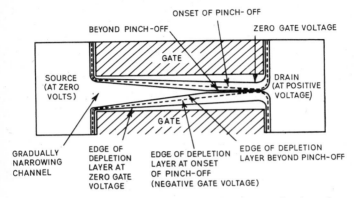

Figure 9.6b. Variation of effective channel width along the channel

As a consequence, the reverse bias between gate and channel increases towards the drain. The depletion layer is thus wider at the drain than at the source, as is shown in fig. 9.6b. As the gate voltage is made more negative, the depletion layer widens. The width of the conducting channel is thus reduced at each point along its length. *Pinch-off* occurs when the two depletion layers meet at the drain end of the channel. If the gate voltage is made even more negative, the region over which the two depletion layers meet is extended slightly further towards the source. The conductance of the channel is reduced in such a way that the current saturates beyond *pinch-off*.

The remarks in the last paragraph indicate that the carrier depletion mechanism in the channel is rather more complex than was assumed in the simple theory of the last section. However, Shockley's [9.13] detailed analysis, which allows for a gradual variation of channel width of the kind shown in fig. 9.6b, produces substantially the same results

as were obtained in the last section. Of course, positive gate voltages
cannot be used, for the gate to channel junction must be kept reverse
biased. The operation of the transistor is thus restricted to the *depletion*
mode.

More detailed analyses, allowing for such factors as field dependance
of mobility and non-uniform distributions of doping impurity in the
channel, have been presented by Dacey and Ross [9.18] and Bockmuehl
[9.19], among others.

Conditions on the drain side of the pinch-off point in the channel are
quite complex. The electrons are acted upon by the space-charges of
the two reversed biased junctions, and are thus restricted to the centre
of the channel. The comparatively high longitudinal electric intensity
between the pinch-off point and the drain is, however, in favour of the
electrons moving in the channel, and hence they are rapidly drawn
through this region to the drain. The whole region is thus depleted of
mobile carriers. The extension of the pinch-off region along the channel
is exaggerated in fig. 9.6b for the sake of clarity. In fact, this extension is
very limited and large fields are produced in this region by drain voltages
in excess of pinch-off. Detailed consideration of this region, called the
expop region, has been given by Shockly [9.13], Dacey and Ross [9.18]
Prim and Shockley [9.20] and others.

9.7 The Insulated-Gate Field-Effect Transistor

The insulated-gate field-effect transistor is also known as the metal-
oxide-semiconductor-transistor, or MOST. This transistor has been
described by Hofstein and Heiman [9.12]. The essential features of the
construction of the transistor are shown in fig. 9.7a. It is fabricated by
the same photolithographic, photo-resist, and diffusion techniques as
used in conventional planar technology. The source and drain are
diffused, heavily doped, n^+-type regions. Thermal oxidation of the
$10 \, \Omega$m, p-type substrate, causes a thin n-type *skin* to appear on its surface.
This *skin* can be used as the conducting channel and the oxide above
it, as the insulation under the evaporated metal gate. Evaporated metal
connections are also made to the source and drain regions. Typically,
the channel length L, between source and drain, is 10 micron and its

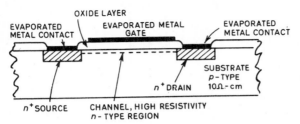

Figure 9.7a. The insulated-gate field-effect transistor

width, normal to the section of fig. 9.7a, is 1 mm. The oxide layer, between the gate and the channel, has a thickness of about 2,000 A.U. that is 0·2 micron. The thickness of the inversion layer itself, that is the channel, is less than 1,000 A.U.

The insulation of the gate electrode from the conducting channel allows this transistor to be operated in either *depletion* or *enhancement* mode. The characteristics of transistors of this type, have the general form of those of fig. 9.5b, but do not completely saturate above *pinch-off*. Hofstein and Heiman [9.12] have offered an explanation for this failure to saturate, but other interpretations are possible [9.21].

The mechanism for carrier depletion, or enhancement, is thought to be as follows. Thermal oxidization of the surface of the p-type semiconductor is believed to introduce *donor*-like surface states. These cause the semiconductor type to change from p to n in the immediate neighbourhood of the surface, thus forming the inversion layer. The energy levels are accordingly bent at the surface. Figure 9.7b(i) shows diagrammatically the surface states and the bending of the energy levels. If the density of the surface *donor* states is high, they will be mostly occupied, if low, they will be mainly ionized. The position of the Fermi level will thus be above, or below, these states, according to their occupation density. In either case, there will be mobile carriers in the conduction band.

When the gate is biased negative, relative to the channel, most of the bias voltage appears across the insulator, as shown in fig. 9.7b(ii). The energy levels of the semiconductor are bent up a little, and the

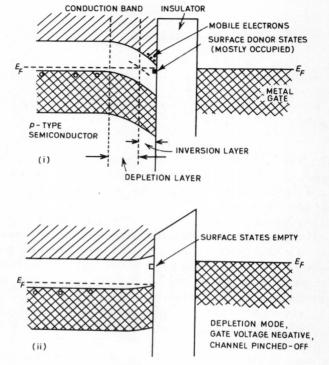

Figure 9.7b. N-type inversion at the surface of a *p*-type semiconductor
(i) In equilibrium, that is zero gate voltage
(ii) Inversion layer biased to pinch-off

Fermi level passes below the surface *donor* states. These states are then largely depleted of electrons, as is also the conduction band. Thus in the depletion mode of operation, and with sufficient negative gate bias, the channel may be *pinched-off*. If the gate is biased positively, relative to the channel, the edge of the conduction band moves closer to the Fermi level, at the surface of the semiconductor. Extra electrons from the source enter the conduction band, and the conductivity of the channel is enhanced. This is the enhancement mode of operation.

Hofstein and Heiman [9.12] predict the characteristics of the device, subject to the assumption that all the gate to channel voltage appears across the insulator. The electric intensity, normal to the surface of the semiconductor, is then given by this voltage divided by the thickness of the insulator. The area density of the induced surface charge is then obtained from this intensity and the permittivity of the insulator, with the aid of the Gauss electrostatic theorem. Subsequently, this approach leads to eqn (9.5-11) and the characteristics of fig. 9.5b, provided the resistances of the source and drain regions are neglected.

Hofstein and Heiman have also produced transistors which operate only in the enhancement mode. In particular, such units may require a minimum positive gate voltage, before any drain conductance can be observed. The *pinch-off* voltage is negative, and the gate must be biased sufficiently positive, to annul this negative *pinch-off* voltage, before conduction can occur. These units are fabricated by compensation of the surface donor states during the growth of the oxide layer. It is believed that the semiconductor then has a net density of *acceptor* surface states. Under this condition, when the gate is forward biased, the electrons drawn in from the source start to fill the *acceptor* centres. Only when all the *acceptors* are full, are electrons available for conduction purposes.

In this section, p-type substrates with n^+-type source and drain regions have been considered. The channel is effectively n-type material and the majority carriers are electrons. There are, of course, exactly analogous devices with all material types changed, and in which holes are the majority carriers.

9.8 The Thin-Film Transistor

The thin-film transistor was first described by Weimer [9.22]. Zuleeg [9.9], Shallcross [9.23] and others have also constructed such devices. The transistor is essentially the same as the insulated-gate field-effect transistor of the last section. It differs from the latter in materials and method of construction. Figure 9.8a shows two geometrical arrange-

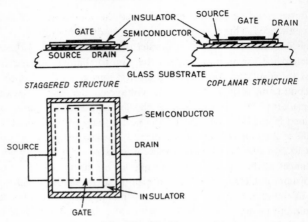

Figure 9.8a. The thin-film transistor

ments of the device, which is produced entirely by vacuum deposition techniques. Typically, the source to drain separation is 10 micron, and the lengths of the source and drain electrodes are 1 mm. The semiconductor, or semi-insulator, in present-day devices is polycrystalline cadmium sulphide or selenide. Its thickness is usually less than 1 micron. Silicon monoxide is usually used for the gate insulation, and the layer is about 500 A.U. thick. The source, drain and gate electrodes are usually gold or aluminium. The source electrode, at least, must have a non-blocking contact with the semiconductor, and it has been reported [9.24] that, while gold is apparently suitable for the staggered structure, fig. 9.8a, aluminium must be used for the coplanar structure. The reasons for this are not apparently fully understood [9.9].

By suitable thermal treatment of the semi-insulator layer, devices can be constructed which will operate in both depletion and enhancement modes, or in simply the latter mode.

Experimental characteristics of thin-film transistors are almost indistinguishable from those of insulated-gate field-effect transistors. This supports the contention that their principles of operation are similar. Theoretical investigations of the characteristics have been carried out by

Borkan and Weimer [9.11] who, for a first approximation, obtain eqn (9.5-11) of this chapter. A more detailed analysis, with some experimental verification, has been given by Haering [9.25] and Miksic, Schlig and Haering [9.26] who consider frequency effects in some detail.

9.9 The Space-Charge-Limited Dielectric Triode

The analogy between the Mott-Gurney law, eqn (9.2-6), governing a space-charge-limited current flowing in an insulator, and the Child-Langmuir law for space-charge-limited currents in a vacuum, suggests that it might be possible to construct a solid-state version of the vacuum triode. Proposals to this effect have been made by G. T. Wright [9.21], [9.27].

Following Wright, and by analogy with the vacuum triode, the drain current in the dielectric triode should have the form:

$$I_d = PK \left[V_g + \left(\frac{V_d}{G} \right)^{\frac{1}{2}} \right]. \qquad (9.9-1)$$

Here, P is the *perveance* of the Mott-Gurney Law, G is an amplification factor which is calculated in a similar way to that for a vacuum valve, and K is a constant, dependant on the geometry of the valve.

In fig. 9.9a, a family of characteristics, given by eqn (9.9-1) with G equal to 24, is plotted. The similarity between these characteristics and those of the vacuum triode is apparent. Zuleeg [9.9] has obtained experimental characteristics which have the general form of those of fig. 9.9a. These were for a thin-film transistor, using a polycrystalline cadmium sulphide thin film, operating in the depletion mode. The principle differences of this device from that discussed in the last section are the use of indium in place of gold for the source, and a source to drain separation which was less than the thickness of the cadmium sulphide layer. It was suggested by Zuleeg that the use of gold for the source produces a blocking contact and that injection into the semiconductor, in this case, is brought about by field emission. This might be possible, in the normal thin-film transistor, because the gate to source voltage across the thin insulating layer, produces a large electric intensity at the

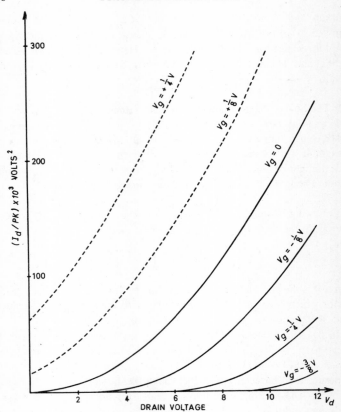

Figure 9.9a. Ideal characteristics of a space-charge-limited triode; negative gate voltages-solid line

injecting contact. In this case, the current in the channel could be *in-jection-limited*. It would therefore be expected to saturate at some drain voltage, giving rise to characteristics similar to those of fig. 9.5b. This saturation is observed for thin-film transistors, with gold or aluminium source electrodes, and insulated-gate field effect transistors, operating in depletion mode. Further investigation as to the nature of metal to semi-insulator contacts is necessary to elucidate this matter.

9.10 The Conduction Law and the Geometry of the Device

In this concluding section, the question as to whether the current flow in the channel of a majority carrier transistor is ohmic or space-charge-limited will be briefly considered. The type of conduction process is greatly influenced by the geometry of the device as well as by the resistivity of the channel material.

In the insulated-gate field-effect and thin-film transistors of sections 9.7 and 9.8 respectively, the channel is very shallow and the gate electrode is everywhere very close to the channel. The charge carriers in the channel are influenced by two perpendicular components of electric intensity, one due to the gate to channel voltage and the other due to the drain to source voltage. Let displacements along the channel be described by an x-co-ordinate and displacements perpendicular to the channel by a y-co-ordinate. Then, because of the geometry of the device, and below the pinch-off point, the magnitude of the intensity component $-(\partial V/\partial y)$ will be much greater than that of $-(\partial V/\partial x)$. It is therefore reasonable to assume, bearing in mind the energy level diagrams of fig. 9.7b, that the magnitude of $(\partial^2 V/\partial y^2)$ will greatly exceed that of $(\partial^2 V/\partial x^2)$. Thus in the two-dimensional form of Poisson's equation, namely (see eqn 7.2-1),

$$\left(\frac{\partial^2 V}{\partial x^2}\right) + \left(\frac{\partial^2 V}{\partial y^2}\right) = -\left(\frac{\rho}{\varepsilon}\right) \tag{9.10-1}$$

that part of the charge density ρ associated with the term $(\partial^2 V/\partial x^2)$ will be small compared with ρ. This latter quantity is the charge density which is responsible for the current-flow; see eqn 9.2-2. The $(\partial^2 V/\partial x^2)$ term therefore approximates to zero and hence $(\partial V/\partial x)$ is nearly constant for the part of the channel below the pinch-off point. The conduction law in the channel is thus approximately ohmic.

For majority carrier transistors with wider channels, for example junction field-effect types, the foregoing intuitive argument is not sound. However, if the resistivity of the channel is not extremely high, which is probably the case for silicon, the transition voltage V_T of eqn (9.3-3) will be very high and the conduction law will still be ohmic.

The structures proposed by Wright [9.21] [9.27] for dielectric triodes, have in effect, wide conducting channels and the voltages on the gate and drain electrodes can be expected to produce fields in approximately the same direction. Provided the channel resistivity is high enough, the current in such devices should be space-charge-limited. Experimental work by Zuleeg [9.9] seems to confirm these general conclusions but there may be other possible explanations of his results.

References

[9.1] MOTT, N. F. and GURNEY, R. W. (1948), *Electronic properties in ionic crystals*, Ch.5, Oxford Univ. Press.

[9.2] See for example: PARKER, P. (1950), *Electronics*, pp. 99–100, Arnold.

[9.3] ROSE, A. (1955), 'Space-charge-limited currents in solids', *Phys. Rev.*, **97**, 1538–1544.

[9.4] LAMPERT, M. A. (1956), 'Simplified theory of space-charge-limited limited currents in an insulator with traps,' *Phys. Rev.*, **103**, 1648—1686.

[9.5] LAMPERT, M. A. (1962), 'Injection currents in insulators', *Proc. I.R.E.*, **50**, 1781–1796.

[9.6] WRIGHT, G. T. (1959), 'Space-charge-limited currents in insulating materials', *Proc. I.E.E.*, **106B**, suppl. 17, paper no. 2928.

[9.7] CONNING, A. M., KAYALI, A. A. and WRIGHT, G. T. (1959), 'Space-charge-limited dielectric diodes', *Journ. I.E.E.*, **5**, 595.

[9.8] DRESNER, J. and SHALLCROSS, F. V. (1962), 'Rectification and space-charge-limited currents in CdS Films', *Solid-state electronics*, **5**, 205–210.

[9.9] ZULEEG, R. (1963), 'CdS thin-film electron devices', *Solid-state electronics*, **6**, 193–196.

[9.10] MIDDLEBROOK, R. D. (1963), 'A simple derivation of field-effect-transistor characteristics', *Proc. I.R.E.*, **51**, 1146–1147.

[9.11] BORKAN, H. and WEIMER, P. K. (1963), 'An analysis of the characteristics of the insulated gate thin-film transistors', *R.C.A. Rev.*, 24, 153–156.

[9.12] HOFSTEIN, S. R. and HEIMAN, F. P. (1963), 'The silicon insulated gate transistor', *Proc. I.E.E.E.*, 51, 1190–1202.

[9.13] SHOCKLEY, W. (1952), 'A unipolar field-effect transistor', *Proc. I.R.E.*, **40**, 1365–1376.

[9.14] DACEY, G. C. and ROSS, I. M. (1953), 'Unipolar field-effect transistor', *Proc. I.R.E.*, **41**, 970–979.

[9.15] WARNER, R. M. (1963), 'Epitaxial FET cut-off voltage', *Proc. I.E.E.E.*, **51**, 939.

[9.16] ROOSILD, S. A., DOLAN, R. P. and O'NEIL, D. O. (1963), 'A unipolar structure applying lateral diffusion', *Proc. I.E.E.E.*, **51**, 1059.

[9.17] STONE, H. A. and WARNER, R. M. (1961), 'The field-effect tetrode', *Proc. I.R.E.*, **49**, 1170.

[9.18] DACEY, G. C. and ROSS, I. M. (1955), 'The field-effect transistor', *Bell Syst. Tech. Journ.*, **34**, 1149–1189.

[9.19] BOCKMUEHL, R. R. (1963), 'Analysis of field-effect transistors with arbitrary charge distributions', *Trans. I.E.E.E.*, Ed-10, 31–34.

[9.20] PRIM, R. C. and SHOCKLEY, W. (1953), 'Joining solutions at the pinch-off point in field-effect transistors', *Trans. I.R.E.*, Ed-4, 1–14.

[9.21] WRIGHT, G. T. (1963), 'Space-charge-limited solid-state devices', *Proc. I.E.E.E.*, **51**, 1642–1652.

[9.22] WEIMER, P. K. (1962), 'The TFT, a new thin-film transistor', *Proc. I.R.E.*, **50**, 1462–1469.

[9.23] SHALLCROSS, F. V. (1963), 'Cadmium selenide thin-film transistors', *Proc. I.E.E.E.*, **51**, 851.

[9.24] WEIMER, P. K., SHALLCROSS, F. V. and BORKAN, H. (1963), 'Coplanar electrode insulated-gate thin-film transistors', *R.C.A. Rev.*, **24**, 661–675.

[9.25] HAERING, R. R. (1964), 'Theory of thin-film transistor operation', *Solid-state electronics*, **7**, 31–38.

[9.26] MIKSIC, M. G., SCHLIG, E. S. and HAERING, R. R. (1964), 'Behaviour of CdS thin-film transistors', *Solid-static electronics*, **7**, 39–48.

[9.27] WRIGHT, G. T. (1960), 'A proposed space-charge-limited dielectric triode', *Journ. Brit. I.R.E.*, **20**, 337–355.

Equivalent Circuits Derived from the Early Circuit

In section 8.6, the equivalent circuit of fig. 8.6b was established for the transistor. Other circuits may be derived from this one by parameter manipulation. Three circuits will be obtained here.

(*i*) *Common-Base T-Equivalent Circuit*
When the components C, C_c and $r_{bb'}$ are omitted from the circuit of fig. 8.6b, the residual circuit has, by inspection, a hybrid matrix:

$$\{h\} = \begin{Bmatrix} r_\varepsilon & , & \mu \\ -\alpha & , & g_c \end{Bmatrix} \tag{A.1-1}$$

where

$$g_c = \frac{2\mu(1-\alpha)}{r_\varepsilon}. \tag{A.1-2}$$

The impedance parameter may be expressed in terms of the hybrid parameters by:

$$\{z\} = \left(\frac{1}{h_{22}}\right) \begin{Bmatrix} h & , & h_{12} \\ -h_{21} & , & 1 \end{Bmatrix} = \left(\frac{1}{g_c}\right) \begin{Bmatrix} \mu(2-\alpha) & ,\mu \\ \alpha & , & 1 \end{Bmatrix} . \tag{A.1-3}$$

This impedance matrix may be split into the sum of two matrices:

$$\{z\} = \left(\frac{1}{g_c}\right) \begin{Bmatrix} \mu(1-\alpha) & , & 0 \\ \alpha-\mu & , & 1-\mu \end{Bmatrix} + \left(\frac{\mu}{g_c}\right) \begin{Bmatrix} 1 & , & 1 \\ 1 & , & 1 \end{Bmatrix}$$

$$\simeq \left(\frac{r_\varepsilon}{2}\right) \begin{Bmatrix} 1 & , & 0 \\ \dfrac{\alpha}{\mu(1-\alpha)} & , & \dfrac{1}{\mu(1-\alpha)} \end{Bmatrix} + \frac{r_\varepsilon}{2(1-\alpha)} \begin{Bmatrix} 1 & , & 1 \\ 1 & , & 1 \end{Bmatrix} \tag{A.1-4}$$

since μ is very small compared with α and unity.

The sum of impedance matrices in this way, corresponds to networks in series-series connection. The second matrix on the right-hand side of this equation, corresponds simply to a single shunt resistance $[r_e/2(1-\alpha)]$. The first matrix corresponds to a network with a forward transfer resistance, but no reverse transfer impedance. Thus, eqn (A.1-4)

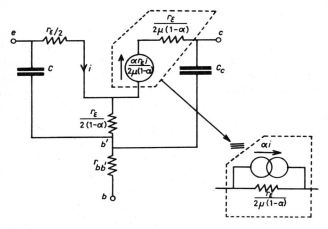

Figure A.1a. Common-base T-equivalent circuit

is the impedance matrix of the network of fig. A.1a, wherein the components C, C_c and $r_{bb'}$ have been included. The conversion to the current generator form of the circuit is readily made as is indicated in the figure.

(ii) The Common-Base π-Equivalent Circuit

If the hybrid matrix of eqn (A.1-1) is converted into admittance parameters, instead of impedance parameters, the admittance matrix is:

$$\{y\} = \left(\frac{1}{h_{11}}\right) \begin{Bmatrix} 1, & -h_{12} \\ h_{21}, & h \end{Bmatrix} = \left(\frac{1}{r_e}\right) \begin{Bmatrix} 1, & -\mu \\ -\alpha, & \mu(2-\alpha) \end{Bmatrix}. \quad \text{(A.1-5)}$$

Splitting this matrix into two parts:

$$\{y\} = \left(\frac{1}{r_\varepsilon}\right)\left\{\begin{matrix} 1-\mu, & 0 \\ -(\alpha-\mu), & \mu(1-\alpha) \end{matrix}\right\} + \left(\frac{\mu}{r_\varepsilon}\right)\left\{\begin{matrix} 1, & -1 \\ -1, & 1 \end{matrix}\right\}$$

$$\simeq \left(\frac{1}{r_\varepsilon}\right)\left\{\begin{matrix} 1, & 0 \\ -\alpha, & \mu(1-\alpha) \end{matrix}\right\} + \left(\frac{\mu}{r_\varepsilon}\right)\left\{\begin{matrix} 1, & -1 \\ -1, & 1 \end{matrix}\right\} \qquad \text{(A.1-6)}$$

since μ is very small compared with α and unity.

The sum of admittance matrices in this way, corresponds to networks in parallel-parallel connection. The second matrix on the right-hand side is simply that of a single series conductance (μ/r_ε). The first matrix corresponds to a network with a forward transfer conductance, but no reverse transfer conductance. Thus, eqn (A.1-6) is the admittance matrix of the network of fig. A.1b, wherein the components C, C_c and $r_{bb'}$ have been included.

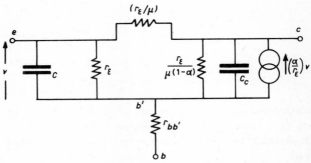

Figure A.1b. Common-base π-equivalent circuit

(iii) *The Common-Emitter Hybrid π-Equivalent-Circuit*

This important circuit is readily obtained from the Early circuit as follows. The admittance matrix of eqn (A.1-5) is *bordered* with an extra row and column, such that each of its rows and each of its columns sums to zero. This gives the *indefinite* admittance matrix:

$$\{y\}_{\text{indef}} = \left(\frac{1}{r_\varepsilon}\right)\begin{Bmatrix} \overset{e}{1} & \overset{c}{-\mu} & \overset{b}{\mu-1} \\ -\alpha & \mu(2-\alpha) & \alpha-\mu(2-\alpha) \\ \alpha-1 & \mu(\alpha-1) & (1+\mu)(1-\alpha) \end{Bmatrix}\begin{matrix} e \\ c \\ b \end{matrix} \qquad \text{(A.1-7)}$$

The extra row and column correspond to the base terminal. The emitter terminal may now be made the common terminal by deleting the first row and first column which correspond to this terminal. The remaining rows and columns are interchanged, so that the first row and column will correspond to the new input terminal, namely the base. The admittance matrix for common-emitter connection is thus:

$$\{y\} = \left(\frac{1}{r_\varepsilon}\right)\begin{Bmatrix} (1+\mu)(1-\alpha), & \mu(\alpha-1) \\ \alpha-\mu(2-\alpha), & \mu(2-\alpha) \end{Bmatrix}. \qquad \text{(A.1-8)}$$

As previously, splitting this matrix into the sum of two matrices:

$$\{y\} = \left(\frac{1}{r_\varepsilon}\right)\begin{Bmatrix} 1-\alpha, & 0 \\ \alpha-\mu, & \mu \end{Bmatrix} + \left[\frac{\mu(1-\alpha)}{r_\varepsilon}\right]\begin{Bmatrix} 1, & -1 \\ -1, & 1 \end{Bmatrix}$$

$$\simeq \left(\frac{1}{r_\varepsilon}\right)\begin{Bmatrix} 1-\alpha, & 0 \\ \alpha, & \mu \end{Bmatrix} + \left[\frac{\mu(1-\alpha)}{r_\varepsilon}\right]\begin{Bmatrix} 1, & -1 \\ -1, & 1 \end{Bmatrix} \qquad \text{(A.1-9)}$$

since μ is very small compared with α.

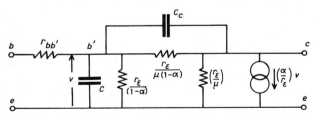

Figure A.1c. Common-emitter hybrid π-equivalent circuit

This corresponds to the network of fig. A.1c, wherein the components C, C_c and $r_{bb'}$ have been included.

Common-Emitter Characteristics

In section 8.2, the form of the d.c. characteristics of a transistor was considered. In this appendix, the manipulation of these characteristics from common-base configuration to common-emitter configuration will be carried out. As in section 8.2, initially, base width variation effects will be ignored. The common-base characteristics are then as given in fig. 8.2b; these were derived from eqn (8.2-23). For common-emitter configuration, a relation between I_C, I_B and V_{CE} is required for the collector characteristic.

The transformation can be effected with the aid of:

$$I_E = -(I_B + I_C) \tag{A.2-1}$$

$$V_{CB} = V_{CE} + V_{EB} . \tag{A.2-2}$$

Both these equations take account of the sign convention. A start is made by isolating an expression for V_{EB} from eqns (8.2-21) and (22), thus multiplying the second by α and adding to the first, gives, with rearrangement:

$$\exp\left(\frac{qV_{EB}}{kT}\right) = \left(\frac{I_E + \alpha I_C + I_{CB0}}{I_{CB0}}\right) = -\left(\frac{(I_B - I_{CB0})(1+\beta) + I_C}{(1+\beta)I_{CB0}}\right) \tag{A.2-3}$$

where eqn (A.2-1) has been used, and β is $(\alpha/1-\alpha)$.

Next, from eqn (8.2-23) and eqns (A.2-1) and (2):

$$-I_C = -\alpha(I_B + I_C) - I_{CB0}\left\{\exp\left[q\left(\frac{V_{EB} + V_{CE}}{kT}\right)\right] - 1\right\} \tag{A.2-4}$$

that is:

$$-I_C = -\beta I_B - (1+\beta)I_{CB0}\left[\exp\left(\frac{qV_{EB}}{kT}\right) . \exp\left(\frac{qV_{CE}}{kT}\right) - 1\right] . \tag{A.2-5}$$

Using eqn (A2.3) and rearranging:

$$-I_C = -\beta I_B \left[\frac{1 - \left(\dfrac{1+\beta}{\beta}\right) \exp\left(\dfrac{qV_{CE}}{kT}\right)}{1 + \exp\left(\dfrac{qV_{CE}}{kT}\right)} \right]$$

$$+ (1+\beta) I_{CB0} \left[\frac{1 - \exp\left(\dfrac{qV_{CE}}{kT}\right)}{1 + \exp\left(\dfrac{qV_{CE}}{kT}\right)} \right]. \qquad \text{(A.2-6)}$$

Because β is very much larger than unity, this last equation may be written:

$$-I_C \simeq \left[-\beta I_B + I_{CE0} \right] \left[\frac{1 - \exp\left(\dfrac{qV_{CE}}{kT}\right)}{1 + \exp\left(\dfrac{qV_{CE}}{kT}\right)} \right]$$

$$= -\left[-\beta I_B + I_{CE0} \right] \tanh\left(\frac{qV_{CE}}{2kT}\right) \qquad \text{(A.2-7)}$$

where I_{CE0} is $(1+\beta) I_{CB0}$ and is called the collector to emitter leakage current.

This gives the form of the collector characteristic. For V_{CE} more negative than about $-8(kT/q)$, that is 0·22 volt at room temperatures, $\tanh(qV_{CE}/2kT)$ is within a few per cent of its asymptotic value of -1, and eqn (A.2-7) then approximates to:

$$-I_C = -\beta I_B + I_{CE0}. \qquad \text{(A.2-8)}$$

A sketch of characteristics given by eqn (A.2-7) is shown in fig. A.2a. Their principle difference, from those for common-base configuration, is the way they saturate for negative values of V_{CE}. According to eqn (A.2-7) the characteristics, for all values of I_B, pass through the origin. In fact, from the exact eqn (A.2-6) the value of I_C for zero V_{CE} is one half of I_B; which is very small in general and justifies drawing the characteristics through the origin.

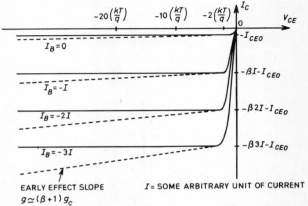

EARLY EFFECT SLOPE I = SOME ARBITRARY UNIT OF CURRENT
$g \simeq (\beta + 1) g_c$

Figure A.2a. Common-emitter collector characteristics

When allowance is made for the base width variation effects, the straight parts of the characteristics have a slope corresponding to the output conductance of the collector. For the common-base configuration, this was shown in fig. 8.3b. The slope of these latter characteristics is the g_c of the Early equivalent circuit, eqn (8.6-19). Defining the output conductance for common-emitter configuration in a similar way:

$$g = \left(\frac{\partial I_C}{\partial V_{CE}}\right)_{I_b} = \left(\frac{\partial I_C}{\partial \beta}\right)_{I_b}\left(\frac{d\beta}{d\alpha}\right)\left(\frac{d\alpha}{dV_{ce}}\right). \qquad (A.2-9)$$

Now α hardly varies at all with V_{eb} and so $(d\alpha/dV_{ce})$ can be replaced by $(d\alpha/dV_{cb})$ with negligible error. Then, from eqn (A.2-8) and the expression for β:

$$g \simeq (I_B - I_{CB0})\frac{1}{(1-\alpha)^2}\left(\frac{d\alpha}{dV_{cb}}\right) = (I_B - I_{CB0})(\beta + 1)^2\left(\frac{d\alpha}{dV_{cb}}\right). \qquad (A.2-10)$$

Using eqn (A.2-8) again, this is:

$$g \simeq (\beta + 1)(I_C - I_{CB0})\left(\frac{d\alpha}{dV_{cb}}\right) = -(\beta + 1)I_E\left(\frac{d\alpha}{dV_{cb}}\right) = (\beta + 1)g_c \qquad (A.2-11)$$

with reference to eqns (8.6-13) and (14).

The slope of the collector characteristics is thus approximately β times greater for common-emitter configuration than for common base. These slopes are indicated by the dotted curves of fig. A.2a.

It is also possible to convert the common-base characteristics to common-emitter characteristics by a purely graphical technique. Thus consider the common-base collector and emitter characteristics given in figs. 8.3b and c respectively. Starting with fig. 8.3b, select an emitter current, I_E, that is a particular characteristic, and a collector-base voltage V_{CB}, that is a point on the particular characteristic. The current I_C corresponding to this point is then found from fig. 8.3b. The emitter-base voltage V_{EB} corresponding to the point can be found from fig. 8.3c, for I_E and V_{CB} are known. The base current I_B and the collector-emitter voltage V_{CE}, corresponding to the selected point, can now be determined from eqns (A.2-1) and (2). This information can then be used to plot a point on the collector characteristic and a point on the base characteristic, both for common-emitter configuration. In this way, point by point, the common-emitter characteristics can be constructed. The process is, however, very tedious and in practice, the characteristics would be determined experimentally.

The Transistor as a Charge Controlled Device: Circuit Problems

The basic equations governing the operation of a transistor as a charge controlled device were established in section 8.9. In this appendix, a few simple solutions of these equations, relevant to particular circuit configurations, will be considered.

(i) Transistor Switched from Cut-Off to Conduction; No Saturation, Constant Base Current $-I_0$

Let it be supposed that a *pnp* transistor is in the cut-off condition with both of its junctions reverse biased. Leakage currents will be neglected. Now let a constant current $-I_0$ be drawn from the base. Equation (8.9-9) is therefore:

$$\left(\frac{dQ_b}{dt}\right) + \left(\frac{Q_b}{T_B}\right) = I_0 . \qquad (A.3\text{-}1)$$

Integrating:

$$Q_b = I_0 T_B \left[1 - \exp\left(-\frac{t}{T_B}\right)\right] \qquad (A.3\text{-}2)$$

where $Q_b(0)$ has been put equal to zero.

From eqn (8.9-8), the collector current is:

$$I_C = -I_0 \left(\frac{T_B}{T_C}\right)\left[1 - \exp\left(-\frac{t}{T_B}\right)\right] . \qquad (A.3\text{-}3)$$

Note (T_B/T_C) is approximately equal to β. The base charge and the collector current thus rise, exponentially, towards their final values, with time constant T_B. The transistor might be considered to be switched on after, say, a time $3T_B$.

(ii)   Transistor Switched from Cut-Off to Point of Saturation; Constant Base Current $-I_0$

Let it be supposed that the collector current is limited, in magnitude, to a current I, given by the collector supply voltage and collector load resistance. In order that the transistor may be switched into saturation by the base current $-I_0$, it is required that:

$$I_0 \left(\frac{T_B}{T_C} \right) \geqslant I . \tag{A.3-4}$$

The time to switch the transistor to the saturation point is then given by eqn (A.3-3) as:

$$T = T_B \ln \left(\frac{I_0 \, T_B}{I_0 \, T_B - I \, T_C} \right) . \tag{A.3-5}$$

(iii)   Transistor Switched from Point of Saturation, Initial Collector Current $-I$, *to Cut-Off; Constant Base Current* I_0

In this case, eqn (8.9-8) shows that:

$$Q_b(0) = I T_C . \tag{A.3-6}$$

The equation to be solved is eqn (8.9-9) with I_b equal to I_0.

$$\left(\frac{dQ_b}{dt} \right) + \left(\frac{Q_b}{T_B} \right) = -I_0 . \tag{A.3-7}$$

Integrating, and using eqn (A.3-6):

$$Q_b = -I_0 \, T_B + (I T_C + I_0 \, T_B) \exp \left(-\frac{t}{T_B} \right) . \tag{A.3-8}$$

The time for Q_b to decay to zero is:

$$T = T_B \ln \left(\frac{I T_C + I_0 \, T_B}{I_0 \, T_B} \right) . \tag{A.3-9}$$

(iv)   Transistor Switched from Some Degree of Saturation to Point of Saturation: Collector Current Constant at $-I$; *Base Current Before Switching, Constant at* $-I_1$, *Switched at t Equals Zero to Constant value* I_0

For this example, it is convenient to use the set of equations in terms of Q_c and Q_s, see fig. 8.9a(ii), that is, eqns (8.9-23), (24) and (25). For simplicity, a symmetrical transistor will be assumed, so that T_E and T_C will be equal, as will also be T_{Bf} and T_{Br}. The latter will be denoted by T_B. The values of Q_s and Q_c prior to switching can be obtained from eqns (8.9-23) and (24), with time varying quantities put to zero: thus:

$$-I = \left(\frac{1}{2T_B}\right)Q_s(0) - \left(\frac{Q_c(0)}{T_C}\right) \tag{A.3-10}$$

$$I_1 = \left(\frac{1}{T_B}\right)Q_s(0) + \left(\frac{Q_c(0)}{T_B}\right). \tag{A.3-11}$$

Solving for $Q_s(0)$ and $Q_c(0)$:

$$Q_c(0) = T_C(I + \tfrac{1}{2}I_1) \tag{A.3-12}$$

$$Q_s(0) = \left[\frac{I_1 T_B - I T_C}{1 + \left(\dfrac{T_C}{2T_B}\right)}\right]. \tag{A.3-13}$$

Note that $Q_c(0)$ is not $T_C I$ as might be expected intuitively, and also that $I_1 T_B$ must exceed $I T_C$ if $Q_s(0)$ is to be positive. This latter condition is eqn (A.3-4) again. When the base current is switched to I_0 at t equal to zero, eqns (8.9-23) and (24) become:

$$-I = \left(\frac{1}{2T_B}\right)Q_s + \tfrac{1}{2}\left(\frac{dQ_s}{dt}\right) - \left(\frac{Q_c}{T_C}\right) \tag{A.3-14}$$

$$-I_0 = \left(\frac{1}{T_B}\right)Q_s + \left(\frac{dQ_s}{dt}\right) + \left(\frac{Q_c}{T_B}\right) + \left(\frac{dQ_c}{dt}\right). \tag{A.3-15}$$

Eliminating the terms in Q_s:

$$\left(\frac{dQ_c}{dt}\right) + \left(\frac{2}{T_C} + \frac{1}{T_B}\right)Q_c = (2I - I_0). \tag{A.3-16}$$

Examination of this equation shows that Q_c tends towards the steady value:

$$Q_c \simeq (I - \tfrac{1}{2}I_0)T_C \tag{A.3-17}$$

since T_B is much larger than T_C. Further, the change from its initial value, eqn (A.3-12), to this value occurs quite rapidly, for the time constant of eqn (A.3-16) is approximately $(\frac{1}{2}T_C)$.

A good engineering approximation results when Q_c is taken equal to the constant value given by eqn (A.3-17). Substituting into eqn (A.3-15), the following differential equation for Q_s is obtained:

$$\left(\frac{dQ_s}{dt}\right) + \left(\frac{Q_s}{T_B}\right) = -I_0 - (I - \tfrac{1}{2}I_0)\left(\frac{T_C}{T_B}\right)$$

$$\simeq -\left[I_0 + \left(\frac{T_C}{T_B}\right)I\right]. \qquad (A.3\text{-}18)$$

This latter approximation also results if eqn (A.3-17) is substituted into eqn (A.3-14). Integration yields:

$$Q_s = (Q_s(0) + I_0 T_B + I T_C)\exp\left(-\frac{t}{T_B}\right) - (I_0 T_B + I T_C). \quad (A.3\text{-}19)$$

Using the approximate form of eqn (A.3-13):

$$Q_s = (I_0 + I_1)T_B \exp\left(-\frac{t}{T_B}\right) - (I_0 T_B + I T_C). \qquad (A.3\text{-}20)$$

The time for the saturation charge to decay to zero is therefore:

$$T = T_B \ln\left(\frac{I_0 T_B + I_1 T_B}{I_0 T_B + I T_C}\right). \qquad (A.3\text{-}21)$$

It will be apparent that an exact solution of the eqns (A.3-14) and (15) is very involved indeed. The particular advantage of the Q_c and Q_s representation for the saturation condition for the transistor lies in the fact that Q_c changes quickly to its new value, and that the change is small provided I_0 and I_1 are small compared with I. It is often assumed that Q_c remains equal to $I T_c$, but the example shows that this is not justified if I_0 is an appreciable fraction of I. Rather, Q_c should be taken as $(I - \frac{1}{2}I_0)T_C$.

The whole topic is rather more involved for a non-symmetrical transistor.

Index